TA O
THE SKIES

Graham Smith

COUNTRYSIDE BOOKS

NEWBURY, BERKSHIRE

COUNTRYSIDE BOOKS
3 Catherine Road
Newbury, Berkshire

To view our complete range of books,
please visit us at
www.countrysidebooks.co.uk

ISBN 1 85306 815 2

*To the memory of
all those brave and determined aviators*

The cover painting is from an original by
Colin Doggett and shows the Armstrong Whitworth
Argosy I-G-EBLF *City of Glasgow*, of
Imperial Airways, in 1926

Designed by Mon Mohan

Produced through MRM Associates Ltd., Reading
Typeset by Techniset Typesetters, Newton-le-Willows
Printed by Woolnough Bookbinding Ltd., Irthlingborough

CONTENTS

Leonard Bridgman's Programme Cover for 1926 RAF Display showing Siskin IIIs. (RAF Museum)

I

SETTING
THE SCENE

On 17th December 1903 a deep and cherished ambition, almost as old as recorded history, was realised – man had gained mastery of the air; Orville Wright, with his brother Wilbur anxiously watching, achieved the world's first powered flight in a heavier-than-air machine. In the hundred years since that historic event the progress of aviation has been astounding. Each year millions upon millions of people travel by air to all corners of the world, some even beyond the speed of sound, with barely a passing thought for the determination and bravery of all those pioneer aeronauts and aviators, whose remarkable endeavours and sacrifices helped to make this seemingly improbable form of transport so commonplace and such an essential part of today's world.

From time immemorial mankind had dreamed of flying, to move through the air as free as the birds. The ancient Greeks had their legends of Daedalus and his son Icarus and the Persians their magic carpets. Such was the importance attached to flight that most of the supernatural beings conceived by human imagination were endowed with the power of flight, either by magic or by wings. Through the centuries there were many instances of foolhardy but brave attempts to emulate birds with fabricated cloth and feathered wings. In pre-Roman Britain (circa 843 BC) King Bladud is reputed to have been killed whilst trying to fly from the Temple of Apollo in Trinavantum (London) using wings made of leather. Perhaps the most famous 'tower-jumper', as they were later called, was an English Benedictine monk, Oliver of Malmesbury ('the Flying Monk'); in about 1020 he jumped from Malmesbury Abbey with wings made of wood and covered with linen and was fortunate to survive the experiment with broken legs. Nevertheless over the centuries many still tried with various types of wings but sadly died in their attempts. Even now British 'birdmen' are still attempting to win a prize for a hundred metre flight; the 24th annual contest was held off Bognor Pier in August 2002 but the record 'flight' of 89.2 metres was not surpassed.

In 1270 another monk and noted scientist, the Franciscan Roger Bacon, wrote rather presciently of '... an instrument to flie withall, so that one sitting in the midst of the Instrument, and turning about an Engine, by which the wings being artifically composed may beate the ayre after the fashion of a flying bird ...'. But it was Leonardo da Vinci, some two centuries later, who designed the first ornithopter – a flying machine with flapping wings – and the first glider. His designs, now recognised for their technical innovation, were not translated until the end of the eighteenth century.

Man first managed to escape the confines of earth in 1783 by ascending into the air in a lighter-than-air apparatus – a balloon – sustained by hot-air. Joseph and Étienne Montgolfier gave the first public demonstration of their balloon in Avignon, France in June 1783. The honour of becoming the world's first aeronaut fell to François Pilâtre de Rozier when on 15th October he ascended in the Montgolfier balloon to a height of 84 feet, the limit of the retaining rope, and was airborne for almost 4½ minutes. On 21st November de Rozier, accompanied by the Marquis d'Arlandes, left the Bois de Boulogne in Paris for the first free flight. The brightly coloured balloon rose some 300 feet, was airborne for 25 minutes and travelled about 5½ miles. Poor de Rozier was killed in June 1785 whilst attempting to cross the English Channel in a composite hot-air/hydrogen balloon – the first of many aerial fatalities.

Ballooning arrived in Britain on 15th September 1784 when Vincenzo Lunardi, an attaché with the Neapolitan Embassy in London, ascended in a *Charlière* – a hydrogen filled balloon. Lunardi left Moorfields in London and drifted north-east, finally landing safely at Standon Green End near Ware in Hertfordshire, where there is a stone monument recording the feat. James Sadler became the first English aeronaut, he made an ascent from Oxford on 4th October. During the next two years Lunardi made provincial tours with his balloon; in August 1786 he was in York, where according to reports '... the balloon rose to a prodigious height to the great acclamations of several thousands spectators ...' – the balloon craze had spread to Britain.

During the nineteenth century ballooning gained in popularity especially with members of society when it became fashionable to take 'an aerial ride'. It was not solely the preserve of men; on 29th June 1785 Mrs Letitia Sage was the first of many women to take to the skies in a balloon. Balloon displays became an exciting spectator sport, especially with the added attraction of parachute descents. The inherent disadvantage of these lighter-than-air balloons was the aeronaut's inability to steer and control them in flight, which led to attempts to make these 'aerial ships' capable of being navigated. At Brompton Hall near Scarborough George Cayley was engaged in defining the principles and theory of flight. He was a remarkable amateur scientist and talented engineer, who spent his whole life studying all aspects of flight. Sir George ultimately laid down the basis of the science of aerodynamics, and is universally recognised as the 'Father of Aerial Navigation'.

Sir George Cayley (1773–1857) – Pioneer of Aerial Navigation and Founder of Aerodynamics. (Science & Society Picture Library)

7

In 1796, at the age of 23, Cayley built a powered model helicopter, adapted from an earlier French design, this and his later models are really the true ancestors of modern helicopters. Three years later he produced the first known design for an aeroplane with fixed wings, a fuselage, tail unit and a paddle propulsion system. It was engraved on a silver disc, which on the reverse showed the physical forces acting upon a wing. In 1804 he constructed his first monoplane model glider and five years later his first full-scale glider was completed and successfully flown but unmanned. During 1809/10 he published his thoughts and findings in several papers entitled *On Aerial Navigation*; he envisaged a time when '... we shall be able to transport ourselves and our families and their goods and chattels, more securely by air than by water and with a velocity of from 20 to 100 miles per hour.'

Some thirty years later in Chard, Somerset, the next development of the aeroplane took place. William Henson, a lace manufacturer, designed a large passenger-carrying steam-powered aeroplane, originally named the *Aerial Steam Carriage* and later the *Ariel*. In 1843 Henson received a patent for his design expected to be built for service with a proposed Aerial Transit Company. Because of the ambitious nature of the project it attracted much public attention; several engravings were made of the proposed monoplane and they were well publicised. Henson assisted by a friend in Chard, John Stringfellow, proceeded to construct a large working model with a twenty-foot wing span powered by a single cylinder steam engine. During 1847 Stringfellow trialled the model at Bewley Down near Chard, but unsuccessfully, although the engine performed well. In the following year Henson, beset by financial problems, abandoned the experiments and left for the USA. However, Stringfellow, now known in Chard as the 'Flying Man', continued the experiments.

In 1848 he built a ten-foot monoplane, which weighed only nine pounds, and was fitted with a lighter and more powerful steam engine along with two four-blade propellers. The curved wings were pointed and streamlined. To negate the vagaries of the weather Stringfellow hired a large room in a disused lace mill. The model, which had no undercarriage, was launched from a sloping wire, it climbed steadily for several yards after launching. He then successfully demonstrated his monoplane to the members of the local Institute along with guests from London – it was the world's first powered flight. Hence why Chard proudly claims to be 'The birthplace of powered flight'.

Sir George Cayley was still experimenting; in 1843 he designed an

John Stringfellow's 1848 Monoplane. (Chard & District Museum)

'Aerial Carriage' with four circular rotating wings, the first attempt at a 'convertiplane' – the original name for a vertical landing and take-off aeroplane. Six years later a ten-year-old boy living on the estate became airborne for several yards in one of his gliders after being towed by manpower down a hill and into a breeze. This lad was the first person to fly in a heavier-than-air machine. Towards the end of his life Sir George constructed a large triplane glider and in the summer of 1853 he 'persuaded' his coachman to take a ride in it! The glider was airborne for some four hundred feet across a local valley. The reluctant aviator broke his leg on landing and is reputed to have told Sir George, '... I wish to give notice. I was hired to drive not fly!' Four years later Cayley died at the age of seventy-four. A celebrated aviation historian wrote of him, 'His name should be placed in letters of gold at the beginning of the history of the aeroplane.'

Although ballooning remained in the ascendancy there were a number of professional engineers in the country greatly interested in the science of heavier-than-air flight. On 12th January 1866 they established an Aeronautical Society and in its early years the Society flourished under the guidance and encouragement of Frederick W. Brearey, who had designed a glider. He was the Society's active

The first ever Aeronautical Show – Crystal Palace, 1868. (Science & Society Picture Library)

Honorary Secretary until his death in 1896. In 1868 the Society staged the first-ever aeronautical exhibition at the Crystal Palace. Prizes were offered for the best models and Stringfellow was invited to submit a model for display. His large steam-powered triplane had pride of place in the exhibition and it was said that the Prince of Wales, one of the many important visitors, was most impressed with the triplane. Stringfellow was awarded £150 for his model and its lightweight 1 h.p. engine. The Society's report of the exhibition fully acknowledged that '... it [the Society] was prepared to expect some of the ridicule that has ever been attached to this subject, by those that are apt to mistake sarcasm for sound argument, but this cannot influence the

Colonel James L. B. Templar in the car of an Army balloon. (Museum of Army Flying)

success or failure of a particular question in science.' It was the absence of a light but powerful engine that impeded the development of powered flight; existing steam engines were far too heavy and cumbersome.

The War Office, never particularly progressive, decided in 1878 that there might well be a future for the use of balloons for reconnaissance and artillery spotting; thus £150 – the first 'Air Estimates' – was allocated for the construction of a balloon. James L. B. Templar, then Captain of the 2nd Middlesex Militia, and Captain H.P. Lee of the Royal Engineers were appointed to carry out the development work. Templar was an enthusiastic aeronaut and with his own balloon, *Crusader*, he trained Royal Engineer officers on the basis of 10 shillings for every day of instruction. The first Army coal-gas balloon, aptly named *Pioneer*, was constructed at Woolwich Arsenal for the cost of £71, and was first used on military manoeuvres at Aldershot in June 1880. The balloon detachment moved into the R.E. base at Chatham, Kent two years later, where under Templar a staff of instructors, scientists and craftsmen was assembled, all dedicated to their new duties.

Despite numerous accidents and several fatalities the popularity of ballooning had not diminished, thousands regularly attended the many public displays and the sight of balloons in the skies, if not quite commonplace, was at least a fairly familiar occurrence. The attraction of this novel form of 'aerial transport' was probably best captured by Sir Claude de Crespigny, an ardent balloonist, '... if some of the least adventurous people could only realise the unspeakable splendour which so swiftly opens out to the gaze of the aerial traveller, they would admit that ballooning has great and natural attractions. The sensations the aeronaut experiences in the ascent, during his voyage through the skies are pleasurable beyond description ... and moreover the most profound and indescribable silence prevails ...'. Sentiments surely expressed by those who travel in today's hot-air balloons.

Nevertheless the War Office was not really convinced of the military value of balloons and prolonged discussions on the matter delayed a balloon detachment joining the Sudan campaign in 1882. After considerable pressure by Templar a detachment was despatched to an expedition to Bechuanaland in November 1884, where the appearance of its balloon suggested to the native chiefs that 'The English have indeed great power'! Three years later a Balloon Establishment and Factory was formed at Chatham and James Templar was appointed instructor and Superintendent of the Factory. It later moved to a permanent base at Aldershot and a School of Ballooning was formed. The first balloons were produced in 1893 and the following year a second factory was established at South Farnborough, Hampshire.

During the late nineteenth century there was a revival in heavier-than-air flight. Most of these intrepid aviators followed closely in the footsteps of Cayley and Stringfellow. Stringfellow died in December 1883 but his pioneering work was continued by his son Frederick, who exhibited in the Aeronautical Exhibition held at Alexandra Palace in 1903. The three airmen that were the major influences on the development of flight in the 1890s were involved in the design and construction of manned gliders.

The most dominant was Otto Lilienthal, a German civil engineer, who considered the problems of human flight in a most methodical and scientific manner. He published the result of his experiments in 1889 – *Birdflight As the Basis of Aviation* – which influenced many early

12

pioneers. Lilienthal was the first actively to control a glider by swinging his legs and shifting his weight during his glides. Between 1891 and 1896 he made several monoplane and biplane gliders, testing them with amazing bravery mainly from a man-made hill near Berlin. Lilienthal completed over 2,500 flights achieving distances ranging from 330 to 1,150 feet; he was killed in August 1896 when a sudden gust of wind threw his frail craft out of control. Lilienthal, certainly 'the first true flying man', wrote, 'It is easy to invent a flying machine; more difficult to build one; to make it fly is everything.' A maxim that many aspiring aviators found to be so true.

In America the French-born Octave Chanute, a successful railroad engineer, became interested in flight in 1889, and five years later he published *Progress in Flying Machines*, the first comprehensive history and theory of heavier-than-air flight – essential reading for any further research into the subject. Chanute also developed his own biplane gliders, which were tested at Indian Dunes Park near Chicago, and their success convinced him that it was possible to build a stable machine that could maintain its balance in the air with movements made by the pilot.

The pre-eminent British glider designer was Percy Pilcher, a marine engineer who built his first machine in 1895, the *Bat*, after visiting Lilienthal; he flew it that year from Cardross on the banks of the Clyde. Several other gliders followed – *Beetle*, *Gull* and *Hawk* – the latter being constructed in 1896 at Eynsford, Kent. *Hawk* was complete with a tailplane and a wheel undercarriage, and Pilcher was in the process of developing a light engine for probable use in this glider. Unfortunately he crashed on 30th September 1899 whilst giving a public demonstration with the *Hawk* at Stanford Park, Market Harborough and died two days later.

Perhaps the most bizarre flying machine developed and trialled in Britain during the 1890s was devised by Hiram Maxim, an American who had come to England in 1881. He was an engineer, instrument maker and latterly a professional inventor, famed for the machine gun that bears his name. Maxim devoted the profits from this invention to finance his abiding interest – powered flight. Characteristically Maxim started virtually from scratch, paying scant regard to previous developments. In 1893 he constructed a giant biplane with a wingspan of 104 feet, two huge propellers and powered by two 180 h.p. steam engines. It was variously described as '... massive and ungainly ... a truly awesome sight ...'. Maxim built a large shed and a long test track

A replica of Sir Hiram Maxim's Flying Machine of 1894.

at Baldwyns Park, Bexley, Kent. On 31st July 1894 he tested his biplane, crewed by three men, and it careered along the track at some 40 m.p.h. and briefly left the rails. His experiments attracted wide interest and many distinguished people came to view his machine. The trials continued until the following summer when the biplane was damaged by an axle becoming entangled with the upper restraining rails. Maxim now abandoned the machine, which was reputed to have cost £30,000. The large shed was dismantled and re-erected at Eynsford where Pilcher, who had assisted Maxim, built his *Hawk* glider. However, Maxim did not lose his enthusiasm for aviation; in December 1901 he addressed the Aeronautical Society on 'Aerial Navigation'. The previous year he became a British citizen and was knighted in 1901. Sir Hiram was now convinced that '... a practical aeroplane will be developed and will be used for military purposes ...'.

In faraway Australia, Lawrence Hargrave was developing his box-kite. In 1894 he was lifted some sixteen feet in the air by four of his kites. Hargrave published his findings both at home and in Europe. His design provided excellent lift and stability and would become the basis of some of the early French aeroplanes. Hargrave briefly re-visited England in 1899 (he had been born in Greenwich) and gave a series of lectures on his experiments.

The first Englishman to experiment with box-kites was Captain B.F.S. Baden-Powell of the Scots Guards; he already had some experience of military ballooning and in June 1894 a system of his box-kites managed to lift a man. Indeed a man-lifting section was briefly established at the Balloon Establishment at Aldershot. Baden-Powell, brother of the founder of the Boy Scouts, became President of the Aeronautical Society and was deeply involved in early aviation. During his Presidential address in January 1903 Baden-Powell declared 'we are on the threshold of manned powered flight ... primarily it would form an incalculably valuable engine of war. One could scarcely imagine any invention, which would have a greater effect on the conduct of warfare ...' With the outbreak of the South African war in 1899, two balloon detachments were despatched closely followed by a third; balloons were employed to direct artillery fire during the seige of Mafeking and later Ladysmith, and were considered to have made an important contribution during the initial phases of the war. Nevertheless many Army officers considered their use to be 'unfair ... against a chivalrous opponent'!

Oblivious of developments taking place in America, the progress of powered flight in Europe concentrated on dirigible (steerable) airships. Foremost in airship design was Alberto Santos-Dumont, a wealthy Brazilian living in Paris. His first airship flew in 1898 and in October 1901 an improved No V1 machine gained the Deutsch Prize of 100,000 francs for a flight from St Cloud to the Eiffel Tower and back in less than half an hour. He subsequently designed and constructed other airships and convinced those in Europe, at least, that the age of flying had finally arrived.

Perhaps a more ominous event was the first flight on 2nd July 1900 of the great cigar-shaped airship that sailed above Lake Constance in southern Germany. It was the *Luftschiff Zeppelin* (LZ1) designed by Count Ferdinard von Zeppelin, a former army general. His name would become synonymous with large rigid airships. All were driven by petrol engines, which had been developed in the last decades of the century with the utmost significance to powered flight. Daimler's first petrol engine was built in 1884 and a year later Carl Benz produced his first automobile, which he named after his daughter – Mercedes.

In Britain it was mostly the hardy pioneer motorists that were also enthusiastic aeronauts dedicated to the sport of ballooning. Amongst these were the Hon. Charles S. Rolls, third son of Lord Llangattock, Frank Hedges Butler, a wealthy wine merchant, and his daughter Vera, who were members of the Automobile Club. On 24th September 1901 whilst taking a flight in the Spencer's *City of York* balloon, they discussed Santos-Dumont's recent success with his airship; thereupon they decided to form the Aero Club of Great Britain, really as an adjunct to the Automobile Club. Its objects were '... the encouragement of aerial-automobilism and ballooning as a sport ... and to develop the science of aerial navigation in all its forms and applications ...'. Less scientific than the more learned members of the Aeronautical Society, its members were nevertheless avid balloonists and also blessed with

Balloon, City of York, – *24th September 1901. Stanley Spencer in uniform, Miss Vera Butler, Frank Hedges Butler & the Hon. C. S. Rolls. (Rolls-Royce Heritage Trust)*

the finance to fund their new expensive passion. It was later suggested that the Aeronautical Society and the Aero Club should amalgamate, but the Society members rather pompously dismissed the proposal as 'highly inappropriate to join a social club'! The Aero Club was officially formed on 29th October 1901 and controlled 'the science and sport of balloons, airships and aeroplanes in Great Britain.'

The most flamboyant pioneer aviator was Samuel Franklin Cody, who, like Maxim, was American, and his life was as bizarre as the many legends that surrounded him. His real name was Franklin Samuel Cowdrey, the family adopted Cody maybe to imply a connection with Colonel 'Buffalo Bill' Cody of 'Wild West' fame. He sedulously adopted the appearance of a cowboy, wearing buckskin chaps and a stetson hat; he had been a cowboy, a gold prospector as well as a performer in a minor 'Wild West' show. Cody and his wife, Maud, arrived in England in the late 1880s and were soon appearing in music halls as 'Captain Cody and Miss Cody, Buffalo Bill's son and daughter'. Maud returned to America and Cody formed a relationship with Lela Davis; they, along with her three sons and daughter from her former marriage, appeared on stage as 'The Cody Family' and later in Cody's own spectacular show – *The Klondike Nugget*. Lela was always known as 'Mrs' Cody and he referred to her as 'Madame' Cody; she and her sons became deeply involved in his aviation experiments.

In October 1901 Cody wrote to the War Office '... I believe I possess certain secrets which would be of use to the Government in the way of Kite-Flying ...' In November he publicly demonstrated his large kite, *Viva*, at Wanstead Flats, East London, and more successfully at Bury St Edmunds where he was lifted to a height of 300 feet. Cody applied for a patent for his kites and Major Frank Trollope was deputed to view Cody's kites on behalf of the War Office. In mid-December he viewed a demonstration at Leeds, was impressed and recommended Cody to Colonel Templar at Farnborough. Templar witnessed a demonstration at Seaham but despite his recommendation the War Office were not impressed, but the Admiralty were and their kites were made at the Alexandra Palace. Cody advertised his 'War Kites' by showing a photograph of 'Mrs' Cody ascending to show how easy is 'the controlling or steering apparatus'. Cody had several brushes with death whilst trialling his 'war kite', notably in April 1903 when ascending from H.M.S. *Seahorse* off Portsmouth, he and the kite were flung into the sea. In June he became a member of the Aeronautical Society, as did Lieutenant-Colonel John E. Capper of the Royal

Samuel Franklin Cody – the most charismatic pioneer aviator. (Smithsonian Institution)

Engineers; both men had a great influence on military aviation.

Certain developments in manned flight were taking place in America; Professor Samuel Langley, a distinguished mathematician and secretary of the Smithsonian Institution, had been experimenting with steam-powered model aeroplanes from his houseboat on the Potamac river at Quantico, Virginia for several years. On 6th May 1896 he launched his *Aerodrome No 5* from a catapult on the roof of his houseboat, it flew for ninety seconds and a distance of one hundred feet. Two other trials were conducted when the *Aerodrome* flew for nearly a mile. Alexander Graham Bell, the inventor of the telephone and a kiting enthusiast, witnessed the trials and said, '... the experiment was of such historical importance that it should be made public...' Ten days later his report was published in *The World*. Professor Langley believed that the Greek word *aerodrome* meant 'air runner'; however, *dromos* was rightly a 'running or race track', hence why aerodrome became the universal name for landing grounds.

Two years later the U.S. War Department considered that there might be some military potential for flying machines, and $50,000 was allocated to Professor Langley to continue his experiments. His brief was 'to build a manned flying machine which would have a practicable application in war'. Considering the rudimentary state of heavier-than-air flight this sponsorship shows commendable vision and foresight by the U.S. War Department.

It was about this time that Orville and Wilbur Wright in Dayton, Ohio became actively involved in aviation matters. Their first joint business venture, in 1889, was a local newspaper printed on a press made by Orville but four years later they started selling and building bicycles from their shop in Dayton. Through their engineering skills the Wright Cycle Company prospered; but their abiding interest in aviation was rekindled by the writings of Lilienthal and Chanute. In May, Wilbur wrote to the Smithsonian Institution for current information on aerial navigation and their first tentative experiments were made with a large kite that they had constructed. In May 1900 Wilbur wrote to Chanute admitting that '... For some years I have been afflicted with the belief that flight is possible to man ...'; thus started a long correspondence and close friendship between the pioneer airmen.

By August 1900 they had built their first biplane glider and following advice from the U.S. Weather Board about suitable wind conditions along the Atlantic coast, they selected the remote sand hills at Kitty Hawk, North Carolina to test the glider. During September and

Man-lifting kites developed by S. F. Cody.

October they experimented with their glider, mostly tethered like a kite and methodically recorded their findings. In July of the following year they returned to Kitty Hawk with a larger glider with a wingspan of twenty-two feet, which was tested from the nearby Kill Devil Hills with Wilbur at the controls. Some thirty flights were made, the longest lasting seventeen seconds. After a third period at Kitty Hawk in 1902 they had completed some 1,000 flights, both were skilled pilots and able to handle their glider in most weather conditions; their longest flight covered more than six hundred feet and lasted twenty-six seconds. They now felt ready to return home to Dayton and seriously think about adding power to their machine.

Despite official financial support and the resources of the Smithsonian Institution at his disposal, it took Professor Langley five years to obtain a suitable lightweight petrol engine built by Charles M. Manly, his engineer and prospective pilot. By late 1903 Langley's large *Aerodrome* was ready for its first manned trials. On 8th October it was launched from the houseboat with Manly at the controls but the machine snagged the launching mechanism and plunged into the river; miraculously Manly managed to extricate himself from the wreckage. The press reports were scathing; the *Washington Post* described the event '... There was a roaring, grinding noise ... it simply slid into the water like a handful of mortar'! The machine was recovered, rebuilt and on 8th December a second launching was tried. Yet again the machine failed, its flimsy wings collapsed and it plummeted into the river. Although the newspapers were slightly kinder to Langley, they still held out little hope for human flight. The U.S. War Department swiftly abandoned the project and Langley, now aged sixty-nine, embittered by public ridicule gave up his aeronautical experiments; he died in 1906.

Meanwhile, in March 1903, quite unheralded the Wright brothers applied for a patent for an aeroplane based on their No.3 Glider but it was refused on the grounds that they had bypassed the legal profession. Late in 1902 they had written to a dozen small and nascent American motor-car manufacturers but without success, the engines were too heavy and lacked power; the only alternative was to design and build their own. Charles Taylor, a young mechanic working in their bicycle shop, developed a four cylinder 12 h.p. engine, which drove twin propellers with simple bicycle chains; it now needed to be tested.

In late August they returned to Kitty Hawk with their machine. After engine tests and some problems with the propeller shafts, the *Flyer* was ready for its trials at the end of November, but the weather was too calm. They patiently waited for a fortnight until a mild breeze was blowing and made their first attempt on 14th December, which was not successful. Then on the morning of 17th December with five local men from the nearby lifesaving station present as witnesses, the brothers calmly tossed a coin to decide which of them would pilot the *Flyer* – Wilbur lost! At 10.35 a.m. the *Flyer* took to the air, it travelled one hundred and twenty feet and the flight lasted twelve seconds. One of the lifeguards, John T. Daniells, took the dramatic photograph of the historic event, capturing the moment of lift-off at the end of the

'Damned if they ain't flew' – The Wright Brothers' historic flight, 17th December, 1903. (Smithsonian Institution)

launching rail. Another three flights were made during the morning, the final one by Wilbur covered eight hundred and fifty-two feet and lasted fifty-nine seconds. After landing, a sudden gust of wind caught the *Flyer*, it turned over and was damaged; this historic aeroplane would never fly again.

The famous telegram was sent to their father, Bishop Milton Wright in Dayton; 'Success four flights thursday morning all against twenty one wind started from Level with engine power alone. average speed through air thirty one miles longest 57 seconds [sic] inform Press. home Christmas. Orevelle Wright [sic]'; he gave a copy to the Dayton reporter for the Association Press. Thus, just nine days after Professor Langley's final abortive trial, the Wright brothers had achieved the world's first powered and controlled flight. As one of the witnesses is reported to have said, 'Damned if they ain't flew!'

2
THE AERIAL
MOTOR CARS
(1904–1908)

The news of the Wright brothers' historic flights was greeted – 'not to a fanfare of trumpets but rather with a sad whimper'. There was little notice in the press on both sides of the Atlantic, maybe due to disbelief but more likely by a lack of interest. The few reports that appeared in America were found by the Wrights to be '... incorrect in almost every detail ... and contained statements that were false pure and simple ...'. They issued a written statement giving the accurate facts, which closed with an unequivocable message – 'the age of the flying machine had come at last.'

In England *The Times* ignored the news from Kitty Hawk but the junior and 'upstart' newspaper – *Daily Mail* – recorded the event two days later. In a small paragraph headed Balloonless Airship the bare facts were recorded and ended with the information that 'the idea of the box-kite was used in the construction of the airship.'. This popular newspaper, which sold for $\frac{1}{2}$d, had been founded by Alfred Harmsworth in May 1896, who was a most ardent promoter of motor-cars and also became the foremost advocate and generous sponsor of British aviation.

It is unlikely that any of the august members of the Aeronautical Society were readers of this newspaper but from March 1904 they could not claim to be unaware of the Wrights' flights, because they were addressed on the subject by Patrick Alexander, who had visited the Wrights only two months earlier. He had a diverse range of scientific interests and had particularly immersed himself in all aspects of flight. It was said that he was '... probably better acquainted with all who are interested in aeronautics in Europe and America than any other living individual.' This reputation, allied to the fact that his father had been one of the founders of the Society, should have added gravitas to his lecture; nevertheless his words fell mostly on disbelieving or deaf ears, the members greeted his information with considerable scepticism. The more pressing news engaging their attention was the recent report of the Committee, set up in 1903, to examine military ballooning as a result of inadequacies experienced during the Boer War.

The report recommended that the Army should develop dirigible airships and the newly promoted Colonel Templar's budget (see previous chapter) was increased to £14,600 though this figure barely covered his Balloon Establishment, let alone finance a new project. Nevertheless Templar considered that the major objective was the construction of an Army airship and he left for France to discuss the undertaking with the leading authority – Alberto Santos-Dumont. He returned convinced of the military potential of airships compared with the obvious limitations of balloons.

There was at least one senior Army officer who considered that there might be some military significance in 'flying machines' – Lieutenant-Colonel John E. Capper. He had served in the Boer War and was an experienced aeronaut. In 1903 Capper had been given command of the Balloon Section at its new quarters at Laffan Plain, Farnborough and he had persuaded the War Office to extend the length of secondment of personnel to the Section to five years in order to widen its expertise, also approval was obtained to train more Royal Artillery men in aerial observation. Capper deemed that the forthcoming St Louis World Fair and Exposition, hosting the first International Aeronautics Congress, would be an ideal opportunity to ascertain the progress of aeronautics in America. Largely due to Templar's influence at the War Office, Capper was authorised to attend as the British official delegate. Alexander provided him with letters of introduction to his 'aviation' friends in America, and in June Capper attended the Fair. The Wrights were not competing, they had visited the site earlier in the year and decided that the layout of the course was more suitable to airships. During the summer they had constructed an improved *Flyer II*, which they tested at Huffman Prairie, some eight miles out of Dayton.

In October Capper visited the Wrights at Dayton, only a week after they had completed their 71st flight. He was shown photographs of their two flying machines in flight, also their engine but not a sight of *Flyer II*, which was said to be under repair; they were already becoming secretive about their machine for fear of copying. Nevertheless Capper was convinced of the potential of their machine and enquired whether they would submit proposals to the British Government for 'an aerial scouting machine'. On his return to London Capper wrote to the War Office advocating the Wrights' aeroplane as well as informing them of the development of 'flying machines' in America, 'England is very backward. There are strong hopes of success in this direction ... and small machines may come much earlier than is generally anticipated ... but America is leading the way whilst in England practically nothing is being done.' He could have added that the country also lagged far behind France in such matters.

Without doubt France, with its long tradition of ballooning, was the leading European country in the development of heavier-than-air machines. Captain Ferdinard Ferber, an Artillery officer, had been experimenting with Wright-type gliders for several years and had been in contact with the Wrights regarding purchase of one of their machines. In Ernest Archdeacon, the President of the *Aéro-Club de France* (founded in 1898), the country had an active supporter and generous sponsor. There was already a prize of 1,500 francs for the first flying machine to make a flight of 100 metres into the wind. In 1905 the Voisin brothers, Gabriel and Charles, formed the *Syndicat d'Aviation* to build aeroplanes at Billancourt. Their first float-gliders, one for Archdeacon and the other for Louis Blériot, were tested not very successfully on the Seine in Paris. Blériot, a prosperous motor-car headlight manufacturer, had been interested in aviation for several years. He and Gabriel Voisin would form a brief partnership to construct aeroplanes. Santos-Dumont, although still engaged on airships, was turning his talents to flying machines and was already designing his first aeroplane. But of greater significance was the development of a remarkable fuel-injected engine by Léon Levasseur, an art student turned engineer. His engine, *Antoinette*, named after his sponsor's daughter, had originally been designed for motor-boats, but he developed two engines – 24 h.p. and 50 h.p. – that would power several early aeroplanes and airships. Levasseur later designed and built *Antoinette* monoplanes, perhaps the most elegant of all the early aeroplanes.

The French pioneer aviators had their own centre to conduct trials. In March 1905 a military parade ground at Issy-les-Moulineaux (or 'Issy'), a suburb of Paris, was made available for their use on certain days; the centre had ample facilities for spectators. Unlike other countries the French were most supportive of the early aviators, it was claimed that

Paris was 'the aviation centre of the world'. It was therefore not surprising that Paris was the venue, in October, for delegates from seven European countries and the U.S.A. to meet and establish an International body 'to regulate the various aviation meetings and advance the science and sport of aeronautics.'. It was named the *Fédération Aéronautique Internationale* (F.A.I.), with Great Britain as one of the founding members – powered flight was at last being taken seriously.

Cody, aided by his step-sons, Leon and Vivian, was still engaged in kite building. Early In 1905 the War Office purchased two sets of Cody's box-kites, one for observation and the other for transmitting signals. During February he was given a three-month contract as Chief Kiting Instructor and in April (27th) a member of the Balloon Section, Sapper Moreton, reached a height of 2,600 feet beneath one of his kites. Cody now turned his talents to gliders, building a large biplane which strongly resembled a kite; it was trialled at Aldershot but in September it crashed, badly injuring Vivian.

In January 1905 the U.S. Army refused the Wrights' offer to sell them one of their machines, on the grounds that they were not interested in designs '... until they had been brought to a state of practical operation ...'! They now opened negotiations with the War Office, which dragged on for most of the year. The major problem was that the War Office wanted to examine the machine and witness it fly before agreeing to a formal offer. The Wrights could not agree to this proposal, they were deeply concerned that their technology would be copied or stolen without any financial return to themselves. In October they offered an aeroplane that could carry two people for fifty miles at a speed of 30 m.p.h. at a cost of $2,500 (some £1,100) per mile to include pilot training and technical assistance. However, in December Colonel H. J. Foster, the British military attache in Washington, was directed to break off negotiations with the Wrights.

The advancements made by the Wrights during the summer of 1905 only emphasised what a golden opportunity had been missed. Their improved *Flyer III* first flew in June and proved to be the world's first practicable aeroplane – it could bank, circle and land with ease. By early October they had completed forty-eight flights from Huffman Prairie each of longer duration and on the 5th October *Flyer III* flew for an incredible 39$\frac{1}{2}$ minutes and over twenty-four miles before the fuel was exhausted; small wonder that Wilbur claimed 'There is no sport equal to that which aviators enjoy while being carried through the air on great white wings.' The U.S. Government rejected their second offer of an aeroplane and faced with no response from Britain, the Wrights calmly decided to cease flying, they locked away *Flyer III* and waited until the world was ready to accept their remarkable flying machine. Neither would fly again until May 1908, this moratorium described by one historian as 'the astonishing interregnum', resulted in them losing some of the advantage of their innovative technology.

In England Alliott Verdon Roe was utterly convinced of their achievements and could not understand all the scepticism. The son of a Manchester doctor, Roe was a much travelled young man. He had trained as a civil engineer in Canada, spent two years aboard ship as a marine engineer and was now working as a draughtsman/designer in the motor-car industry. For several years he had built and flown model gliders after studying the flight of albatrosses whilst at sea. In January 1906 Roe wrote to *The Times* drawing attention to the Wrights' flights. 'It may be news to some of your readers to learn that flying with heavier-than-air type of machine is an accomplished fact. I allude to the Wright brothers' 24¼ miles in a motor-driven aeroplane. Although great publicity does not seem to have been given to the fact it is nevertheless one of the greatest achievements of the times ... If immediate steps were taken I see no reason why a motor-driven aeroplane should not be gliding over England by the middle of next summer.'. The letter was not published; the Engineering Editor noted '... all attempts at artificial aviation on the basis he describes are not only dangerous to human life, but foredoomed to failure from the engineering standpoint'! He must have felt a trifle foolish when Blériot flew the English Channel some three years later.

In March the Committee of the Aero Club, strongly urged by Charles Rolls, issued an invitation to the Wrights to come to England to demonstrate their flying machine – they politely declined. Later in December Rolls was introduced to the Wrights in New York, when he was exhibiting Rolls-Royce cars at the New York Automobile Show. On his return Rolls wrote '... I am quite convinced and perfectly satisfied that they had attained in flight even more than has been published in the newspapers.' Rolls was probably the staunchest supporter of the Wright brothers in Britain. He was also a member of the Aero Club's Technical Committee, formed in February, to examine the 'development of flying machines'; other members were Alexander, Baden-Powell, and Capper.

Nevertheless the Club, which now had some 200 members, was

almost solely devoted to ballooning. It regulated the sport and since June 1905 had been issuing certificates of competence to balloon pilots. Ballooning – 'the Sport of the Gods' – was even more expensive than motoring and those members that had not purchased balloons (varying from £135 to £220) could use the Club's balloons. Most ascents were made from either Crystal Palace or the polo/croquet grounds of Ranelagh Club near Barnes, where it was said 'the whole of London in its best kit came down to see the start of a balloon race.' Such was the social standing of ballooning that one aeronaut maintained, 'To go up in a balloon is the only way to go into the air like a gentleman'!

Most British pioneer aviators gained their first taste of flight by ballooning – Grahame-White, Moore-Brabazon, Baden-Powell, Sopwith, Grace and, of course, Rolls. He was perhaps the foremost aeronaut of the day with his *Midget* and *Venus* balloons. The Aero Club organised the first balloon race in Britain on 7th July, when seven balloons ascended from Ranelagh Club and the winner was Frank Butler accompanied by Colonel and Mrs Capper. The Spencer family had a virtual monopoly of balloon manufacture but now it was being challenged by Eustace and Oswald Short. They had recently moved into new premises at the Battersea railway arches adjoining the gas works to facilitate easier inflating. It was in a Shorts-built balloon, *Britannia*, that Rolls competed in the first International race for the Gordon Bennett Trophy, he was placed a credible third. Bennett was the wealthy proprietor of the *New York Herald*, and later sponsored a prestigious International Trophy for aeroplanes.

On the military front Colonel Templar retired in April but was retained as an adviser, and Colonel Capper took over as Superintendent of the Balloon Factory. In May Lieutenant John W. Dunne of the Wiltshire Regiment, who was on half-pay due to injuries suffered in the Boer War, was appointed as a kite designer. Dunne was dedicated to the development of an inherently stable flying machine, and had designed a tail-less aeroplane with swept back wings. Capper afforded Dunne every encouragement and support to further his experiments at Farnborough.

In the autumn the European aviation world was surprised by the reported flights of Santos-Dumont at Bagatelle on the outskirts of Paris. On 13th September, in his rather improbable tail-first (canard) monoplane *Bis-14*, he made 'hops' of thirty-three feet. He then replaced the 24 h.p. *Antoinette* engine with a more powerful model and finally on 12th November he flew 722 feet and was airborne for over 21

Santos-Dumont's 14-Bis – *1906.* (via J. M. Curry)

seconds. This flight was officially witnessed and became the first F.A.I. recognised world record for distance and time. *Le Petit Santos,* as he was fondly called (he was only five feet tall), once again became the toast of all France and a banquet was held in his honour. He was considered 'the greatest aviator in France if not the whole world'! Blériot later told him 'You are the pathfinder. We who come after merely follow.' *Le Figaro* claimed '... The air is truly conquered. Santos has flown. Everybody will fly.' The Wrights' achievements were conveniently ignored!

Sir Alfred Harmsworth (or Lord Northcliffe since December 1905) seized on these flights as an opportunity to make the conquest of the air essentially a *Daily Mail* exclusive. He told his news editor, who had 'buried' the story, 'It does not matter how far he has flown. He has shown what can be done. In a year's time, mark my words, that fellow will be flying over here from France. Britain is no longer an island. Nothing so important has happened for a very long time. We must get hold of this thing and make it our own ...' Soon the *Mail* was speculating that 'aerial motor cars', as Lord Northcliffe liked to call them, would be so familiar that the very roads would disappear when it became 'possible to voyage through space'.

Northcliffe further demonstrated his strong belief in powered flight by offering a prize of £10,000 (an enormous sum in those days) for the

Lord Northcliffe (on the left), a very generous sponsor of pioneer aviation, with Orville Wright in France. (via J. M. Curry)

first flight from London to Manchester, a distance of some 180 miles. This caused considerable derision in the London Press. The *Punch* magazine was particularly biting in its satire, offering its own prizes including one for 'a genuine flight of fancy' – to fly to Mars and return within a week! Northcliffe joined the Aero Club but further emphasised his complete faith in 'aerial motor cars' by appointing the first Air Correspondent. Harry Harper, an entertainments critic with a London journal, had approached Northcliffe to sponsor the construction of a glider he had designed. 'The Chief', as he was known, was impressed with Hawker's knowledge and his contacts in the aviation world. He declined to finance his glider but instead offered him the post of air correspondent of the *Daily Mail*. Harper gladly accepted not least because his monthly salary increased fourfold to £33! He would be present to report all the great pioneer flying events, as well as writing a number of popular books on aviation notably as joint-author with Grahame-White.

Largely due to Harper's prompting Lord Northcliffe decided to sponsor the Model Aeroplane Exhibition and Competition held at the Agricultural Hall in April 1907. The *Daily Mail* offered £250 in prize money for models capable of mechanical flight. The newspaper's advance publicity ensured that the Exhibition was not only well-attended but also attracted over 200 entrants to the competition, some of which were bizarre and fantastic pieces of apparatus. Harper recalled '... it was a mystery to me how the judges managed to maintain a solemn aspect.' Nevertheless the large response showed just how many people were experimenting throughout the country.

Since his letter to *The Times* A. V. Roe had sought a position with the Aeronautical Society and the Aero Club but then he left for the U.S.A.; however, he returned in time to enter three models. The models, which were tested at the Alexandra Palace, were required to complete a distance of one hundred feet to qualify for the first prize of £150. The judges, in their wisdom, decided that none had performed well enough to merit this prize but they awarded Roe £75 for his eight-foot model biplane. It was generally felt that Roe had deserved the first prize, nevertheless he gratefully accepted, the money would help to finance the construction of a full scale biplane. Roe returned to his brother's house (Dr S. Verdon Roe) at Putney and started to build his biplane in the stables at the rear of the property. Earlier in the year both the Admiralty and the War Office again rejected the Wright brothers. In March the Admiralty stated '... aeroplanes would not be of any practical use to the Naval Service', and the War Office replied '... it was not disposed to enter into relations at present with any manufacturers of Aeroplanes ...' Another chance missed.

Colonel Capper had finally persuaded the War Office to finance the construction of an Army airship. Cody was engaged on the work, conducted under great secrecy at Farnborough; his direct responsibility was the engine – a 50 h.p. *Antoinette*. The Dirigible No 1 (known as

Nulli Secundus *flew over central London in October, 1907.* (Science & Society Picture Library)

Nulli Secundus or 'Second to None') was 122 feet long and 26 feet in diameter with a capacity of 55,000 cubic feet and was first flown at Farnborough Common in September. On 10th October it appeared in the skies above London to the loud accompaniment of a klaxon horn. The airship, crewed by Capper and Cody with the latter acting as pilot, flew low over Buckingham Palace and circled St Paul's Cathedral but strong head-winds frustrated its return to Farnborough in triumph; Cody landed it safely in the grounds of the Crystal Palace. The following morning the newspapers proclaimed 'Mastery of the Air', *Nulli Secundus* had completed fifty miles in 3 hours and 25 minutes. Five days later it was still marooned at Crystal Palace when a storm blew up and in a hurried attempt to secure the airship the skin envelope was cut and it deflated. In 1908 a larger airship, *Nulli Secundus II*, was built and first flown in July but by the end of August it was also dismantled.

In July Horatio F. Phillips is reputed to have made a flight of almost five hundred feet in his *Multi-plane* at Streatham. Phillips, a veteran inventor aged sixty-two, had been experimenting with flying machines since the 1860s. His distinctly odd machine had two hundred tiny aerofoils slatted in four tandem frames, somewhat resembling venetian

32

blinds. There were claims that Phillips achieved the first powered flight in the United Kingdom, though it was certainly not widely nor officially recognised as such, as the machine lacked any real control and there was insufficient evidence to warrant the claim.

By September, Roe had completed his aeroplane – *Roe I*; a canard biplane mounted on an undercarriage consisting of two pairs of main wheels spaced well apart. The twin-bladed propeller was driven by a 6 h.p. JAP motor-cycle engine built by J. A. Prestwich of Tottenham and situated behind the pilot. He required a large but secluded open space to test the machine and was fortunate to obtain permission to use the new motor-car racing track at Brooklands near Weybridge, Surrey.

The many enthusiastic motorists who wished to race their motor-cars had been compelled to travel to Europe in order to take advantage of the higher speed limits, that is until Hugh F. Locke King decided to transform his large estate at Brooklands into the first purpose-built racing track complete with high banked curves and facilities for drivers and spectators. The track was formally opened on 17th June 1907 with races and a splendid motorcade. For thirty-two years Brooklands was the Mecca for motor-car racing and in 1910 it also became renowned as a major centre of aviation.

Horatio F. Phillips' odd Multi-plane of 1907. (Science & Society Picture Library)

A.V. Roe's Biplane at Brooklands, 1908. (Via L. Harris)

The Clerk of the Course, E. de Rodakowski, somewhat reluctantly allowed Roe to erect a small hut alongside the finishing straight to house his machine and act as his workshop; it was only twenty feet wide so the biplane with a wing span of thirty-six feet had to go in sideways! By December Roe began his first trials of the biplane; he was keen to claim the latest *Daily Mail* prize – £100 for the first *British* aviator to complete a round flight of a quarter of a mile and back. It soon was apparent that the engine was not powerful enough to get the biplane airborne and Roe had to rely on friendly motorists to tow it like a glider behind their cars. As he could not afford to purchase a larger engine, he sought other ways out of his dilemma.

Roe was not the only aspiring aviator at Brooklands. John T. C. Moore-Brabazon was also engaged in trials. He recalled that Brooklands was then 'wholly unsuitable for aviation experiments, it consisted of the track alone with spiked railings to the side.' Moore-Brabazon had asked the Short brothers to make him a glider, which they completed for £25, and it was the first heavier-than-air machine built by them. A motoring friend and fellow Aero Club member, Howard Wright, adapted the glider to carry a 16/18 h.p. *Buchet* engine with a four-bladed propeller. The tests were unsuccessful and it was converted back to a glider. Moore-Brabazon, an aeronaut and motor-car racing driver, was a close friend of Rolls and had acted as his mechanic. Not far away at Farnborough Cody had also started constructing a biplane under great secrecy. He had been granted £50 by the War Office, and at first he utilised the *Antoinette* engine, which had powered *Nulli Secundus I.* Roe was probably blissfully unaware of Cody's project. Thus the year closed with at least some tentative if painful steps being taken to achieve powered flight in Great Britain.

Across the Channel French aviators were forging ahead. Earlier in 1907 a new figure had appeared on the scene – Léon Delagrange; a sculptor who had purchased one of the Voisins' first aeroplanes. In April he was airborne for about forty seconds at Bagatelle, though the machine was totally destroyed on landing! Throughout the summer and well into the autumn Blériot had been persevering with great determination and courage with his various monoplanes, but had also gained an unenviable reputation for his many spectacular accidents. By mid-December he had completed no less than six flights. Both airmen were rather eclipsed by the appearance and exploits in October of a most influential pioneer aviator – Henry (or Henri as he was known in France) Farman. He was born in Paris of English parents, educated in France and knew little English; he later made it clear that he considered himself thoroughly French although he did not become a French citizen until 1937. Farman, a motor-car racing driver, owned a large and successful motor-car business in Paris in partnership with his brothers

A Voisin biplane of 1908.

35

Maurice and Richard. After several gliding experiments Farman purchased a Voisin biplane and on 26th October he flew 2,530 feet at Issy, thus achieving the second officially recognised distance record. A longer flight was made on 13th January 1908 when he completed a circuit of 1,625 feet lasting one minute and twenty-eight seconds; it gained him the *Deutsch/Archdeacon* prize of 50,000 francs (about £2,000) for the first flight to cover a kilometre.

The Times, which barely two years earlier had ridiculed powered flight, now claimed 'The Conquest of the Air ... success of an Englishman! ... nothing of this kind has ever been accomplished ...' – so much for the Wright brothers! During 1908 Farman and Delagrange, who were close friends, would take Europe by storm, setting distance and time records, making the first flights in Belgium and Italy and taking up the first passengers in Europe.

With all this great enthusiasm for the remarkable new form of transport, H. G. Wells warned of the possible aggressive use of both aeroplanes and airships in a future war. The first part of his new serial, *War in the Air*, – appeared in January 1908 and later episodes contained stark and dire warnings of the perils that might lay ahead; they vividly described 'death and destruction to civilians – men, women and children – in cities far from the front line.' Few people at the time heeded such prophecies, after all in those exciting and innocent pioneer days, flying was considered nothing more than a daring, amazing and exciting if somewhat dangerous sport.

By the spring Cody was almost ready to trial his biplane and Roe had managed to secure the loan of a 24 h.p. *Antoinette* engine and was eagerly awaiting its arrival. It was clear to him that the Brooklands track manager barely suffered his presence there; he restricted his trials to either early morning or late evening, and Roe had to lift his fragile machine over the spiked railings to get onto the track. Rodakowski considered that Roe's 'rickety flying machine' brought his track into disrepute. When the engine finally arrived Roe had to make modifications to his biplane, not least to extend the wing area to account for the greater engine weight. By early June he began his first tentative taxiing trials and on the 8th he was up at dawn as usual. It was on this day as Roe later recalled, 'I was able to realise my dreams by making some of the first short aeroplane flights in England' – 'hop flights' covering distances of 75 to 150 feet; they were not officially recognised because of the lack of official witnesses. Nevertheless there is a stone pillar with a plaque at Brooklands commemorating his experiments at this time and also a modern replica of the biplane and its shed.

The honour of being the first person to fly in Britain fell to Cody with his large biplane, *British Army Aeroplane No 1*. On 19th September he is reputed to have been airborne for a distance of two hundred feet, but it was his flight from Laffan's Plain on 16th October when he reached a height of thirty feet and a distance of 1,390 feet that is officially recognised as the first powered flight in Great Britain. The flight unfortunately ended with a heavy crash-landing but Cody escaped relatively unharmed.

These first flights in Britain were as nothing compared with what the Wright brothers achieved in America and more especially in France. On 6th May they finally resumed flying with a vengeance with their *Flyer III*, known as Type A, at Kitty Hawk. It had been provided with a more powerful engine and had been variously modified, most noticeably with a seat for a passenger alongside the pilot, both sitting upright – the prone position had been abandoned. There were two reasons to explain their return to flying. The U.S. Signals Corps had established an Aeronautical Division in the previous August and it was now seeking tenders for a flying machine that would carry a passenger and sufficient fuel for 125 miles and be capable of flying at least ten miles at a speed of 40 m.p.h.; the Wrights had been asked to submit a machine for trial. Secondly the brothers had finally come to an agreement with a syndicate of French businessmen to build and sell their machines in France under licence, providing that satisfactory demonstration flights were made in France.

For eight days the brothers completed a number of flights all exceeding 1,000 feet and on the 14th Charles W. Furnas, a mechanic from Dayton, became the first person to be carried as a passenger. Orville returned home to Dayton to prepare for the Signal Corps' trials at Fort Meyer, Virginia in September, whilst Wilbur left for France. They were on the brink of international fame and recognition. Wilbur arrived in France on 28th May and set up a workshop on the edge of Hunaudières racecourse at Le Mans some 120 miles south-west of Paris. *Flyer III* finally arrived at Le Havre during June and to Wilbur's dismay the machine was virtually in pieces; however, he set about rebuilding it, working night and day. Fortunately close by was the motor-car factory owned by Léon Bollée, who generously placed his facilities at Wilbur's disposal. The French press had previously described the Wrights as *blaffeurs* and 'bicycle peddlers' and the

Cody's large biplane – British Army Aeroplane No 1 – *at Farnborough.*

inordinate long delay before attempting a flight in France only increased their scepticism, bets were being taken as to whether Wilbur Wright would even get off the ground let alone fly any distance!

At long last Wilbur intimated that he was ready for his first flight on Saturday 8th August. The news travelled fast, crowds flocked to the racecourse and all the leading figures in French aviation gathered to witness the event. Although he was only airborne for one minute and forty-five seconds, he nevertheless astonished and captivated the spectators with the consummate skill and ease by which he banked, turned, circled and landed, it was a complete and utter revelation to them – 'We beheld the great white bird soar above the racecourse'. The reporter from *Le Figaro* could barely contain his excitement, 'I've seen him. Yes! I have today seen Wilbur Wright and his great white bird.' *The Times* more soberly judged 'The Wrights deserved conclusively the first place in the history of flying ...' Blériot was deeply impressed by his mastery of control, 'Monsieur Wright has us all in his hands ... we are as children compared to the Wrights ...', and Delagrange soberly observed '... Well we are all beaten.'

Wilbur made a number of flights from the racecourse 'to satisfy the crowds' before he was invited by the military to move his camp to the more spacious military field at nearby Camp d'Auvours, which became the mecca for anybody interested in flying, as well as the cream of Parisian society. The French public took *Vilbare* to their hearts, he became 'the Hero of the Hour' or 'the poet of flight' – the most celebrated person of the day. Wilbur was modest and unassuming, he declined an invitation to speak at an *Aéro-Club* with the famous comment: 'I know of only one bird – the parrot – that talks: and it can't fly very high'! His flying attire was a neat black business suit with a stiff collar and black tie but always wearing an old green peaked cap, which was copied and sold in its thousands – known as *Veelburs*.

The news from Orville in America during early September was equally encouraging. He had completed many successful flights in the process setting nine world records and greatly impressing the military men, several had flown as passengers. On 17th September disaster struck, whilst Orville was flying with Lieutenant Thomas E. Selfridge of the Signals Corps, the biplane suffered a propeller failure and

Wilbur Wright with a passenger flying his 'Great White Bird' – France, 1908.
(via J. M. Curry)

crashed. Orville was seriously injured and tragically Selfridge was killed, the first person to die in an aeroplane accident. Orville spent almost two months in hospital. Despite the disturbing news Wilbur carried on doggedly from Camp d'Auvours, indeed on 21st September he completed a major endurance flight of forty-one miles. Up to the end of the year Wilbur completed one hundred flights and carried over sixty passengers.

Perhaps his most important passengers, at least as far as British aviation was concerned, were four members of the Aero Club; on 8th October they became the first resident Englishmen to fly with Wilbur. They were Griffith Brewer, Charles Rolls, Frank H. Butler and Major Baden-Powell; the latter maintained 'that Wilbur Wright is in possession of a power which controls the fate of nations is beyond doubt.' Rolls had already ordered a *Flyer* from the production company formed by the French syndicate. He later described his first flight '... there is nothing so fascinating or exhilarating as flying. It gives one an entirely new lease of life ... the fact of accomplishing what several eminent scientists have "proved" impossible gave also an added satisfaction.' The four men returned to England to spread the news to anybody that cared to listen; the Short brothers wisely judged that '... this means the end of ballooning'!

With the renewed interest engendered by Wilbur's flights in France, Lord Northcliffe once again came to the fore to encourage flying. On 5th October the *Daily Mail* offered a prize of £500 for the first aviator to fly across the English Channel in either direction before the end of the year. The *Mail's* representative in France was instructed to approach Wright and offer him a sum *just* to enter the competition. He refused on the advice of Orville as there was some doubt about the reliability of their engine.

After Cody's successful flight from Laffan's Plain, further funds were requested to continue the Balloon Factory's experiments with aeroplanes, including Dunne's trials with gliders and his tail-less aeroplane. In July 1907 in order to preserve the secrecy of the project, Capper arranged with his friend the Marquess of Tullibardine for Dunne to use the secluded Scottish estate at Blair Atholl for further trials. Dunne was not particularly successful, although in December 1908 he claimed that his 'test' pilot, Lieutenant Lancelot D. Gibbs, had flown for a distance of 120 feet. However, the Treasury was not predisposed to approve further funds for research yet. In October a sub-committee of the Committee for Imperial Defence was formed under the chairmanship of Viscount Esher, its brief was to examine all aspects of aerial navigation and the military advantages that might accrue from airships and aeroplanes. The sub-committee welcomed written evidence but Sir Hiram Maxim, Charles Rolls, Colonel Capper and Major Baden-Powell were specifically called upon to give their expert opinions in person. The report did not appear until late February 1909 and its recommendations had a considerable impact on military aviation.

For some months the Aeronautical Society had been actively seeking a suitable site close to London to use as an Experimental Flying Ground for its members. The most ardent proponent in the matter was Baden-Powell. By December an area of reclaimed land near Dagenham Dock, Essex had been selected and members were requested to subscribe to a fund for the preparation of the land, the erection of sheds and a clubhouse. On November 9th the Society granted honorary membership to the Wright brothers; four days earlier Wilbur had received the Grand Gold Medal from the *Aéro-Club de France*.

Besides Cody, Roe and Dunne the Aero Club reckoned that at least

41

Moore-Brabazon's Voisin biplane – The Bird of Passage.

thirty flying machines had been or were in the process of being constructed throughout the country and it was thought that several may be capable of 'short hops'. Some of these pioneer constructors became celebrated in the world of aviation – Frederick Handley Page, Geoffrey de Havilland, Howard Wright and Robert Blackburn – whilst others disappeared almost without trace. No British machine was exhibited at the Automobile Salon of the Grand Palais in Paris on 24th December 1908 – the first time aeroplanes were displayed. The number of French machines on show only emphasised just how far Britain lagged behind in the aviation field. However, there was one aspiring British aviator who was taking positive steps to join the exclusive European 'birdmen' – Moore-Brabazon. After his unsuccessful trials at Brooklands, he travelled to Paris and bought a machine from the Voisins, which he named *The Bird of Passage*. Moore-Brabazon received flying instruction at Issy as well as gaining experience alongside Farman at his airfield near Châlons.

It was fitting that Wilbur Wright brought a memorable year to a close with a remarkable flight. On 31st December he flew for seventy-seven miles and was airborne for over two hours and ten minutes – a world record – gaining the *Michelin Trophy*, (donated by André and

Edouard – French tyre manufacturers) and 20,000 francs for the longest circuit flight of the year. Orville, almost fully recovered from his injuries, accompanied by their sister Katherine, arrived in France a few days later to share in Wilbur's success. It had taken almost five years for the world to accept their achievements and accord them the credit and recognition they richly deserved. During 1908 they had proved beyond doubt that they were the 'true masters of flight'.

3

THE AIR IS
CONQUERED
(1909)

'In the history of the aeroplane, no year stands out more prominently than does 1909. It was a year of such remarkable achievements aerially, that ordinary people, as well as those specially interested in aviation, began to realize that the air had really been conquered and that a new era in transportation was dawning' – so wrote Claude Grahame-White, the celebrated pioneer aviator, in his *Flying* published in 1930.

1909 was a year of unprecedented 'aerial' activity throughout the country; Cody, Roe and Moore-Brabazon dominated the flying scene. The first Aeronautical Show opened at Olympia in the spring and the first Air Shows (or Meetings) in Britain were held at Blackpool and Doncaster. Landing grounds were established on the Isle of Sheppey, Brooklands, and briefly at Dagenham and North Fambridge in Essex. The Short brothers became the first aeroplane manufacturers in the country, closely followed by Handley Page. But the highlight was Blériot's successful crossing of the English Channel in July; this not only stimulated countless aspiring aviators but it also captured the public's imagination.

The increased public awareness of aviation was further enlivened by the appearance of a number of specialised journals: *Aeronautics*, *Aerocraft* and *The Airship*; hitherto the subject had been largely covered by motor-car magazines. In January the first edition of *Flight* (now *Flight International*) was published with Moore-Brabazon's biplane featuring on the cover. Later *The Aero* arrived on the scene with Charles G. Grey as joint-editor. Grey, a trained engineer, had reported on aviation for *The Autocar* since 1906. In 1911 he founded *The Aeroplane*, the most popular aviation magazine, which he edited until 1939 and in the process became a living legend; his was the dominant voice in all matters concerning flying – both military and civil. His trenchant and forthright views carried considerable influence and he witnessed and commented on British aviation matters from the first flights to the inaugural turbo-jet passenger service in 1952. He died the following year aged seventy-eight.

France was undoubtedly in the vanguard of aviation. On 7th January its *Aéro-Club* issued its first *brevets* (certificates) to *pilote-aviateurs*. Blériot and Farman were among the first to be accredited, Wilbur Wright received 'No 15'. He had moved to winter quarters at Pau in south-west France, where a large flying field at Pont-Long had been provided for him and he established a flying school. Hopeful aviators, celebrities, politicians and royalty flocked there to meet the Wrights; Lord Northcliffe presented Wilbur to King Edward VII, who was wintering at nearby Biarritz, but he declined the offer of a flight! Roe made 'the pilgrimage' to Pau, he gamely cycled the four hundred or so miles from Calais.

Cody was continuing his experiments at Farnborough and on 9th January he flew his biplane with streamers attached to check the airflow; eleven days later he achieved a flight of 1,200 feet but damaged the machine on landing. Towards the end of January Viscount Esher presented his report on military aviation to the Government. It recommended that £35,000 be allocated to the Admiralty for non-rigid airships and £10,000 to the War Office for them to replace captive balloons. As far as aeroplanes were concerned, the report concluded that the experiments at Farnborough should be discontinued and 'advantage be taken of private enterprise in this form of aviation'. The report was approved on 25th February, thus from March Cody and Dunne were released from their posts and allowed to retain their machines but not the engines! Winston Churchill, then President of the Board of Trade, considered this proposal was '... too amateurish. The problem of the use of aeroplanes is a most important one, and we should place ourselves in communication with Mr Wright and avail ourselves of his knowledge.' Churchill became the most dedicated supporter and advocate of military aeroplanes. Rolls, who was a Captain in the Army Motor Reserve, proposed that he should be given facilities at Farnborough for his French-Wright Flyer (still on order) and he would then place his experience and aeroplane at the disposal of the War Office; it was another year before a Flyer was bought by the Government.

During February Griffith Brewer finally secured some suitable land for the Aero Club's flying ground – at Shellbeach near Leysdown on the Isle of Sheppey. The Club set up its headquarters at nearby Mussel Manor and Brewer persuaded the Shorts to move from Battersea to Leysdown. William Harbrow Ltd of St Mary Cray, Kent erected a factory building for the Shorts and also a couple of 'sheds' for the use of Club members. Harbrow 'sheds' were later used by many pioneer airmen throughout the country. The term 'hangar' had not yet come into common usage, it was derived from a French word, which originally described a covered space for a carriage.

Oswald and Eustace had been joined by their elder brother Horace, a talented engineer and designer, and the brothers founded the first company in Britain to build aeroplanes; their breakthrough came when they were contracted to build six Wright Flyer Type As under licence. Brewer was instrumental in this contract as he was the Wrights' Patent Agent in Britain. Horace travelled to France to make accurate drawings of the French-Wright aeroplane.

The first International Aeronautical Show held in Britain opened on 19th March at Olympia under the auspices of the Aero Club. It became an annual event of increasing importance in the coming years as the British aeroplane industry developed. There were eleven full-scale models on view, of which only three were British and only one had actually flown – Moore-Brabazon's *The Bird of Passage*. There were thirty-six engines displayed as well as numerous other exhibits. The British machines were constructed by Howard Wright, the Shorts and Frederick Handley Page. Wright also worked from a railway arch at Battersea and he displayed a Voisin-type biplane; he was one of the country's leading designers albeit for a brief period. The Shorts showed their biplane, S.1, which had been designed for Frank McLean. Handley Page exhibited an incomplete small monoplane that he had built for José Weiss. Page, an electrical engineer, had joined the somewhat moribund Aeronautical Society in 1907. He was co-opted onto its technical 'Wings Committee' where he met Weiss, a Hungarian living at Amberley, Sussex. Weiss had experimented with gliders with swept-back wings and because of his advancing years had used Eric G. England as his trials pilot. In July 1916 *The Aeroplane* listed some thirty influential pioneers of British aviation prior to 1910 and Weiss as 'the real pioneer of inherent stability' was placed by Charles Grey as second in importance to A. V. Roe – some standing! Handley Page operated from a small workshop in Woolwich, where he made a precarious living from making propellers for airships and aeroplanes, but he had far greater ambitions. In June (17th) he formed the first *Limited* Company to design and manufacture aeroplanes, which would be in the forefront of British aviation until its demise in 1970. Despite the paucity of aeroplanes on display, the Show, which lasted nine days, was considered a modest success, it certainly generated considerable interest. Lord Northcliffe through his *Daily Mail* decided later to offer £1,000 for the first *British* aviator to complete a circuit of one mile in an *all-British* aeroplane.

Although the Wrights had rather stolen the thunder from French aviators, Blériot, Levasseur, Farman and Santos Dumont were determined to equal or even surpass their technical advantage. On 23rd January Blériot first flew his latest monoplane – XI – powered by an Italian Anzani engine; it was the first really successful 'tractor' aeroplane, that is the propeller pulling the machine and placed in front of the engine and the main wings, as opposed to the 'pusher' aeroplane where the propeller was sited behind the engine, the wings and the aviator. The Blériot XI became one of the most popular monoplanes of the day, flown by many early airmen. Farman, displeased with the Voisins for their duplicity in selling the biplane they were building for him to another customer (Moore-Brabazon), set about designing and

Blériot XI – one of the most popular monoplanes of the day. On display at the White City, Manchester – March 1910?

47

Farman III – a classic aeroplane of all time.

building his own biplane, really a modified Voisin. However, it was the first to be fitted with ailerons (moveable surfaces fitted to the trailing edges of wings to control rolling movements) and first flew on 6th April; in the summer it was fitted with the revolutionary Gnôme rotary engine designed by the Seguin brothers, Louis and Laurent. This engine developed a remarkable amount of power for its weight and powered many early aeroplanes. The Farman III became one of the classic aeroplanes and was copied the world over.

Moore-Brabazon, or 'Brab' to his friends, erected two small sheds on Lord Carnarvon's estate at Seven Barrows near Beacon Hill to the south of Newbury, Berkshire, to house and trial his Voisin. However, he thought it more convenient to install *The Bird of Passage* at Shorts' works at Leysdown, and it was from here during 29th April/2nd May that he completed three flights of 450, 600 and 1,500 feet at a height of about 50 feet; his final landing practically destroyed the biplane but he 'survived without a scratch'. They were the first recognised flights by a *resident* Englishman in Britain. 'Brab' was now determined to claim the *Mail*'s £1,000 prize and approached the Shorts to build him a machine, S.2, powered by a British engine.

In early May the Wrights arrived in England *en route* to the States; they were dined, feted and presented with two awards. On 4th May they were taken by Rolls to visit the Aero Club's flying ground and Shorts' factory. Their visit was recorded by the now famous photograph – a unique group of pioneer airmen. When they returned to America it was to a heroes' welcome in New York, Washington and

A unique group of pioneer airmen – 4th May 1909. Back row from left: T.D.F. Andrews (Owner of Mussel Manor), Oswald, Horace and Eustace Short, Francis McClean, Griffith Brewer, Frank Butler, W.S. Lockyer, Warwick Wright. Front row from left: Moore-Brabazon, Wilbur and Orville Wright, the Hon. C.S. Rolls. (via M. Murray)

in their hometown Dayton. During July they were back at Fort Meyer, Virginia giving further flying demonstrations to the U.S. Army. On 2nd August the U.S. Signals Unit purchased its first Wright aeroplane for $25,000 plus an additional $5,000 because it had exceeded 40 m.p.h.! Finally they had been accepted as 'prophets in their own country'.

Britain's 'own' American, Cody, had been granted a short-term contract by the War Office, along with a 'portable' shed at Laffan's Plain and the 'loan' of the *Antoinette* engine to continue his work on his biplane. His fellow experimenter, Dunne had gained financial backing from the Blair Atholl Syndicate and continued his experiments over the next few years. On 14th May Cody flew a distance of just over a mile and landed safely. Nevertheless he continued to modify and improve his biplane and in August he tried out a more powerful French ENV engine. Cody had added a passenger seat and was ready for his next venture. On 14th August Colonel Capper came to see the progress he had made, after all Cody was still being supported by the War Office. A larger crowd than normal gathered to watch his flight; Capper was treated to a mile-long passenger flight no doubt in grateful appreciation for his steadfast and loyal support. When they landed Lela volunteered to take a flight with him. She was dressed in what would become *de rigueur* for the many fashionable ladies who would 'take to

'Madame' Cody was the first woman in Britain to fly as a passenger.

the air with a flying man' in the near future. 'Madame' Cody's hat was firmly secured with a scarf and her long and full skirt tightly fastened by a cord around the ankles, which is reputed to have directly led to a new fashion – the hobble skirt. She became the first woman to fly as a passenger in Britain. A week later Leon and Frank, Cody's fourteen-year old son, were taken up and soon people queued for the privilege of a flight with Cody, who jokingly dubbed his aeroplane 'The World's first aerial omnibus'. In September Cody covered over forty miles – a world record for a cross-country flight – declaring that he was ready to bid for the *Daily Mail*'s London to Manchester prize – he was then well ahead of anybody else in Britain.

Roe had been beavering away at Putney designing a triplane. John Prestwich, a motor-cycle engineer, entered into partnership with him providing a much-needed £100. They had received an order for another triplane from George Friswell, the British agent for Peugeot motor-cars. Roe had built most of the two machines in sections and now needed space to assemble and trial them. He was no longer welcome at Brooklands but was convinced that the War Office would allow him to share Farnborough Common with Cody. However, it was made clear that the War Office was 'not disposed to provide facilities for amateur

Bull's Eye *Triplane at Lea Marshes in July 1909.* (Science & Society Picture Library)

51

experimenters of aeroplanes ... they were a waste of time ... '! With grim determination Roe cycled around the outskirts of London looking at every available stretch of open land; Hackney Marshes, Wimbledon Common and Wormwood Scrubs were all considered but permission was refused by the various authorities. Finally he discovered a couple of derelict railway arches close to Lea Marshes, Essex, which the Great Eastern Railway agreed to lease at a nominal rent. Shortly after Roe moved there, he was in dispute with Friswell and his triplane was never completed. During May he tested his machine, his trials created considerable local interest, the many spectators, who watched his antics with a certain amazement and no small amusement, dubbed him 'The Hopper'. Notwithstanding the £100 investment Roe still could not afford a lighter and more powerful engine, and in order to compensate for the heavy JAP engine, he had constructed the triplane of wood and covered it with yellow oiled paper. It had a wing-span of twenty feet and was twenty feet long; it really was a most flimsy and fragile machine.

On 13th July after many setbacks Roe managed to coax his triplane off the ground and was airborne for about one hundred feet. Two days later he made another short flight but damaged the undercarriage on landing. Then on the 23rd he achieved a flight of nine hundred feet at a height of ten feet and could have travelled farther but for a row of trees directly in his path, he was forced to land swiftly as he had not yet mastered the art of turning! The triplane landed gently, Roe had become the first Briton to fly in an all-British aeroplane. After months upon months of careful and patient tests he had achieved his dream, but he still had a very long way to go before he could lay claim to the various prizes on offer. As the newspapers commented '... that he is able to fly at all with such little power shows that Mr Roe is on the right lines ...'. In August Roe proudly painted *Avroplane* onto the fuselage, the first of so many successful Avro aircraft.

By coincidence not many miles from Lea Marshes, Handley Page was establishing the foundations of Handley Page Limited. In June he moved from Woolwich to a large workshop at Creekmouth near Barking, Essex where some adjacent open land was available for trials. With considerable enterprise he advertised freely in the aviation journals that he was prepared to construct aeroplanes directly based on clients' designs and moreover was actively seeking and appointing agents in all parts of the country. In fact Handley Page was willing to undertake any aeronautical work in order to develop his Company.

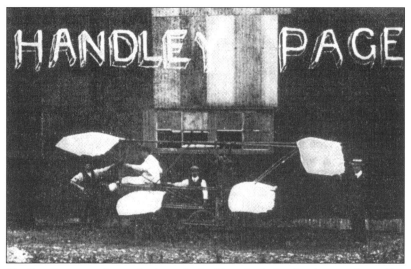

Handley Page's works at Creekmouth, Barking. Saul Quadruplane on its trolley. (via B. Smith)

Over the other side of the Thames Estuary several Aero Club members were waiting patiently for their Short-Wright aeroplanes that were still under construction. The airframes had been completed in June but the engines, built by Léon Bollée to a Wright design, did not arrive for another three months. Rolls had ordered two, Frank McLean, the Hon. Maurice Egerton, Alec Ogilvie and Cecil Grace the other four; each cost £1,000. There is no doubt that Roe would have dearly wished to have such a large sum available to advance his experiments; clear evidence of the chasm in British aviation then between the struggling designers such as Cody, Roe, de Havilland and Blackburn compared with the wealthy aviators – Rolls, Moore-Brabazon, McClean *et al*.

Several members were unhappy with the uneven surface of the Club's landing ground as it was crossed by drainage dykes. By the autumn Frank McLean had located and acquired a more favourable site at Eastchurch just a few miles away, it provided a clear run of a mile or so free of ruts and dykes. He leased it to the Club on very nominal terms – £1 per annum. In October, 1910 the Short Brothers also moved into Eastchurch to share the landing ground, which Brab considered 'a decent aerodrome'. Eastchurch quickly became a hub of aviation activity and manufacture and there is a fine memorial in the village commemorating this home of pioneer aviation.

The Aeronautical Society were not so fortunate in their choice of a Testing Ground at Dagenham; although it would be fair to say that it had not been universally approved by members and there was considerable debate about the site and the costs involved in its preparation. By June much of the work had been completed and four members were already in residence. G. Deverall Saul's rather strange tandem biplane, built by Handley Page, had already been trialled there with Page as 'operator' and it was reputed to have made some 'hops'. Major Baden-Powell's quadruplane was housed in a shed that he shared with Saul. C. A. Moreing, an Australian mining engineer, had his Voisin biplane in another shed and John V. Neale had selected Dagenham in preference to the Aero Club's ground at Shellbeach to trial his monoplane – *Pup*.

A 'Special Day' was arranged for 18th August and some seventy or so members along with guests attended as well as 'lots of newspaper photographers'. Many travelled from London in the Society's 'Aeronautical special train' – a rather grandiloquent title for what was basically open goods wagons from which the elegantly dressed gentlemen and ladies had to dismount by way of a ladder! The weather was not favourable and there was no flying but the various machines were on display and Moreing's airship was on view but deflated. Really the most positive outcome of the 'Special Day' was that the members agreed to award Cody the Society's silver medal for 'his services to aeronautics'. The Dagenham Experimental Ground was unsuitable in many respects, one member described it scathingly as 'a weed preserve' and *The Aero* reported that 'the grounds will need a great deal of improving before they can be considered good … not a blade of grass was visible …'! By the end of the year it had fallen into disuse and of the four resident experimenters only Neale later produced a successful machine at Brooklands. Handley Page bought some of the buildings for his nearby Barking factory but the financial loss was still being hotly debated by members in the following year. In 1925 the Ford Motor Company Ltd. built their large car factory on part of the site.

Another landing ground in Essex also proved to be 'a white elephant'. Noel Pemberton-Billing, a yacht salesman, sometime gun-runner and entrepreneur of some style, had experimented with kites as well as designing a few monoplanes. He acquired a considerable stretch of marshland at Fambridge with the intention of offering facilities to aeroplane experimenters; two large sheds were erected and plans were in hand to establish a flying school with a row of cottages to house the airmen. This rather isolated landing ground did attract Howard Wright and José Weiss but the most active tenant was Robert F. Macfie. He was born in America of Scottish parents and had spent some time in France studying the methods of Wright and Blériot. Within six weeks Macfie had completed his monoplane powered by a 35 h.p. JAP engine and it was thought that he managed a short flight at Fambridge but also suffered several crashes. His monoplane was considered 'comparable with the best of the period'. Macfie, like the other aviators, found the marshy land unsuitable for trials and he moved to Foulness Island, Essex but the War Office moved him out. He was not allowed to experiment in France, so he returned to England to try his luck at Portholme, Huntingdon and later settled at Brooklands. As for Pemberton-Billing, this setback did not deter such an ebulliant character, he remained in aviation and later established Pemberton-Billing Ltd at Woolston, Southampton to build 'Surpermarine' Flying Lifeboats.

All this aviation activity, such as it was, paled into insignificance compared with what happened over the English Channel in July. The *Daily Mail* had increased its prize money to £1,000 for the first aerial crossing. Four aviators had expressed their interest – Blériot, Farman, the Comte de Lambert and Hubert Latham – although in the event only Blériot and Latham attempted the crossing. There was great interest and speculation in the newspapers on both sides of the Channel. Charles, Comte de Lambert, who had been instructed by the Wrights at Pau, brought his French-Wright Flyer to Wissant, where he set up his headquarters. Latham was an Englishman permanently residing in Paris, he was a great adventurer, who had the means to live life to the full – motor-boat racing, big-game hunting and now flying; he bought an *Antoinette* and learned to fly at Issy, proving to be a 'natural' pilot. Accompanied by Levasseur, Latham set up camp at Sangatte near Calais. Blériot was the last to appear; on 13th July he had completed a cross-country flight of over twenty-five miles to win a prize of 4,500 francs but he suffered burns on his foot as a result of his petrol tank exploding. When he did arrive at Les Baracques, just north of Calais, he was walking with the aid of crutches but as he told a reporter, 'If I cannot walk, I will show the world that I can fly'!

Latham stole a march on his competitors when early on 19th July he

Hubert Latham's Antoinette *over the English Channel.*

made his attempt. Flying at an altitude of about 1,000 feet he seemed to be going well until after about seven miles the engine failed and Latham ditched in the Channel. It was said that he was sitting on his floating machine calmly smoking a cigarette, whilst waiting to be rescued by his escort vessel, *Harpon*. He returned to Calais and immediately ordered another *Antoinette* from Paris.

Blériot waited for favourable weather conditions and early in the morning of 25th July he decided they were right. He made a short test flight before setting off at 4.35 a.m. for the English coast preceded by his escort vessel, the French destroyer *Essopette*, which had on board a concerned Madame Blériot; because of the number of accidents and mishaps he had suffered during his flying career, Blériot had promised that this would be his last flight. He soon passed the *Essopette* but the English coast was shrouded in mist. As he recalled for the *Daily Mail* '... I am alone I can see nothing at all – *rien du tout*! For ten minutes I am lost. It is a strange position to be alone, unguided, without compass, in the air over the middle of the Channel ... A break in the coast appeared to my right, just before Dover Castle. I was madly happy. I headed for it. I was above ground! ...' Blériot landed heavily on Northfall Meadow to the east of the Castle, his flight had lasted thirty-seven minutes. He was met by a policeman and a few soldiers but a little later he was interviewed by a Customs officer from Dover, who

Louis and Madame Blériot at Les Baracques before his epic flight. The wings detached for easy storage.

with some initiative issued him with a quarantine certificate treating his aeroplane as if it was a yacht and Blériot the owner and master! The Customs Collector at Dover wrote to his Board in London '... a time may come when this Dept. will have to treat their arrival seriously and take steps to ensure that no opportunity be given for the Revenue interest to suffer through indiscriminate landings of airships [sic] in this country.' Obviously he was convinced about the future of aeroplanes.'

The Comte de Lambert abandoned his attempt but Latham saw no objection to being the *second* aviator to cross the Channel. Two days later he set off on his second attempt, and when news of his proposed flight became known thousands of spectators crammed the pier and seafront at Dover. There was great excitement when his small aeroplane was sighted but when it was less than a mile from the coast, the engine failed and Latham had again to suffer the ignominy of being pulled out of the sea. These flights created immense public interest and when Gordon Selfridge displayed Blériot's monoplane in his new store in Oxford Street over 120,000 queued and paid to view it. Crowds waited at Victoria station for Blériot's arrival from Dover and many lined the streets to the Savoy Hotel, where a reception was held in his honour. A rapturous welcome awaited him on his return to Paris and orders for his monoplane flooded in. Blériot's fame quickly spread world-wide assuring his place in aviation history.

Blériot's flight also created anxiety in some quarters. The *Daily Graphic* commented '... a machine which can fly from Calais to Dover is not a toy but an instrument of warfare of which soldiers and statesmen must take account ...' H. G. Wells warned: '... we are no longer, from a military point of view, an inaccessible island ...'. Indeed the message 'Britain is no longer an Island' became the banner-cry of the *Daily Mail* as Lord Northcliffe continually exhorted the military authorities to take aeroplanes seriously as weapons of war.

On 22nd August the first International Aviation Meeting (*La Grande Semaine D'Aviation de la Champagne*) opened on the plains of Bétheny near Reims. All the leading French aviators attended to compete for the most generous of prizes donated by the local champagne industry. Latham was there as was Glenn H. Curtiss, an American aviator then barely known in Europe. The only *resident* Briton to enter was George B. Cockburn, who had learned to fly just a month or so earlier. There were thirty-eight entries of which twenty-three managed to get airborne. During the seven days of competitions the large crowds, estimated at over $\frac{1}{2}$ million, were treated to a splendid feast of flying, some 120 successful flights of which most were over three miles. Farman, Latham and Blériot (so much for his last flight!) were the leading prize-winners but Curtiss won the Gordon Bennett trophy with his *Golden Flyer* at a speed of just under 47 m.p.h. He and the Wrights were deadly and bitter rivals and were deeply involved in a legal battle in the States concerning infringements of the Wrights' patents. The meeting attracted many influential political, military and financial figures from all over Europe and marked the beginning of the acceptance of aeroplanes as a serious form of aerial transport rather than 'wealthy men's toys'. It also set the standard for similar events held throughout Europe and the U.S.A. during the next few years. Many of those who attended and witnessed the splendid flying were inspired to enter this brave new world of aviation, be they aspiring airmen, designers, manufacturers or financiers.

Sadly, in September, French aviation lost two leading airmen. On the 7th Eugène Lefevbre, chief pilot of the French Ariel-Wright Company, was killed at Port-Aviation aerodrome at Juvisy outside Paris whilst testing a new Flyer – the first pilot to be killed in a flying accident. Fifteen days later Captain Ferber was killed whilst flying his Voisin biplane at an air show in Boulogne. Both had competed at Reims. In December another French airman, Ferdanez, was killed and early in January 1910 the most experienced Delagrange lost his life in an aerial accident. This new exciting sport had claimed its first victims.

In late September there were signs that the War Office had at long last grudgingly accepted that aeroplanes might have some military use. Three officers, Captains John Fulton, Lancelot Gibbs and Bertram Dickson, were allowed to use their personal aeroplanes for aerial observation during the autumn maneouvres on Salisbury Plain. Nevertheless there were still many senior Army officers opposed to military aeroplanes and cavalry officers claimed that they frightened their horses! Some months earlier Richard Haldane, the Secretary of State for War, had formed an Advisory Committee for Aeronautics with Lord Rayleigh as its Chairman. It is doubtful that this decision had been influenced by the formation, in April, of the Aerial League of the British Empire, pledged to campaign for adequate air defences.

Haldane had long considered that experimental work on aeroplanes should be conducted in a more 'scientific manner' and controlled by a civilian rather than a serving officer. Thus in October the Balloon Factory was removed from control by the War Office and placed directly under the Secretary of State with Mervyn O'Gorman appointed as its first civilian Superintendent. 'O'G', as he was universally known, was a highly qualified and experienced engineer and he selected another talented engineer as his assistant or Works Manager, Frederick Green, who had previously been employed by the Daimler Company at Coventry. Together they established Farnborough as a centre of excellence for experiment and research into all aeronautical matters.

Because of growing public interest two towns, Blackpool and Doncaster, decided to host aviation meetings. Blackpool was organised by the Lancashire Aero Club and the Blackpool Corporation and was officially recognised by the Aero Club as being conducted under F.A.I. rules. Doncaster was not recognised although it was billed as 'England's First Aviation Races'. The Aero Club issued dire warnings to the competitors that if they flew at Doncaster they would be barred from subsequent competitions. Cody was incensed by such threats and became even more determined to fulfil his obligations to the Doncaster Corporation. His appearance alone would ensure large crowds as the British public had taken this most colourful and courageous American to their hearts.

The Doncaster meeting was held at the racecourse and opened on

'England's First Aviation Races' – G.N.R. Poster, 1909. (Science & Society Picture Library)

15th October, a day of high winds and torrential rain. Cody's biplane dwarfed those of his fellow competitors, the large shed in which it was housed was christened *The Cathedral* and the press mistakenly applied this name to his biplane; it almost became Cody's trademark. On the 16th, Cody managed a flight of about 600 yards but crashed heavily on landing, causing considerable damage to his biplane and suffering severe cuts to his face. Nevertheless being the consummate showman, Cody stole the plaudits of the crowd when he swore the Oath of Allegiance and duly signed his British naturalisation papers in full view of the public. He immediately notified the *Daily Mail* of his intention of claiming the £1,000 prize for the first Briton to fly a circular flight of one mile.

Blackpool opened three days later and was blessed initially with good weather. Twelve competitors had entered – mostly French – but only seven managed to fly. Roe brought his triplane, *Bull's-eye*, named in recognition of his brother Humphrey's support; he owned a factory in Manchester making webbing, as well as the famous *Bull's-eye* elastic braces. Unfortunately Roe was unable to get airborne and Farman gained the honour of making the first circuit of the course to the thunderous applause of the large crowd. He gained most of the awards – some £2,400 in total; one flight covered forty-five miles, a British record. But it was Latham who really stole the show with an amazing and fearless flight in the teeth of a gale – acknowledged by fellow airmen to be a remarkable exhibition of flying. Although these two meetings were minor affairs, at least compared with Reims, they demonstrated that there was a demand in Britain for such competitions.

George Holt Thomas, the proprietor of the *Daily Graphic*, was utterly convinced of the bright future for aeroplanes. When he attended the Reims meeting he was so impressed with the spectacle that he contracted Louis Paulhan, one of the competitors, to come to London to display his flying abilities. Paulhan had been involved in ballooning since the turn of the century but it was Santos-Dumont's historic flight in 1906 that first interested him in aeroplanes. He won a model aeroplane competition and his prize was a Voisin biplane, but without an engine. His friends clubbed together to help him buy a new engine, he learned to fly in July 1909 and a month later he was competing at Reims. Thomas persuaded the Locke Kings to make their Brooklands course available to Paulhan. About thirty acres of land in the centre of the course was cleared and a small shed erected. Paulhan, fresh from

61

competing at Blackpool, gave his flying exhibitions on 29/30th October and 11th November. The moderate success of the displays convinced the Locke Kings that aviation would provide an extra attraction, at least when no motor-car racing was taking place. Obstacles were removed, the ground levelled, a number of sheds erected and in December the new Track manager, Major Lindsay Lloyd, who was more sympathetic to aviation, advertised the facilities available at Brooklands '... exclusive occupation of the sheds [rental £10 per month] and the right to use the interior of the track as an aviation ground ...' Over the next twelve months many aspiring aviators took up the offer.

French airmen dominated the European skies and in this respect Farman must be considered French. In September he was awarded the *Légion D'Honneur*, again emphasising that he considered himself 'a Frenchman in every acceptance of the word.'. Cody (since October), Roe, Moore-Brabazon and Latham (and he still resided in France) were the only British airmen of any consequence. In December the Aeronautical Society honoured Cody, at the ceremony Baden-Powell said, 'We were behindhand in England, but Cody has made up that lost ground, and now he has become an Englishman I feel that it is the wish of all members of the Society to honour him as being the first Englishman to have satisfactorily flown in England.'! Roe had grounds to dispute such a claim. Since the Blackpool meeting he had been forced to find another landing field, the local council had forbidden his continued use of Lea Marshes. Through the good offices of the Aeroplane Club, founded by Captain Walter Windham as a rival to the 'exclusive' Aero Club, Roe used open land at Wembley Park for trialling his Triplane 2, although he soon found the field too restricting and in 1910 he returned to Brooklands in more congenial circumstances.

By October, Moore-Brabazon had taken delivery of his Short S.2 biplane; it had no undercarriage but rather skids and he was compelled to use a Wright-type launching track to get airborne. He managed to steal the march on Cody because on the 30th he made a one-mile flight in two minutes and thirty-six seconds from Leysdown, there was a *Daily Mail* representative as witness; thus he won the £1,000 prize and the flight was officially recognised as the first exceeding one mile by a British airman in a British machine. He used the prize-money to buy a cup as a permanent memento of this flight. Five days later in a rather jocular frame of mind Brab wanted to prove that 'pigs might fly'; no

Moore-Brabazon's Short S.2 Biplane.

doubt he had frequently been the recipient of this adage during his short flying career! He fixed a wicker cage to his Voisin biplane to carry a piglet bearing the message 'I am the first pig to fly.' He left from Leysdown on a short three-mile flight, a photographer was conveniently present to record the unique event for posterity! Later Moore-Brabazon also claimed the British Empire Michelin Cup for the longest distance – nineteen miles – within a closed circuit awarded to an 'all-British' aviator; the Cup was valued at £500 and there was additionally a £500 prize; he was clearly Britain's leading airman.

Charlie Rolls was desperately eager to join 'the flying elite'. For some reason the proposal that he would be taught at Wrights' flying school at Pau had come to nothing. In May, Rolls sought Orville Wright's advice about learning to fly and he suggested that he should 'Buy a glider and learn the same way we did.' Rolls asked the Shorts to build him a glider to a Wright design. After it was delivered at the end of July he began gliding experiments at Standford Hill, Eastchurch – virtually the site of the Aero Club's new landing ground. By the time the first Short-Wright Flyer was delivered on 1st October, Rolls had completed over forty successful glides. On the following day he made his first powered flight and admitted that he '... went up with a wallop and came down with a thud ...' – the biplane was returned to Shorts for repairs. Later in the month (22nd) he completed a flight of 250 yards to claim a £25 prize from the Aero Club. On 1st November Rolls, whilst flying from Leysdown, made a flight of a ½ mile there and back, which entitled him to claim the Sir David Salomons Cup. This trophy had been presented to the Aero Club by Sir David back in 1906; he was a committed motor-car enthusiast and founder member of the Aero Club. It should be said that the required distance was well within Moore-Brabazon's command but he had graciously allowed his friend seven days to compete for it. Rolls now went from strength to strength and on 30th December he set a record for a British aviator whilst completing a flight lasting fifty-five minutes and later took up fellow aviator, Cecil Grace, for a flight of twenty minutes, described as 'the longest yet passenger flight in England.'

There was another British airman coming on to the scene – Claude Grahame-White; a trained engineer, who was now a motor-car dealer of some substance in London. Like Rolls he had ballooning experience and had been inspired by Wilbur Wright and the flying at Reims. Grahame-White ordered a Blériot Monoplane XII, which he named *White Eagle*, and even persuaded Blériot to allow him to spend eight weeks at his factory whilst it was being constructed, quite an honour considering that manufacturers were notoriously secretive about their methods of construction. On 6th November he astonished spectators at Issy by flying solo without any prior flying instruction – another 'born airman'. He and Rolls became Britain's leading airmen in the coming year, but tragically Rolls' fame would be all too brief.

As far as British designers were concerned, the Barnwell brothers, Harold and Frank, of the Grampian Company at Stirling, Scotland, had achieved short hops in their large canard biplane. On 31st December Harry Ferguson made the first aeroplane flight in Ireland in a monoplane of his own design. Also 'the Grand Old Man' of British aviation, Sir Hiram Maxim, had nearly completed another flying machine of all metal construction. Geoffrey de Havilland and Frank Hearle had been busy designing a biplane at workshops in Fulham and had taken over Moore-Brabazon's sheds at Seven Barrows for trials. Robert Blackburn was engaged on his designs in Leeds, but his trials from the beach at Marske-by-the-Sea, Yorkshire had so far been unsuccessful. In June, Horatio Barber founded the Aeronautical Syndicate Ltd. at Larkhill on Salisbury Plain, ultimately producing his *Valkyrie* monoplanes and *Viking* biplanes. Three months later

Claude Grahame-White: a rising star of British aviation.

Humber Ltd., the established motor-car manufacturer, announced their intention of producing monoplanes at £400 per machine, although their time as aeroplane manufacturers would be rather brief. Sir George Stanley White had already formulated plans for his entry into the aviation world, to manufacture aeroplanes from Filton near Bristol.

There were countless earnest and dedicated experimenters up and down the land designing and building machines of various shapes and sizes in sheds, small workshops and back gardens. Most were considered 'eccentric cranks' by their neighbours, some would be successful in getting airborne, if only briefly, but the majority would fail and fall by the wayside to be largely forgotten. Nevertheless there were encouraging signs that British aviation was at last waking up from its lethargy. During the year numerous aero clubs had been formed around the country, but there was still a long and uphill road ahead for British designers and airmen to claw back the superiority held by France in all aviation matters.

4

MEETINGS, RACES AND FLYING CLUBS

(1910–1911)

Although 1909 could be considered an *annus mirabilis* for British aviation, 1910 was also rather remarkable. Cross-country flights of increasing distance became frequent, a number of flying schools were established and the English Channel was crossed several times, clearly Blériot had broken through the psychological barrier. The public perceived flying as an expensive pastime for rich young men, those with the leisure and money to indulge themselves in this amazing form of transport. That they should be able to enter this new world was far beyond their wildest dreams; but nevertheless thousands attended the various events up and down the country to gaze in awe and wonderment at 'the magnificent men in their flying machines'. By the end of the year there were fifty certificated British aviators, some had been awarded their *brevets* by the *Aéro-Club de France*.

One impecunious 'flying man' – Roe – had his feet firmly placed on the ground, he realised that he urgently needed additional finance to develop his machines. With the financial help of his brother, Humphrey, an astute business man, A. V. Roe & Company was duly registered in January, with a workshop in the basement of Brownsfield Mills, Manchester and sheds at Brooklands. Thus Roe followed the Shorts, Handley Page, Horatio Barber and Howard Wright into the precarious world of commercial manufacture. But these pioneers were mere novices compared with the French; the Voisins produced over sixty machines, Blériot and Farman were close behind and there were numerous other smaller producers.

One Englishman, Sir George S. White, had ambitious plans to challenge the French monopoly. He was a talented entrepreneur, who had revolutionised Bristol's public transport system. In 1908 he had established a factory at Filton, a few miles out of Bristol, to build lorries and omnibuses and now announced his intention to build aeroplanes at the Filton omnibus depot. Sir George had obtained a licence to manufacture French Zodiac biplanes and he registered four companies: The British & Colonial Aeroplane/Aviation Company Ltd. and the Bristol Aeroplane/Aviation Company Ltd. He first traded as the British & Colonial Aeroplane Company, although the famous *Bristol* insignia soon appeared on the Company's letterheads and became universally recognised throughout the world of aviation.

The Aero Club's ground at Eastchurch was well established with seven sheds and a repair shop and considering its members were drawn from the upper echelons of Edwardian society, it was not surprising that on 16th February King Edward VII granted the Club permission to use the 'Royal' prefix. In March it awarded the first aviator certificates; on the 8th Moore-Brabazon received 'No 1', followed by Rolls, Cody qualified as 'No 9' in June and a month later Roe became the eighteenth certificated pilot. *The Aero* maintained that 'the crack flyer of this country at present is undoubtedly the Hon. C. S. Rolls....' In March the War Office bought his Short-Wright 1 for £1,000 and it was transported to Farnborough – the first aeroplane built by a private constructor purchased for military use.

The undisputed 'star' of British aviation over the next few years, Claude Grahame-White, made his first flight in Britain on 13th January from Brooklands; nine days earlier he had received his French *brevet*. *The Aero* was impressed with his flying '...His style is quite equal to that of the crack French flyers [praise indeed!] ... We look forward to some very fine flights by Mr Grahame-White before long'. Within a week he had found the ideal site for his proposed flying school – Hendon. The two hundred or so acres of meadows bordered on one side by the Midland Railway offered boundless opportunities for development into an 'aviation centre'. It had good rail and road access and was conveniently close to London. Grahame-White acquired the option to purchase the land. By the end of January he had also found eight pupils eager to learn to fly at a fee of £105 and by mid-February his 'British Aviation School' opened at Pau – the first British flying school – albeit on foreign soil.

The second Aeronautical Show at Olympia opened on 11th March and attracted large press attention, especially as the Prince and Princess of Wales (soon King George V and Queen Mary) attended. Reports suggested that '... the displays of aeroplanes are undoubtedly the finest the world has yet seen, not only in numbers [eighteen] but in design, workmanship and practicality ... British constructors have every reason to be very proud of the display they make ...'. Handley Page showed his Type A monoplane with its crescent-shaped wing, it was dubbed the *Bluebird* because of the colour of its fabric. Rolls' Short-Wright was displayed as was the new biplane – S.27 – designed by Oswald for Cecil Grace, their twelfth successful machine. British & Colonial had a Bristol-Zodiac on show though in fact it was French-built!

About a week later news arrived from France of yet another aviation 'first'. Henri Fabre, who had not previously flown, managed to take-off from water at La Mède harbour near Marseilles in his Hydravion, to add a novel dimension to aviation; although almost twelve months elapsed before Glenn Curtiss designed and flew the first *practical* hydroplane or waterplane.

By the spring Brooklands landing ground was being used by many well-known aviators – J. V. Neale, James Radley, Graham Gilmour, H. J. D. Astley, the Hon. Alan Boyle, Jack Humphreys, Robert McFie, C. E. Moering, and A. V. Roe. Charles Lane had established a 'Gliding School' and his manager was Eardley Billing, brother of Noel Pemberton-Billing; Billing and his wife ran the famous 'Bluebird' cafe, which was located in the centre of a row of aeroplane sheds. It became the social centre of the fast-growing 'aviation village'; as Roe recalled, 'Few places can have seen such visions and dreams created under the sign "Refreshments at Popular Prices". By the end of the year there were six flying schools in operation, the most successful was the Bristol School of the British & Colonial Company. The Hewlett & Blondeau School also opened for business, it was unique in that one partner was a redoubtable lady – Mrs Hilda Hewlett, the wife of the novelist Maurice Hewlett. She had met Blondeau at the Farman School at Mourmelon-le-Grand and they decided that there was a great potential for flying in Britain. They bought a Farman biplane and rented Shed 32 at Brooklands advertising tuition for £75 (inclusive of breakages!) as 'the FIRST Established School in England'.

With his 'British Aviation School' at Pau now well established, Grahame-White returned to Britain, he was determined to attempt the London-Manchester flight for the *Daily Mail's* £10,000 prize. Aware that his Blériot XI with its somewhat unreliable Anzani engine was not suitable for such a long flight, he bought a Farman biplane with a 50 h.p. Gnôme engine for £1,500. News reached him that Holt Thomas

A scene at Brooklands. (via J. Adams)

was sponsoring Louis Paulhan for the prize. To Lord Northcliffe's obvious delight the event thus developed into a race, which captured the public's imagination and gripped the country's attention more especially as it was a novice English aviator pitted against a celebrated French 'ace'.

When Grahame-White arrived in London he was relatively unknown in aviation circles let alone to the public at large, but this would swiftly change. The competition rules decreed that take-off and landing had to

69

Louis Paulhan – winner of the London to Manchester Race.

be within a five miles radius of the *Mail*'s offices in London and Manchester and only two stops for rest and refuelling were allowed. Grahame-White left early on 23rd April from the Royal Agricultural Society's showground at Park Royal, Ealing and was compelled to fly to Kensal Green (within the five-mile radius) before striking out for Manchester. He completed 117 miles before engine failure forced him to land at Lichfield. Unfortunately his machine was damaged whilst on the ground and it had to be brought back to London for repairs; he would have to start again.

By now Paulhan had arrived in London and on the afternoon of 27th April he left from Hendon also flying a Farman. The Press called it 'The Race, not of the century but the centuries'. By the time darkness fell Paulhan landed at Lichfield with some seventy miles still to go, whereas Grahame-White, about an hour or so behind, was obliged to land at Roade, Northamptonshire – some fifty miles adrift. In a valiant attempt to make up the leeway Grahame-White decided to take-off in complete darkness. Harper of the *Daily Mail*, who was following by car,

Claude Grahame-White landing at Ranelagh Gardens.

thought it would be '... sheer suicide. No one has ever made a cross-country flight by night'; Paulhan took-off at dawn and was now about ten miles in the lead. Both had to fly through difficult head winds and Grahame-White was compelled to land at Polesworth. The experienced Paulhan coped better with the conditions and finally landed near Didsbury station, completing 185 miles in 4 hours and 12 minutes at an average speed of 44 m.p.h. Grahame-White's brave attempt had failed.

The airmen were guests at a banquet held in the Savoy, where Paulhan confessed that he would not repeat such a flight 'not for ten times £10,000'. Grahame-White was given a silver rose bowl as a consolation; however his fame was assured, he was recognised in the streets, his effigy appeared in Madame Tussauds and he was in great demand to give exhibition flights throughout the country. He became the country's first aviation hero. Blessed with good looks and a natural charm Grahame-White was a great favourite with the ladies, who vied to be his passenger. He took up so many passengers at the Ranelagh and Hurlingham Clubs and other exhibition venues that his Farman was dubbed the 'Aero Bus'!

The excitement of the race had barely died down when the English Channel was crossed by air for the second time. On 21st May Jacques de Lessups, the son of the French constructor of the Suez Canal, landed his Blériot at Dover to win 12,500 francs and the *Daily Mail* £100 cup for the second crossing. He was met on arrival by Rolls, who had just returned from successfully competing at Nice and had established a camp at Swingate, Dover for his Channel attempt. His biplane had been fitted with flotation bags. On 2nd June Rolls, wearing a Falmouth floating jacket, took-off for France; ninety-five minutes later he returned and landed safely, having completed the first non-stop two-way crossing. This flight provided just the tonic that the country and British aviation needed; King Edward VII had died on 6th May and the country was still in mourning. *Punch* published a cartoon captioned 'Well done, my boy! You have given us a lift we sadly needed.' *Flight* maintained '... the Hon. Charles Rolls has won back British prestige in the art of flying ...' Rolls was presented with the Ruinart Cup and gold medals from the Royal Aero Club and the Aerial League; the country now had two flying heroes!

There were other signs that British aviation was gaining some momentum. In June the British & Colonial Company leased two hundred acres of Salisbury Plain at Larkhill, Wiltshire. Sheds were erected and in the autumn a Bristol school of flying was established conveniently close to the Army's large Bulford Camp. The Zodiac had proved to be a dismal failure; Sydney Smith, Sir George's nephew and the Company manager, had tried to get it airborne from Brooklands without success; the problem was the underpowered Darracq engine. Sir George was advised by several experts to forget it and build instead a modified Farman biplane. George Challenger, the Company's chief engineer and works manager, was given the task. He quickly produced drawings clearly based on a Farman but with certain essential modifications. Sir George was so impressed that he ordered twenty to be built at Filton; known simply as the Bristol biplane, it later acquired the name *Boxkite*, one of the famous early aeroplanes.

As a reminder that airships had not been forgotten, the Army's *Beta I*, a reconstruction of the earlier *Baby*, first flew on 26th May. At 104 feet long with a capacity of 33,000 cubic feet it made a night-flight from Farnborough to London and back under the command of Colonel Capper. *Beta 1* was the Army's first really efficient airship and the first to be fitted with wireless. Later in the year *Gamma* appeared and in October the Army acquired two French airships – *Clement-Bayard II* and *Morning Post*, the latter so named because that newspaper had raised £18,000 for its purchase.

The numbers of British aviators prepared to compete at the various meetings were slowly increasing. In the last week of June the Midland Aero Club organised a meeting at Dunstall racecourse, Wolverhampton *solely* for British airmen. Nineteen entered but three failed the preliminary trials. Most of those based at Brooklands entered as did a few who operated from Eastchurch, but a notable absentee was Cody, who was recovering from injuries sustained a few days earlier whilst testing his Biplane III. The meeting was marred by unfavourable flying conditions and several machines were wrecked or heavily damaged. Rolls, Grahame-White and Radley shared the majority of the prize money. The meeting closed on 2nd July and nine days later many competitors moved down to Bournemouth for a meeting planned as part of the town's centenary celebrations. Although billed as an 'International' meeting only five foreign aviators competed, including one American, J. Armstrong 'Chips' Drexel, who had been taught at Grahame-White's school at Pau.

It was held on a specially prepared landing ground at Southbourne to the east of the town and opened on 11th July, attended by thousands of spectators and several important guests including Blériot. Sadly the meeting is almost solely remembered for the tragic death of Charles Rolls. He was killed on the second day when his French-Wright biplane suffered a structural failure – part of the upper tailplane broke away as Rolls was correcting his height prior to landing in the spot-landing competition. It dived vertically from about eighty feet plunging Rolls to his death. Harper wrote '... there was silence. The crowd seemed numbed, no one spoke until ambulance men ran to the wreck ...' Rolls was the first British aviator to be killed in a flying accident. Moore-Brabazon was devastated: 'This terrible disaster to aviation and also the loss of so dear a friend sickened me and my wife of aviation altogether and I never flew again until the war.' Rolls' obituary in *Flight* stated '... With the passing of the Hon. C. S. Rolls there has been removed from the actual field of flight one of its most brilliant supporters – Motoring, ballooning, aviation, all owe much to the pioneer work of Charles Rolls.' He is the most commemorated pioneer aviator with statues at Monmouth (his hometown) and Dover, a memorial window at All Saint's Church, Eastchurch, and plaques at Derby and Southbourne.

Despite this tragedy, Bournemouth was the most successful meeting mounted in Britain so far. French aviators and machines dominated proceedings with Léon Morane, the competition manager of the Blériot Company, winning £3,525, Grahame-White came second with £1,335. In July he sold his Bleriot XII to the War Office, although it was hardly the ideal machine for novice pilots, its large engine and erratic flying habits made it difficult to control. Nevertheless Grahame-White remained utterly dismayed by the Government's apparent lack of enthusiasm in the military potential of aeroplanes. In late July he took his Farman down to Penzance and made a dramatic and audacious

C.S. Rolls on his French-Wright at Bournemouth – July 1910. (Rolls-Royce Heritage Trust)

flight over the Combined Fleets anchored in Mounts Bay for an informal review by H.M. King George V. He singled out the flagship H.M.S. *Dreadnought* for a remarkable display of low-flying. When the Fleets moved to Tor Bay a few days later he repeated the flight. Grahame-White wanted to demonstrate the Fleets' vulnerability to aerial attack, he seriously embarrassed the Admiralty and made front-page news but it is doubtful whether his daring flights had any material effect on Government policy.

The next aviation meetings were held in early August at Squires Gate, Blackpool and Lanark; the latter, sponsored by the Scottish Aeronautical Society, was the first to be held in Scotland. Both attracted a number of European aviators and some competitors experienced difficulties with the railway companies, several machines were delayed in transit. But none were so unfortunate as Roe, his two triplanes were destroyed by fire on the journey from Brooklands to Blackpool, caused by sparks thrown back by the engine. Roe returned to Manchester in an attempt to prepare another machine in time for the meeting. At Blackpool Grahame-White again tried to impress the military of the value of aeroplanes. He demonstrated a delivery of 'despatches and urgent medical supplies' from Squires Gate to 'military headquarters' at Lytham Hall about six miles away. On a second flight a photographer accompanied him, to take photographs of 'enemy positions'. They were perhaps a little more impressed this time because a few aeroplanes were allowed to take part in the Army manoeuvres in September. As a result of the Blackpool meeting both Grahame-White and Roe were invited to compete at the first Harvard/Boston Aero 'Meet' in the States – the first British aviators to challenge the Americans in their own 'backyard'.

September was an eventful month for British aviation. Geoffrey de Havilland, assisted by his engineer Frank Hearle, finally achieved success with his Biplane II at Seven Barrows. On the 10th he remained airborne for about a quarter of a mile; he later took Hearle up, and then his wife, Louie, who carried their eight-week old son Geoffrey in her arms. The local newspaper at Newbury greeted the news with a fulsome report under the headline 'The All British Biplane: the de Havilland Aeroplane Flies at Beacon Hill'; it was powered by an engine built by the Iris Car Company to de Havilland's design. In December, Frederick Green at Farnborough persuaded O'Gorman to buy the biplane for £400 and to employ de Havilland as a designer/test pilot with Hearle as his engineer. Another celebrated designer/airman was on the first rung of the ladder of success.

On 11th September the first attempt was made to cross the Irish Sea by air. Robert Loraine, a well-known actor and notable aviator, took-off from Holyhead in his Farman; the distance to Dublin was about sixty-five miles and Loraine experienced considerable problems with his engine during the flight, it gave up when Loraine was barely forty yards from dry land – a valiant attempt. Another aerial sea-crossing made the news during the month. John Moisant landed at Tilmanstone, Kent in a Blériot after completing the first Channel crossing accompanied by a passenger – Albert Filieux his engineer. They had left Issy back in mid-August to attempt the first Paris-London flight but were dogged by a series of mishaps. Moisant was a wealthy American with business interests in central America and had come to France to buy a Blériot for the Nicaraguan President, with six free flying lessons as part of the sale. In order to gain experience of the aeroplane, he decided to fly across the Channel! Moisant was awarded the *Daily Mail*'s £50 prize for the first Paris-London flight; he was killed at the end of the year whilst competing in America.

In late September Captain Dickson demonstrated a Bristol biplane to the military on Salisbury Plain; he was allowed to take an active part in the Army manoeuvres, flying as 'observation scout'. After the manoeuvres the War Office announced that Colonel Capper would be replaced by Major Sir Alexander Bannerman, Royal Engineers, as commander of the Balloon Factory and his command was extended 'to afford opportunities for aeroplaning'. There were hints that the War Office may well be considering the formation of an 'Army Air Corps'. Bannerman, although experienced in ballooning, was directed to qualify as a pilot, which he finally did in March 1912. The War Office had just two aeroplanes – a Short-Wright 1 and Blériot XII – but because of strong Press pressure, it purchased a Farman militaire biplane and a new and largely untried biplane produced by Paulhan.

Cody was back flying at Laffan's Plain in September, his ambition was to capture the British Empire Michelin Trophy. He was aware that he would have to cover at least two hundred miles such was the advance of flying in just twelve months. Cody completed several long flights during the month as well as carrying a number of passengers, also he advertised his Flying School at Laffan's Plain. He was quite prepared to go into commercial production, offering 'The Cody Flyer' for sale as 'the Perfection of British workmanship'! Little did he know then that his closest rival for the Trophy would be a young man who, as yet, had not flown even as a passenger – Thomas Sopwith.

Thomas Sopwith in his Howard Wright Biplane. (via M. Murray)

Sopwith was just twenty-two years old and born into a comfortably well-off family, which enabled him to take up motoring, motor-racing, ballooning and yachting. He had visited Issy and was determined to experience this new form of transport. On his return he went to Brooklands, where he gladly 'paid a fiver to Mrs Hewlett' for Blondeau to take him on a flight of two circuits of the track; this flight became in his words 'the start of the bug'. He bought a new Howard Wright Avis for £630 and on 22nd October, with no previous instruction, flew a short distance but crashed heavily on landing. After repairs he was flying almost daily to improve his skills. On 21st November he presented himself for testing by Harold Perrin of the Royal Aero Club. Candidates were required to make three circular flights of three miles, each finishing with a landing within 150 yards of a prescribed spot. Sopwith passed the test and was issued with his certificate (No 31). With that unbridled confidence of youth he set his sights on the Michelin Trophy.

Meanwhile across the Atlantic Grahame-White had taken the American aviation scene by storm. He swept the board at Boston winning $22,500 in prize money. Overnight the debonair and handsome airman was in great demand for exhibition flights and

Claude Grahame-White taking-off from Washington – 14th October, 1910. A remarkable demonstration of precise and controlled flying. (Smithsonian Institution)

passenger rides, society ladies were prepared to pay $500 for a five-minute flight with 'the matinee idol of the air'. One particularly daring flight was made on 14th October when he circled the Washington Memorial in his Farman and then calmly and impeccably landed in Executive Avenue alongside the White House to call on President Taft, whom he had met in Boston. The President was not at home so quite nonchalantly Grahame-White took-off from Executive Avenue as if '... he was driving away in an automobile!' A plaque was erected recording: '... the first time that a heavier-than-air flying machine ever alighted in the streets of any city in the world' – a remarkable demonstration of precise and controlled flying; the plaque has since 'disappeared' from the street!

By the time he arrived in New York for the Belmont Park International Meet he was the most celebrated airman in the States, and had been selected to compete for Britain in the Gordon Bennett International Cup along with Radley and Ogilvie. Grahame-White completed the twenty laps (62½ miles) in his Blériot racer at an average speed of 61.2 m.p.h.; he was the individual winner by some margin over Moisant with Radley finishing a credible third. He won $5,000 and the Cup for Great Britain – its first International aviation trophy. Grahame-White returned to England having amassed over $250,000 in prize money and exhibition fees, and was awarded a Gold Medal by the Aerial League for 'his services to Aviation'.

Grahame-White's next challenge was to compete for the Baron de Forest prize for the longest non-stop flight from England to the Continent by a British airman in a British machine before the end of the year. Another seven were also in the field – Clement Greswell, Loraine, Lieutenant H. E. Watkins, Cody, Ogilvie, Grace and Sopwith. Despite being such a novice, Sopwith had recently flown 130 miles non-stop and so was a genuine contender. During early December a week of gales and heavy rain delayed any attempts and several machines were damaged in the storms. On the 18th, when there was a lull in the weather, Grahame-White took a Boxkite he had on loan for a test flight and crashed into a stone-wall; he was taken to hospital with a fractured leg and ankle. Sopwith left on the same day from Eastchurch and made a remarkable flight lasting 3 hours and 40 minutes landing in Belgium – a distance of 169 miles. But there were still thirteen days to go; Ogilvie crashed at Camber Sands, Watkins at Shorncliffe and Loraine had a mishap at Eastchurch. On 22nd Cecil Grace left from Dover but when over Calais he decided to return because the wind had freshened and changed direction; he was blown out over the North Sea and was never seen again – the second British aviator killed in the air. Cody was too pre-occupied by the Michelin contest to make an attempt. On 16th December he was airborne for just under three hours for a flight of 115 miles but Sopwith was still in the lead. Ogilvie completed 139 miles in under three hours twelve days later. The three airmen made their final flights on the last day of the year; Sopwith managed to complete 150 miles at Brooklands, Ogilvie covered 50 miles before his engine broke down, whereas Cody at Laffan's Plain remained airborne for 4 hours 46 minutes – 189.2 miles – a new British record. The Royal Aero Club formally announced that he had won the Michelin Trophy; nobody surpassed Sopwith's flight so he won the Baron de Forest competition and £4,000.

It seemed appropriate that the year should close with the oldest and most experienced aviator and the youngest and most inexperienced airman winning the two major prizes – Cody echoing the past and Sopwith presaging the future. The perceptive H. G. Wells commented at the end of the year '... I am impressed with the fact that the type of

James Radley's Blériot Monoplane at Portholme, Huntingdon. Radley on the left &
W.B. Rhodes-Moorhouse. (Cambridgeshire County Council)

flying machine we now have is not that which is likely to prevail
ultimately ... The time will come when flying will be the ordinary
means of rapid locomotion all over the world for long distances ...'
    The steady advance of flying during 1910 had left its mark; a number
of Aero Clubs had been formed and there were new centres of aviation
activity blossoming throughout the country. 'Chips' Drexel had teamed
up with William McCardle of Bournemouth establishing the New
Forest Aviation School at Beaulieu, Hampshire. Further along the coast
Fort George, Gosport was used by the Hampshire Aero Club. In Sussex
both Shoreham and Eastbourne boasted flying schools. James Radley
had settled in at Portholme, Huntingdon where he devoted his time
to designing aeroplanes rather than flying them. In the north-west
C. Compton Paterson was the driving force behind aviation in the area
with a flying school at Southport and trials conducted at Freshfields
near Formby. To the north the Admiralty's first rigid airship, Vickers
R1 *Mayfly* was being completed at Cavendish Dock, Barrow-in-Furness
and the banks of Lake Windermere were active with the development
of hydroplanes and floatplanes with the Lakes Flying Company under
E.W. Wakefield and Oscar Gnosspelius; at the end of the year a school
was established there for tuition on hydroplanes. But nevertheless **the**
centre of aviation in the country was still Brooklands, although it
would soon be rivalled by Hendon.
    Grahame-White was busy raising funds to develop Hendon into a
major aviation venue. There was a poor response to his attempt to float
a Company with Blériot and Sir Hiram Maxim, so with the backing of

81

family and friends he formed the Grahame-White Aviation Company. He obtained a ten-year lease and proceeded to have the ground levelled and drained to provide a landing ground of some two miles in circumference. Hendon was already used by the Blériot Flying School and Barber's Aeronautical Syndicate. He moved his flying school from Brooklands and appointed Richard Gates as General Manager of 'London Aerodrome' as the new centre was named. On 24th March to celebrate its completion Grahame-White rather mischievously organised an air race to his rival Brooklands, he did not compete but many of his staff pilots did and the winner was Gustav Hamel in a time of fifty-eight minutes. This young man was destined to become the new star of British aviation, rivalling Grahame-White and Sopwith in popularity and success. Despite his name, he was British-born, the son of a doctor, and had been educated at Westminster and Cambridge; Hamel had only recently learned to fly at the Blériot School at Pau.

Meanwhile, on 1st February, Sir George White opened the gates of his aeroplane factory at Filton to the Press. Five machines were under construction and over the previous eight months the Company had completed forty machines and now employed eighty men. Sir George reported that eight biplanes had been sold to a 'great foreign power' (Russia) and that they were also being demonstrated in India. He also revealed that the Company had been asked to tender machines for the War Office (four Boxkites were ordered in March). Additionally the Company was the sole agent for the successful Gnôme aero-engines; without doubt he and his Company were major forces in British aviation.

On the same day Sopwith responded to a Royal command by flying to Windsor Castle and landing on the East Lawn. He had been in the habit of flying from Brooklands to Datchet Golf Course to have coffee with his sister May at a local hotel. These flights attracted large crowds and on hearing this King George V invited him to fly to Windsor. Sopwith and his friend and engineer Fred Sigrist were presented to the King and three Royal Princes – Henry, George and John. Sopwith was now an accomplished airman. He bought a Martin-Handasyde monoplane, *Dragonfly*, for £1,000 and also acquired a 70 h.p. Blériot; to recoup some of this expenditure he was attracted, like Grahame-White, by the flying competitions in America. During the summer he competed successfully in the States.

At the end of February the War Office issued an Army Order that from 1st April an 'Air Battalion Royal Engineers' would be established, comprising No 1 (Airship, Balloon & Kite) Company and No 2 (Aeroplane) Company. No 1 Company, commanded by Captain E. M. Maitland of the Essex Regiment, was based at Farnborough and Captain J. D. B. Fulton of the Royal Field Artillery was placed in charge of No 2 Company at Larkhill, part of its purpose was to train pilots. Major Bannerman was given the command of the Battalion; he is later quoted as saying 'For military purposes I doubt whether the aeroplane is very far ahead of what it was at the time of Wrights' first flight' – not very inspiring views for a Commander of the first Air Battalion.

Army officers were invited to apply for flying training. They were required to have previous aeronautical experience and not less than two years' service, good map-reading skills, be medically fit with good eyesight, unmarried and under the age of thirty, a good 'sailor' (poor stability of early aeroplanes), mechanically inclined and with a knowledge of foreign languages. They received a compensatory payment of £75 for arranging their private flying tuition – a figure which barely covered their expenditure. About forty came forward although they were aware that they were jeopardising their future promotion prospects considering the military hierachy's opinion of aeroplanes.

Not to be up-staged by the Army, the Admiralty gladly accepted a generous offer from Frank McLean to make available two of his Shorts' biplanes to enable naval officers to learn to fly at Eastchurch and fellow Club member, George Cockburn, freely offered his services as flying instructor. Lieutenants R. Gregory, C. R. Samson and A.M. Longmore of the Royal Navy and E. L. Gerrard of the Royal Marines were selected. They also received instruction in design and construction at Shorts factory. By May all four had received their certificates.

The third Aero and Motor-Boat Exhibition was held at Olympia during the last week of March. Twelve British constructors exhibited twenty machines and needless to say the British & Colonial Company had the largest stand proclaiming 'Second to no Aeroplane Company in the World'! The Blackburn Aeroplane Company was able to display, at last, an aeroplane with the claim that it had flown. Robert Blackburn, like Roe and Handley Page, had recognised that his forte was designing aeroplanes rather than flying them. Thus it was his 'test' pilot, Bentfield C. Hucks, previously a mechanic with Grahame-White, who managed to get airborne in Monoplane II – Mercury – at Filey Beach, Yorkshire on 8th March. Blackburn had rented a large shed there, also a bungalow to house his pilots and mechanics and later set

Robert Blackburn's Mercury *at Filey Beach in early 1911.*

up a flying school. During the summer Hucks flew the latest Mercury on an exhibition tour of the West Country and in the process made the first aerial crossing of the Bristol Channel. Grahame-White Aviation exhibited a new biplane, which had recently arrived from America, where it had been built by W.S. Burgess of Marblehead to Grahame-White's design. With a wing-span of just twenty-seven feet it was aptly named Baby and considered 'one of the lightest and fastest biplanes at present flying'. The latest Handley Page – Type D – with its distinctive crescent wings, was on sale for £450 but remained unsold probably because it had not yet flown. Although *Flight* dismissed several of the British machines on display as 'Farman copies', the Show clearly demonstrated the growing strength and depth of British aeroplane construction.

On 19th April Pierre Prier, chief instructor at the Blériot School, flew non-stop from Hendon to Issy in a time of 3 hours and 56 minutes; perhaps there were commercial possibilities for this novel form of transport? Certainly Grahame-White would have subscribed to this view. During the month he was asked to address an informal gathering of both Houses of Parliament on 'the future of aviation'. He used the occasion to advocate the aeroplane as a military weapon – his pet subject. Indeed his name was hardly out of the newspapers, what with Hendon, exhibition flights and romantic links with the American actress Pauline Chase. In April he displayed another talent – writing;

84

his first book *The Aeroplane, Past, Present and Future* was published. It had been written jointly with Harry Harper, they had become firm friends during his epic London-Manchester race, and was the first book on aviation written for the layman.

Grahame-White arranged an aerial display at Hendon on 12th May under the auspices of the Parliamentary Aerial Defence Committee. There was an impressive programme of events to demonstrate the military potential of aeroplanes – despatch-carrying, reconnaissance, aerial scouting and bombing – with Drexel, Hamel, Loraine, Cody, Prier, and Grahame-White taking part. The meeting was attended by the Prime Minister, members of his Cabinet (including Winston Churchill), the Leader of the Opposition and over 200 M.P.s. The public also came along in their droves, the roads around Hendon were said to resemble 'Derby Day crowds'. The meeting was described as 'the most important British flying meeting yet mounted', it heralded Hendon as a major venue for aviation events.

In direct contrast de Havilland's introduction to military aviation at Farnborough was far less public. His first task was to repair his Biplane II, which had crashed on its first flight there and in January he flew it for over an hour, duly gaining its air-worthiness certificate; it was designated F.E.1 or Farman Experimental. Cody who was 'ploughing his lonely furrow' at nearby Laffan's Plain was well aware of its existence. Perhaps 'lonely' is not really accurate because whenever he flew, he always attracted large crowds of local supporters. However, the War Office preferred to ignore his existence, as he was involved in a prolonged battle with them to obtain proper recompense for his expenditure on box-kites, an eight-year dispute that was not resolved until 1912.

Geoffrey de Havilland's first Army design was an improved F.E.1, which received its certificate in August. He was also engaged on reconstructing a damaged Blériot known as a 'man-killer'. He fitted an E.N.V. engine and styled it a S.E.1 (Santos Experimental), but in August it crashed killing its Army pilot. Now that the Balloon Factory was actively involved in designing aeroplanes, O'Gorman thought that 'H. M. Aircraft Factory' would be a more apposite name and from April this became its official designation. The Blériot Experimental aeroplane or B.E.1 was according to de Havilland – '. . . my most ambitious and successful design so far'. Originally a Voisin biplane presented to the War Office in pieces by the Duke of Westminster, he converted it into a two-seater of his own design only retaining the original 50 h.p.

Geoffrey de Havilland's Biplane II bought by the War Office for £400.

Wolseley engine. He fitted extended exhausts, which acted as silencers and because it was far quieter than contemporary machines the Press called it 'The New Silent Army Aeroplane'. It was first flown by de Havilland in early December and was described as 'a very modern aeroplane'; in fact it was still in Army service five years later. The B.E.1 was the progenitor of a number of successful 'B.E.' aeroplanes designed by the Factory in the years ahead.

During July the public were treated to a veritable feast of flying. On the first day of the month Eastchurch was the venue for the third Gordon Bennett International Trophy contested by teams from Britain, France and the U.S.A.; it was now regarded as the Blue Riband of Aviation. Large crowds gathered and were perhaps somewhat disappointed that Grahame-White would not defend his title, but pressing commitments at Hendon decreed otherwise. Hamel crashed on take-off but the dependable Ogilvie averaged 51 m.p.h. though he was soundly beaten by the American Charles Weymann in his Nieuport monoplane with a speed of 78 m.p.h. This machine, one of three in action, had been designed and built by Edouard de Niéport, a celebrated French racing motor-cyclist; his Company would produce some of the finest fighters of World War I.

Two days later no less than eleven aviators successfully crossed the Channel, they were the surviving contestants in the long and gruelling European Circuit Race (994 miles), which had started at Paris on 18th

June. They were bound for Hendon (via Shoreham), which was the London control point. Some 10,000 spectators gathered at Hendon to cheer these intrepid airmen, although the only British survivor was James Valentine 'Major Jimmie' in his French-built Deperdussin. The race ended in Paris on 7th July and the winner was 'André Beaumont', really Lieutenant de Vaisseau Conneau of the French Navy, followed by Roland Garros and Jules Védrines.

But it was the *Daily Mail's* 'Circuit of Britain Race' for a prize of £10,000 that proved to be the aviation event of the year; the 'Circuit' covered 1,010 miles from Brooklands to Scotland and back via a western and southern route. The national coverage by the *Mail* ensured that large crowds gathered at each control point, the majority had never seen an aeroplane. Twenty-one airmen competed, many of them British – Hamel, Astley, Fenwick, Hucks, Paterson, Valentine and Cody – and Blackburn, Roe, Handley Page, Howard Wright and the British & Colonial entered machines, the latter no less than six. Over 50,000 spectators gathered at Brooklands in brilliant sunshine for the start of the race on Saturday 22nd July. *Flight* remarked, 'A few years ago crowds used to assemble to see a motor-car, and the generation that introduced the automobile is now assembled in honour of the aeroplane ... and attracts most people to its ground. ...' The 'short hop' to Hendon saw the field reduced to seventeen and even larger crowds thronged Hendon and the hillside overlooking the landing ground – 'the scene was one of incomparable brilliance and fascination ...' The long and gruelling second leg – 383 miles to Edinburgh via Harrogate and Newcastle – started on Monday and fourteen aviators took-off. The capricious British summer now took a hand and the airmen encountered high winds and heavy rain. Jules Védrines in his Morane-Borel held a slight lead over 'André Beaumont' in his Blériot with the other competitors trailing some distance behind. By Edinburgh only Valentine, Hamel and Cody had survived to give chase to the Frenchmen and Hamel soon retired. It was Cody's slow but spirited progression in his Cathedral III that captured the public's imagination, large crowds gathered at each control-point to support and cheer him on. 'Beaumont' was the first to arrive back at Brooklands on 26th, followed by Védrines seventy minutes later. Valentine completed the circuit and Cody finally arrived on 6th August – the deadline for the race. His was the only British machine to complete the race. Although the two Frenchmen won the prizes, many considered that Cody's was 'the finest performance and certainly the pluckiest.'

Most competitors had 'works teams', whereas Cody just had his two step-sons as his 'team'; as Harper commented, 'He carried all his tools in his pockets and did all the running repairs to his machine himself.'. No small wonder he was judged '... the British public's chief and best-loved showman of flight...'

To celebrate King George V's Coronation on 22nd June, Grahame-White arranged with the Postmaster-General to establish the first aerial-mail service from Hendon to Windsor Castle. However, the passing of the Aerial Navigation Act in early June forced its postponement until September. Special envelopes and cards were produced, showing a Farman biplane flying over Windsor Castle and printed 'First U.K. Aerial Post'; they could be posted at a special box at Hendon and most of London's leading stores – 1/1d for letters and 6½d for cards. The first delivery took place on 9th September when Hamel left Hendon for the twenty-five mile flight to the Castle; thirteen minutes later he landed near the Royal Mausoleum at Frogmore where Post Office officials waited to sort and forward the mail. A number of pilots and machines were used until the service was concluded on 26th September. As a rural clergyman recorded in his diary 'Aerial post from Hendon to Windsor – what next?' Perhaps he had missed the news that in early July (4th) Horatio Barber in a *Valkyrie* monoplane (also used for the aerial-post) had carried a box of lamps on behalf of the General Electric Company – the first recorded carriage of goods by air in this country.

Cody was back in the news in the autumn when he won the Michelin trophies on offer. A prize of £400 was awarded for Series 1 – a flight of 125 miles in the fastest time. He made three attempts and on 11th September he completed the distance in 3 hours and 6 minutes, which to his surprise was not bettered. Then on 29th October he flew 255 miles until forced down by high winds. This was a new British long-distance record, which gained him the Trophy for the second successive year. Cody was now forty-four years old, almost twice the age of his rivals; he was 'a living legend' in the world of aviation.

As the year drew to a close it seemed that the military authorities were beginning to take aeroplanes seriously. In October Samson and Longmore persuaded the Admiralty to buy two Short biplanes, S.38 and S.39, to form the nucleus of a Naval Flying School at Eastchurch, where land had been leased from the Royal Aero Club. The School opened in December with the first four officers commencing flying training along with twelve ratings receiving maintenance instruction.

ASL Valkyrie used to fly the first UK Aerial Post – September 1911. (Note the mail bag underneath the pilot.)

The War Office finally bowed to pressure from the aeroplane industry and the national press in particular; it announced a competition for 'machines suitable for military operations' with formal trials to be held in the following summer. If for no other reason it could be said that British aviation had made great strides during 1911.

5

PREPARATIONS
FOR WAR

(1912–August 1914)

The period leading to 'The Great War' was one of significant progress
in all aspects of aviation. Aeroplane manufacture increased markedly
and could now rightly be termed an industry. There were considerable
improvements in the design and performance of British machines,
which began to compare favourably with the French. The prowess of
the aviators also advanced and the popularity of flying as a sport
reached a peak which would not be attained again until the mid-1920s.
This pronounced advancement was somewhat tarnished by the
amount of aerial fatalities, perhaps not unexpected but nevertheless a
sad consequence of the growing numbers of those 'taking to the skies';
by August 1914 there were 881 certificated pilots, of whom over 55%
were military officers.

The increasing strength of military aviation in Britain and Europe
brought in its wake the ominous threat of a more sinister feature of
aeroplanes and airships, as many became convinced that in the event of
war an air attack of some form was quite feasible. Those 'leviathans of
the skies' – Zeppelins – were especially feared and the initial signs of
'Zeppelin mania' surfaced in these last peaceful years. Not surprisingly
the progress and state of military aviation provided the major topics of
news.

On 10th January 1912 Lieutenant C. R. Samson, RN flew a Short S.38
biplane from staging erected over the foredeck of H.M.S. *Africa* at
anchor at Sheerness; the first occasion in this country that an aeroplane
had taken-off from a vessel. However, this feat had been first
accomplished in November 1910 when Eugene Ely flew from U.S.S.
Birmingham in Hampton Roads, Virginia. During the Naval Review
off Portland in early May Samson took-off from a moving vessel

H.M.S. *Hibernia*. Thus Samson, who was described as '... in his element when taking risks ...' heralded the arrival of naval aviation in its true form.

Herbert Asquith, the Prime Minister, asked the Committee of Imperial Defence to consider 'the future development of aerial navigation for naval and military purposes' and 'to propose measures that would create an efficient and effective aerial force'. It was the subject of much debate during the winter of 1911/12 before the Committee arrived at their recommendation – the formation of a unified air service to be called the Royal Flying Corps (RFC) and to include Military and Naval Wings, along with a Central Flying School. On 13th April a Royal Warrant was issued to provide for the constitution of the RFC and one month later it came into being. The 'Royal' appellation was granted 'in consideration of the specially difficult and arduous nature of the flying service.' A budget of £320,000 was allocated to facilitate its formation, considered by many to be 'a meagre and paltry sum'.

The Military Wing was planned to comprise seven companies (later squadrons) – No 1 (Airship and Kite), 2 to 7 (Aeroplanes) – one for each Division of the British Expeditionary Force. No similar system was laid down for the Naval Wing but Eastchurch remained as an Elementary Flying School. The format of the RFC had been largely devised by Brigadier-General David Henderson, D.S.O., C.B., the Director of Military Training, under the overall supervision of Colonel John E. B. Seely, the Under-Secretary of State for War. Henderson, a veteran of the Boer War, had, at the age of 48 years, attained his pilot's certificate the previous August. The first Commander was Captain (temporary Major) Frederick H. Sykes of the 15th Hussars and latterly a Staff officer; like Henderson he had learned to fly at the Bristol School. In order to establish an *esprit de corps* Major Sykes sought a suitable motto for his new command. J.S. Yule, a young Royal Engineer officer, suggested *Per Ardua ad Astra*, which he had read in H. Rider Haggard's book *The People of the Mist*; 'Through Difficulties to the Stars' seemed highly appropriate for the new Service and Royal assent was granted. It is still proudly borne by the Royal Air Force.

In April the male world of aviation was rocked when Harriet Quimby became the first woman to fly across the English Channel. Miss Quimby, known in her native America as the 'Dresden Doll', had gained her American certificate in September 1911 and had competed at several 'meets' in America. She arrived in England during March

Harriet Quimby – the 'Dresden Doll' – the first woman to fly across the English Channel – April 1912. (Smithsonian Institution)

1912 and gained the sponsorship of the *Daily Mirror* for her attempt, as well as engaging Hamel as her adviser. On the 16th she left Dover in her Blériot, missed Calais but landed safely on the beach at Hardelot some thirty miles to the south. Her courageous flight received scant coverage in the British press, it was greatly over-shadowed by dreadful news of the sinking of the *Titanic*. However, *The Aeroplane* thought that she was '. . . a woman of unusual initiative, determination and skill . . .' Shortly after her return to America, she and her passenger were killed whilst competing at Boston in July.

There were a number of British ladies prepared to enter this male preserve. Miss Edith M. Cook, also known as 'Miss Spencer Kavanagh', one of Grahame-White's first pupils at Pau had been the first British woman to fly solo; she was killed whilst parachuting from a balloon in July 1910. A Mrs Gavin was making solo glider flights at Brooklands in the summer of 1910 and Miss Lilian Bland was also flying her glider *Mayfly* at Belfast; she claimed to have flown it under power. Mrs Hewlett of Brooklands fame was the first to obtain an aviator's certificate in August 1911 followed by Mrs C. de Beauvois Stokes in November; in July 1912 she became the first to take up another lady passenger – Mrs Richard Gates – the wife of the manager of Hendon. Sadly Mrs Stokes was severely injured in a flying accident in August 1913 whilst flying as a passenger; although she recovered she never flew again. The Aerial League had an active Ladies Section and such was the growing band that Hendon staged its first Ladies Day meeting on 6th July with Mrs Stokes as the star attraction. One of the most enthusiastic members was Miss Eleanor Trehawke-Davis, her Blériot was invariably flown by Hamel; she considered flying to be 'a most health-giving and nerve-steadying pursuit'! Just two weeks before Harriet Quimby's Channel flight, she became the first woman to cross the Channel by air, albeit as a passenger with Hamel.

On 20th April, Hendon staged its most successful meeting so far, over 15,000 spectators watched displays and races by the leading airmen of the day. The aerodrome boasted some thirty sheds, a splendid club-house and numerous tea-rooms and bars and even a thirty-bedroomed hotel was planned. Grahame-White wanted more people to gain the 'Hendon habit', as he termed it; his personal crusade was to 'Wake Up England!' to the possibilities and realities of the aeroplane. Impromptu air races were organised at Brooklands and flying could be seen on most fine days at these two centres along with Larkhill and Eastchurch.

A fine aerial shot of London Aerodrome in 1912. (RAF Museum)

Roe, along with other manufacturers, was directing his efforts towards the Military Trials to be held in July. His Type E two-seater biplane (later known as Type 500) first flew in March, he maintained that it was his first really successful machine. In May a Type F monoplane appeared, one of the first where the pilot sat enclosed in the fuselage, which was entered from a door in the roof. Later in the year he moved his flying school to Shoreham, where flying trials were also conducted. Handley Page also moved to larger premises, he left Barking for converted riding stables at Cricklewood and used Hendon for trials. The Aircraft Factory at Farnborough acquired the 'Royal' prefix on 1st April and work continued on the development of its Blériot Experimental machines; B.E.2 was first flown by de Havilland on 1st February followed by B.E.3 to 8 during the year. However, it was the B.E.2a that was developed for military use and almost one hundred were ultimately built by a number of contractors, including Vickers, Handley Page, and British & Colonial.

Several new names started aeroplane manufacture during 1912, the most prominent were Sopwith and Airco. Sopwith established a flying school at Brooklands in February and began aeroplane construction there, later founding Sopwith Aviation Company, which moved to premises at Kingston-upon-Thames, Surrey in January 1913. His first original design was a biplane – Hybrid – sold to the Admiralty in November. By the autumn Sopwith had virtually given up competitive flying and employed Harry Hawker as test pilot because he admitted '... Hawker was a much better pilot than I was.' He was one of three Australians who came to England to learn to fly; they were known as 'the Three Harrys' – Busteed flew for British & Colonial and Kauper was an engineer with Sopwith; they made quite an impact in British aviation.

In 1912 George Holt Thomas bought out the A.S.l. Syndicate and established the Aircraft Manufacturing Co. Ltd. (or Airco) at Hendon. He had obtained the British licence to build Maurice Farman machines. Maurice, who had learned to fly before his famous brother Henri, had set up his own aeroplane factory in friendly competition. Airco's first production was the Maurice Farman S.7 Longhorn, a two-seater biplane that proved to be a safe and reliable training machine; several pilots considered it '... an aerial joke ... resembling a Daddy Longlegs ...' The first Longhorn was delivered to the military in September, and was followed in late 1913 by the S.11 Shorthorn; hundreds of military airmen completed their initial flying training on these machines.

Maurice Farman S.7 Longhorn built under licence by Airco.

According to Grahame-White an important feature of aeroplane design in 1912 was '... the production of marine-type machines fitted with pontoon floats instead of landing wheels. These machines, capable of rising from or alighting on the surface of water were called "water planes".' Churchill is reputed to have coined their more familiar name 'seaplanes'. On 1st December 1911 Lieutenant A. M. Longmore, RN successfully landed S.38 on the Medway and in late March the first ever water-plane competition was held in Monaco. Most British manufacturers would build seaplanes over the next few years and the Naval Wing had a fair selection of them; Sopwith was perhaps the most successful in the short term but it was Short Brothers that became the foremost designers and manufacturers of seaplanes and flying boats in the years ahead.

Two pioneer airmen died in the early summer, neither as a result of air accidents. At the end of May the aviation world mourned the loss of Wilbur Wright; he died of typhoid fever at the age of forty-five. Thousands of letters and telegrams from all over the world poured into Dayton. Some six weeks later Hubert Latham was killed whilst big-game hunting in Africa; he had virtually given up competitive flying.

The Aerial Derby that was staged at Hendon on 8th June really marked London Aerodrome as one of **the** places to attend – a social venue to rival Ascot and Henley. The race, sponsored by the *Daily Mail*, was around a circuit of London – approximately 81 miles – with six turning points at Kempton Park, Esher, Purley, Purfleet, Epping and High Barnet. Over 45,000 were present to witness the start and an estimated ½ million around London watched the progress of the race. The first to complete the circuit was Sopwith in 1 hour and 23 minutes, followed by Hamel with Miss Trehawke-Davis as passenger. W. B. Rhodes-Moorhouse came in third in his Radley-Moorhouse monoplane. He had parted company with Radley at Portholme and was now based at Brooklands. In August he made the first Channel crossing with *two* passengers, his wife and a friend. Whilst serving with the RFC in France in 1915 he was the first airman to be awarded the Victoria Cross but sadly posthumously. Sopwith was disqualified for missing a turning point so the Gold Cup and £250 prize went to Hamel. Sopwith appealed and the Royal Aero Club later reversed the decision in his favour.

Nineteen days later Grahame-White was again front-page news when he married Miss Dorothy Taylor, a New York heiress, at Widford near Chelmsford, Essex; the press called it the first 'aero-wedding'! The reception was held at nearby Hylands House and several guests arrived by aeroplane and landed on the lawns of the large country

The start of the Aerial Derby, Hendon – 8th June 1912.

97

How to transport a Blériot! – Rhodes-Moorhouse (seated on the running board) in 1912. (Cambridgeshire County Council)

house. After the ceremony the other guests were treated to an impromptu flying display – a notable first – and as many reports commented 'the aeroplane has truly come of age'!

The Central Flying School (CFS) came into being at Upavon Downs on Salisbury Plain in June, with a complement of twelve officers and sixty-six other ranks and equipped with just seven aeroplanes. Captain Godfrey Paine, RN was appointed as Commandant and the first two instructors were Captain Gerrard of the Royal Marines and Lieutenant Longmore, RN. It was the intention to train pilots for both RFC Wings, although the Admiralty seemed to prefer its existing school at Eastchurch. The target was 180 pilots each year but applicants had to obtain their Royal Aero certificates before acceptance into the School. One of the earliest was Major Hugh Trenchard of the Royal Scots Fusiliers, he learned to fly at Sopwith's school at Brooklands and gained his certificate in August after just a fortnight's instruction. On 12th October Trenchard was appointed an instructor (Squadron

Henri Salmet visited the West Country in 1912 & 1913. (via Colin Cruddas)

Commander) at Upavon, although effectively he was the Adjutant – the start of a glorious career in the RFC/RAF. The School soon gained a fine reputation for its thoroughness, efficiency and discipline.

During the summer, aeroplanes were evident in towns and villages throughout the country, many of which had never before seen such 'flying machines'. Under the sponsorship of Lord Northcliffe and his *Daily Mail*, several aviators were engaged to make extensive exhibition tours to increase the public's awareness of aerial transport, it was also good publicity for the newspaper! These tours created immense public interest, indeed many RFC/RAF airmen revealed that their first interest in flying was kindled by such visits. Henri Salmet, the new Chief Pilot of the Blériot School at Hendon, flew his Blériot to countless places in the West Country whereas Hamel, Hucks, Astley, and Ewen were engaged mainly in the Midlands and eastern and northern England. In July and August Grahame-White and other airmen promoted his 'Wake Up England!' campaign (also backed by the *Mail*) with the emphasis placed on seaplanes, visiting seaside resorts during the height of the holiday season; 120 towns were visited, over 500 exhibition flights were made and over 1,000 passengers were carried. H. G. Wells, who was given his first flight by Grahame-White, was very impressed '. . . I went up in the air with the impression that flying was still an uncomfortable, experimental, and slightly heroic thing to do, and came down to the cheerful gathering crowds on the sands again with the knowledge that it is a thing achieved for everyone. ...' This 'Waterplane Tour' was particularly successful, in fact *The Tatler* magazine complained 'The South Coast just now is over-run with hydro-planes as a seaside lodging house with black beetles and you can see them all over the place; evangels of the *Daily Mail* preaching the gospel of flight.'! These exhibition tours were repeated in 1913 and to a lesser extent in the following year and were the forerunners of the 'flying circuses' that became such a feature of the post-war aviation scene.

The Military Trials took place at Larkhill in August; they had been postponed for a month to allow extra time for the manufacturers to prepare their machines. The closing date was 30th June and thirty-one machines (thirteen biplanes and eighteen monoplanes) were entered; five all British, thirteen British but with foreign engines, eleven foreign and two British-built foreign machines. It was not really the prize money – £4,000 for the overall winner and £1,000 for the best British machine – that attracted the competitors but rather the probability of a military contract.

The only established British company not represented was Short Brothers. Cody entered a biplane and monoplane and as usual 'he cut a lone figure unsupported by the resources of a big factory ...' The Trials commenced on 4th August, by which time a number of machines had been withdrawn and only twenty-two were tested. There was a

Daily Mail *Waterplane Tour 1912.*

rigorous regime of tests. They were required to lift a minimum of 350 lbs (including the pilot and observer), carry sufficient fuel for 4½ hours' flying, fly at a maximum height of 4,500 feet and at 1,500 feet for an hour. Their speed should not be less than 55 m.p.h., pilot facility and vision, noise levels, rate of climb and interchange of parts were all considered as was the ability to land and take-off from various surfaces. Perhaps the most contentious issue was that the Aircraft Factory's B.E.2 was allowed to take part as a 'compare', especially as Mervyn O'Gorman was one of the judges.

There were a number of minor mishaps and several competitors experienced problems with their engines; the most tragic incident was the death of R. C. Fenwick in his Mersey monoplane – other than Cody he was the most experienced airman taking part having qualified in December 1910. Another potential disaster was averted when Lieutenant Wilfred Parke, RN, flying the Avro Type G biplane, along with a military observer, went into a 'dreaded' spin or spiral dive, which had claimed the lives of many pioneer airmen. Parke managed to coolly recover control of the machine at about fifty feet above the ground by pushing the joystick forward and the rudder control against the direction of the spin, quite contrary to the natural reaction. After he had landed safely Parke was able to give a reasoned resume of his corrective action, thus making an immeasurable contribution to flying safety.

The Trials ended on 30th August and the Judging Committee were quick in announcing their findings. Ten machines were placed in order of merit, four were British-built. Two Bristol monoplanes, designed by the Company's new Roumanian engineer Henri Coanda, were placed equally fifth and each awarded £500. Two Deperdussin monoplanes had performed well, one from the French parent company was placed second and thus awarded £2,000 for the best foreign machine and the other built by the British Deperdussin Company, which had been formed in April, was also joint fifth. But perhaps the biggest surprise was that Cody's large Biplane V was declared the overall winner, indeed it was the only British machine to complete all of the tests satisfactorily. Although it had clearly demonstrated that it was an admirable machine, its design was sadly outmoded and was not really suitable for military use. Furthermore it had also been out-performed by de Havilland's B.E.2 – as indeed had most of the other competitors.

Cody received £5,000 and had praise and congratulations showered upon him; it was his finest hour. The Royal Aero Club awarded him

A BE.2 flying past Sir Horace Smith-Dorrien and his staff on Salisbury Plain in May 1913.

'Colonel' Cody beside his winning biplane – Military trials, August 1912.

their highest honour – Gold Medal – and a congratulatory message from King George V was addressed to 'Colonel' Cody. As Cody said: '... if His Majesty has referred to me as 'Colonel' Cody so in future 'Colonel' Cody it has to be.' His good fortune had started back in July when the long legal battle with the War Office was finally settled by the payment of £5,000 for his box-kites. In October he again won the Michelin Trophy 2 with his Trials biplane completing 186 miles in 3 hours and 26 minutes. Two of his biplanes were taken up by the War Office, the original crashed in February 1913 killing the RFC pilot.

Shortly after the completion of the Trials two of the top monoplanes crashed killing their RFC pilots and observers. On 6th September the French Deperdussin came to grief and four days later Lt. E. Hotchkiss and Lt. C. Bettington were killed near Oxford in a Bristol Coanda. These latest fatalities, allied to the loss of Lt. Eustace Loraine, a C.F.S. instructor on 5th July in a Nieuport monoplane, caused the War Office to impose a ban on RFC pilots flying monoplanes but the Admiralty still allowed officers of the Naval Wing to fly them. There was certainly a strong and preconceived impression that monoplanes, although generally faster, were inherently more prone to structural failure. During 1912 there were more disturbing fatal accidents, a number of experienced airmen – Graham Gilmour, E. V. Fisher, H. J. D. Astley, Lt. Parke and Edward Petre – lost their lives whilst flying monoplanes. Although the military ban was lifted in February 1913, long deep-seated prejudices died hard and British manufacturers concentrated on sturdier biplanes mainly to ensure that they would be considered by the military; indeed biplanes would be predominant in military and civil aviation until well into the 1930s.

In November Vickers Ltd. were asked by the Admiralty to produce a biplane armed with a machine gun – the first purpose built armed aeroplane. Since March 1911 Vickers had been engaged in building monoplanes at their factory at Erith, Kent and testing them at their nearby airfield at Joyce Green. The Company had also established a flying school at Brooklands, where several famous RFC/RAF officers learned to fly. Vickers' first biplane crashed into the Thames near Erith on 13th January 1913 killing Leslie F. MacDonald and his passenger; another pioneer airman to lose his life.

The Vickers E.F.B.1 (Experimental Fighting Biplane) was on display at the Olympia Show in February. It crashed on its first flight but nevertheless it was the precursor of a number of models up to the F.B.5 'Gunbus', which saw service with the RFC and the Royal Naval Air

Vickers F.B.5 Gunbus – an early military aircraft. (British Aerospace)

Service. It was not the only 'military' machine on show, Grahame-White Aviation had produced a biplane with a Colt gun mounted over the engine. The Show was considered the first where British machines were able to hold their own with the French 'not only in workmanship but flying ability'. A notable absentee was the Blackburn Aeroplane Company, which was experiencing financial difficulties; not so Avro, which had become a private Limited Company buoyed by orders from the War Office. Indeed the War Office had its own stand modestly displaying its B.E.2, but pride of place was given over to Cody's successful Trials' biplane. It was this machine that particularly attracted the attention of King George V during his visit, although he missed Sopwith Aviation's stand where the Bat Boat hydro-biplane was displayed. It attracted the greatest interest probably because of its fine 'Consuta' hull built by S. E. Saunders of Cowes, Isle of Wight and was the first flying boat as such as well as a successful amphibian; Hawker, in the prototype Bat Boat, won the Mortimer Singer prize of £500 for making twelve alternate landings on land and water. Several versions would be built in the next twelve months, one was bought by the Admiralty.

Towards the end of February, No. 2 squadron moved from Salisbury

Plain, now recognised as 'the Cradle of Military Aviation', to a new airfield at Montrose, Angus. Under Major Charles Burke a handful of B.E.2as and Longhorns set out on the 430 mile journey flying through fog and heavy rain. All the machines arrived safely and over the next few months several B.E.2s were flown from Farnborough to Montrose; one crashed killing Lt. D. L. Arthur, which the Accident Investigation Committee of the R. Aero Club attributed to '... criminally negligent repair work by the Royal Aircraft Factory ...!' It was still producing aeroplanes – fourteen in 1913 – and O'Gorman had a workforce of some one hundred engaged mainly in repair and experimental machines, most notably the B.S.1 and R.E.1 – 3. The Blériot Scout 1 was largely a de Havilland design and was the first to be called a 'Scout', which became the traditional name for a single-seat fighter. It had an impressive performance with a maximum speed of 92 m.p.h., climbing at 900 feet per minute, but it crashed in March injuring de Havilland – his first serious air accident. The R.E.1 (Reconnaissance Experimental) first flew in May piloted by Edward Buck, a Cambridge graduate who specialised in the problems of stability and control. He worked closely with de Havilland on the B.E.2c – the mainstay of the RFC in the early war years.

The Naval Wing also broke away from the confines of its 'Cradle' – Eastchurch; the Wing had already used Carlingnose in Scotland as a temporary seaplane station and the number of aeroplanes and seaplanes slowly increased, stations were established at nearby Isle of Grain at the mouth of the Medway, then at Great Yarmouth and Felixstowe in East Anglia, Gosport and Calshot were used later in the year.

Lord Northcliffe's fervid belief in aviation remained undiminished as indeed did his generosity. In April the *Daily Mail* announced a prize of £5,000 for a Seaplane Circuit of Britain planned to take place in August. The newspaper also offered £10,000 for the first Transatlantic flight, such a concept seemed hardly realistic considering that it was less than three years since Blériot's epic cross-Channel flight. This time Northcliffe's prize was not treated with derision and by September the proposition seemed less far-fetched when Roland Garros crossed the Mediterranean non-stop from France to Tunisia – some 470 miles. Certainly there were at least three airmen bold (or foolish?) enough to consider such a flight providing a large and powerful machine became available, it is perhaps needless to say that Samuel Cody was one of them!

Winston Churchill flies into the Central Flying School, Upavon. (via M. Brown)

The political situation in Europe caused growing unease in the country and there was constant debate in newspapers and Parliament about the strength of British military aviation vis-á-vis France and Germany. This concern was further heightened by the passing of the Aerial Navigation Act, which forbade foreign aeroplanes landing without permission and a total ban on foreign military aeroplanes and airships. Eighty prohibited areas were listed and eight stretches of coastline defined as entry passages for foreign aeroplanes. It all appeared rather ominous.

At the end of July newspapers published what was considered the 'true' strength of the Military Wing of the RFC, the figures caused shock and outrage. Colonel Seely faced constant questions in Parliament about the 'fighting' strength of the Wing and he was finally forced to declare the number to be 126, although at the same time he was busily buying any machine to 'justify' this figure! It was later discovered that out of a total of 120 machines, only 43 were 'ready to fly in the event of a war' and 20 of those were at the Central Flying School, therefore the 'realistic figure' was a mere 23, despite the fact that during the month a new aeroplane squadron, No 5, had been formed. The debate about the strength and effectiveness of the Military Wing continued unabated in the Press and Parliament well into 1914.

It was most noticeable that the respective figures for the Naval Wing did not come under the same close scrutiny. Winston Churchill, the First Sea Lord of the Admiralty, kept the strength of the Wing out of the public domain. His clear objective was to wrest its control of the Wing away from the War Office and place it with the Admiralty as its own Air Service. Churchill took a close personal interest in all aspects of naval aviation, from its aeroplanes and seaplanes, the training of its pilots, fighting tactics and even the planning and siting of seaplane stations. He flew whenever he could despite the unease expressed by his wife and close friends. Churchill also received flying instruction from several Naval instructors and although he had completed over twenty-five hours of instruction, nobody was prepared to allow him to fly solo because of his 'exalted' position as First Lord! His deep and active interest in all aspects of aviation was unique for a politician and proved a great benefit for the RAF in the inter-war years.

Despite the preoccupation with military aviation the public's fascination with flying showed no signs of abatement. They still flocked in their thousands to both Brooklands and Hendon, which was now called 'London's Modern Rendezvous'. On August Bank Holiday Sunday the crowds were thrilled when their 'hero' Cody demonstrated his large Hydro-biplane that he had built for the forthcomimg Seaplane Circuit of Britain. Four days later (7th) he planned to fly to Calshot to get three floats fitted. However, Lt. Charles Keyser and his friend W. H. B. Evans, a former cricketer, prevailed upon him to take them up as passenger. Keyser was taken up first and they landed safely after a twenty-minute flight over Farnborough Common. Cody then left with Evans as passenger and on his return the biplane was passing over Ball Head at about 500 feet when it began to break up and crashed to the ground, killing both men.

It seemed inconceivable that the 'legend' was dead; the news deeply shocked the country – 'to everyone it seemed to be a personal as well as a national loss'; it was the passing of an era. Sopwith commented, '... the death of S. F. Cody is the greatest blow those connected with British aviation have ever felt.' On 11th August 'Colonel' Cody was buried with full military honours in the Military Cemetery at Thorn Hill – a unique honour for a civilian. Over 100,000 people lined the funeral route from his home to the Cemetery, and the funeral cortege stretched for ¹/₂ mile – it was described as 'a farewell fit for royalty'. Cody's son Frank served in the RFC and was killed in action in January 1917, the first father and son to be lost in the air.

The *Daily Mail* Circuit of Britain was still held despite the death of Cody. On 15th August there was just one competitor ready to leave Southampton Water, the other two entrants – Radley-England's

Avro 504 – the most successful pre-war aeroplane. (British Aerospace)

Waterplane and McLean's Short S.68 Biplane – were not ready. Thus Hawker flying the Sopwith Hydro-biplane with his fellow Australian Kauper as mechanic left for Dover with 'an immense feeling of anti-climax'. They managed to complete the 240 miles to Great Yarmouth but then Harper was taken ill with the effects of exhaust fumes and sunstroke. The two tried again on 25th but after a gallant flight up to Aberdeen and down to Dublin, the biplane crash-landed in the sea outside Dublin after covering over 1,040 miles. Kauper broke his arm in the crash and the machine was so damaged that the flight was abandoned. Nevertheless the *Daily Mail* awarded Hawker a special prize of £1,000 in recognition of the quite remarkable flight.

Brooklands and Hendon staged a number of very successful meetings during the late summer, no less than fifty-one meetings at Hendon, often attracting famous celebrities, such as Enrico Caruso, George Robey and Harry Tate. Grahame-White's Company had built a biplane specifically to carry passengers, it was called the Charabanc and was even larger than Cody's last biplane. Four wicker seats were provided behind the pilot and it was later powered by the 120 h.p. Austro-Daimler engine purchased from Cody's estate. In October the Charabanc carried nine passengers, although later it was reported to have taken no less than eleven. In November the large biplane won the Michelin Trophy 1 for covering 315 miles continuously from Hendon to Brooklands.

Perhaps the highlight of the Hendon 'season' was the second Aerial Derby held on 20th September when a record crowd of 65,000 saw Hamel win at an average speed of 75 m.p.h. Fourth placed was Freddie Raynham in an Avro 504; the small biplane had first flown only two days earlier at Brooklands. It had originally been devised back in November 1911 and had been completed finally at Avro's new factory at Miles Platting, Manchester. The 504 was without doubt the most successful pre-War aeroplane, becoming a most reliable and safe trainer – simple to fly and with no vices; it remained in service with the RAF until 1932 – an amazing record. During the 1920s it was also used to give joy-rides to thousands of people.

The devotees who attended flying meetings throughout the country demanded more exciting and spectacular flying to sustain their interest. Moore-Brabazon had scathingly denounced this trend as 'gymkhana flying'! On 25th September 'the great assemblage of spectators at Brooklands witnessed a feat of acrobatic flying never previously seen before ...' The young French airman, Celestin-Adolphe Pégoud, gave a remarkable display of 'looping-the-loop' or literally flying on his head. *Flight* reported '... he took the aeroplane, a dangerous unmanageable thing that had to be treated with the utmost caution, and showed how it could be tamed.' In late November Bennie Hucks became the first British pilot to complete the feat, followed a few days later by Hamel. In no time it became all the rage and no flying meeting was complete without a display by one of the select band of 'loop-the-loopers' as they were known. Hamel received a Royal Command to demonstrate the art at Windsor, and he also took a number of Society ladies as passengers – Miss Trehawke Davis and the Countess of Derby were amongst the first – so that they could boast that they had 'looped-the-loop'.

During September the military airmen were active, many took part in various Army manoeuvres on Salisbury Plain and in Northamptonshire. But the most impressive performance was that of No 2 squadron flying to Ireland to take part in Army exercises. A number of B.E.2s led by Captain Longcroft flew from Montrose to Limerick via Stranraer. Previously only a few civilian airmen had crossed the Irish Sea. It was the first time that the RFC had flown 'overseas' and next time it would be 'the real thing' over to Belgium and France. Recruitment posters for the RFC began to appear inviting 'men aged 18 to 30 of various mechanical trades and others of good education' to apply to join the Military Wing; the rates of pay varied from 2s to 9s per day, the latter for a Warrant Officer. However, men selected to be instructed as 'flyers' would receive an additional 2s or 4s daily rate. This was a completely new departure as hitherto only officers had been considered for flying training; in fact the last military man to be

A Recruitment Poster for the Military Wing, Royal Flying Corps. (Imperial War Museum)

A Sopwith Tabloid won the second Schneider Trophy Race at Monaco in April 1914.

awarded his pilot's certificate pre-war was Sergeant A. F. May. The posters displayed for the first time the pilots' famous badge – wings – which had been introduced with the express approval of King George V. The badge was originally intended to be awarded *only* to pilots who had demonstrated competence in some form, but they were soon awarded to all pilots once they had qualified. They became the most coveted badge in the RFC/RAF and only two persons were allowed to wear them without having qualified to fly – King George V and Winston Churchill – the latter not until April 1943.

In late November another remarkable small Scout biplane was unveiled for public gaze at Brooklands – the Sopwith S.S. – which quickly acquired the name Tabloid from a small and popular medical tablet sold by Burroughs Wellcome. The machine was devised by Harper and Fred Sigrist, who had tried to design the smallest and lightest biplane for transport by sea to Australia, where Hawker wished to revisit and undertake a sales tour for the Sopwith Company. Sopwith later admitted that they had no idea at the time how successful this biplane would be. It was a two-seater with a wing-span of 25½ feet and was just 20 feet long – smaller than the 504 – although powered by the same engine, a 80 h.p. Gnôme. As *The Aeroplane* commented: 'There is no doubt that the machine will astonish those who have been led to believe that we have no manufacturers worthy of consideration in this country ...' The Tabloid's speed, performance, flying qualities, reliability and comfort set the benchmark for other manufacturers to aspire to and was the forerunner of Sopwith's famous WWI fighters. The young Company had a most successful year, almost fifty machines of various models had been constructed, of which twenty-seven had been sold to the military mostly for the Naval Wing. Such pressure of work and an order for nine Tabloids from the War Office had necessitated a move to larger premises in nearby Carbury Park Road; in March 1914 the Company became Limited and grew from strength to strength.

It seemed barely conceivable that it was merely ten years since the Wrights' epic flights and yet aviation had progressed so far. In May the large cabin biplane *Le Grand* or Russian Knight designed by Igor Sikorsky had flown for the first time in Russia powered by *four* engines. In February 1914 it was surpassed by the massive Ilya Murometz with a wing-span of almost one hundred feet, a fully enclosed cabin and accommodation for sixteen passengers in a heated lounge. The first scheduled passenger 'airline' was founded in America between St Petersburg and Tampa in Florida, albeit of short duration but nevertheless the commercial possibilities were plain for all to see. Furthermore aeroplanes were travelling faster, higher and over far greater distances. In September the world speed record stood at 126.6 m.p.h., the altitude at 20,079 feet and the longest recorded distance was 634½ miles – all by French airmen. Indeed France still dominated the world of aviation not only in the numbers of qualified pilots but also in the extent of its aeroplane industry. If such advances had been made in ten years, what did the next decade hold for aviation? The limits appeared boundless.

In January 1914 Geoffrey de Havilland left the Royal Aircraft Factory; he had been invited to join the newly formed Aeronautical Directorate (A.I.D.) as 'Inspector of Aeroplanes' under the Chief Inspector – Colonel Fulton. The A.I.D. was an independent organisation empowered to inspect all aeroplanes and aero-engines, another sign of the growing awareness of safety in aeroplane design and manufacture. By the end of May, de Havilland was back at his true vocation as Chief Designer for AIRCO based at Hendon.

It might be supposed that the one company that would rise to the challenge presented by the 504 and Tabloid would be the British & Colonial. In February it produced a small biplane known originally as the Baby Biplane, designed by Frank Barnwell. It was first trialled by Harry Busteed at Larkhill when he managed to attain a top speed of 96 m.p.h. After it appeared in the Aero Show in March the wing-span was extended to 24½ feet to improve performance and it now became known as a Scout A. Unlike the 504 and Tabloid it was a single-seater with less room for the pilot, in fact Cecil Lewis (of *Sagittarius Rising* fame) described it as '... so small that even an average man had to be eased in with a shoehorn.'! The performance of the improved Scout B was so promising that production went ahead. During the first eighteen months of the war over 160 Bristol Scouts were in service with the RFC in France despite the fact that they were delivered unarmed; the choice of weapons – shotguns, rifles and machine-guns – was left to individual pilots! They were flown by many famous WWI pilots, such as Captain Albert Ball, V.C., Major W.G. Moore and Captain Lanoe Hawker, V.C., who thought it '... a beautiful little toy ...'; it was whilst flying his Scout in July 1915 that Hawker was awarded his V.C.

In April a Tabloid advanced the reputation of Sopwith Aviation by no small measure and in the process became the first *British-built* machine to win an International competition – the Schneider Trophy for seaplanes. It was only the second competition for this Trophy donated by Jacques Schneider, the son of a wealthy French arms-dealer. In the 1920s this International competition became one of the most prestigious events in the aviation calendar – a severe test for new and fast seaplanes. For this competition a Tabloid was fitted with twin-floats and provided with a powerful 100 h.p. Gnôme Monosoupape engine. The contest was held at Monaco on 20th April and because of Hawker's absence in Australia, Harold 'Picky' Pickton, an experienced pilot, was contracted to fly the Tabloid. The race was an out-and-out speed trial comprising twenty-eight laps (about 173 miles) as well as taxiing on the water for a half a mile. The winner received the splendid and ornate Trophy and prize money of 25,000 francs (about £1,000). There were ten entrants, mainly French, including the previous winner – Maurice Prévost. However, Pixton won the Trophy convincingly completing the course in 2 hours and 13 seconds at an average speed of 86.8 m.p.h.; he even flew two additional laps at a speed of 92 m.p.h – then a world record for seaplanes. The British victory was a severe blow to French national pride, and as one British newspaper proclaimed, '... it was the dawning ascendancy of the British aviation industry.' Certainly as a result of the victory the Sopwith Company received over 160 orders for Schneider-type seaplanes.

Despite deepening signs of an impending war the various events and

W.L. Brock – the most successful pilot in the summer of 1914. (Smithsonian Inst.)

races staged at Brooklands and Hendon still attracted thousands of enthusiasts. On 9th May Hendon was the scene of the first parachute drop from an aeroplane in Britain, although parachuting from balloons had become fairly common during the past decade. The intrepid parachutist, William Newell, with the moral support of another parachutist Frank Gooden, was taken up in Grahame-White's Charabanc. Newell was perched precariously on one of the skids and at a height of 2,000 feet he jumped and landed safely about 2½ minutes later using a British Guardian Angel parachute invented by Everard Calthrop. He was awarded a silver medal by the Royal Aero Club. Although parachutes were used by those manning observation balloons during the war, none were issued to RFC pilots; the official view seemed to correspond with that of *Flight* 'A pilot's job is to stick with his aeroplane.'!

Two weeks later one of the 'darlings' of the Hendon crowds – Gustav Hamel – was lost at sea. He had left Villacoublay for Hendon in his new Morane-Saulnier monoplane, which he planned to race in the forthcoming Aerial Derby and was last seen over the English Channel, his eighteenth crossing. Although naval vessels searched the Channel there was no trace of him or his aeroplane and it was assumed that he had been blown out over the North Sea and had run out of fuel. His loss was sadly mourned and allowed an American aviator – Walter L.

Brock – to step in and win all the major flying prizes during June and July. Brock, a twenty-eight year old from Bloomington, Illinois, had learned to fly at Hendon during 1912 and was now instructing at Grahame-White's Flying School. He proceeded to win the third Aerial Derby on 6th June in his 80 h.p. Morane-Saulnier at an average speed of 71 m.p.h. beating an Avro 504 and the Sopwith Schneider Trophy machine. Two weeks later he claimed victory in the Hendon-Manchester-Hendon race (332 miles) in five hours and forty-nine minutes. On 11th July he was placed first in the Hendon-Paris-Hendon race in just over seven hours of flying. In a mere three weeks Brock won £1,750 – the most successful pilot in Europe. Although obviously a fine airmen, he was rather taciturn and unsmiling and lacked the charisma of Gustav Hamel.

In June the Military Wing of the RFC was ordered to Netheravon for a month's training at what was called a 'Camp of Concentration'. There were lectures, discussions of tactics, trials and experiments to test the military potential of the various machines. The Wing was reviewed by His Majesty. No 2 squadron started their long journey from Montrose on 11th May and their machines created great public interest wherever

RNAS seaplanes at Calshot in July 1914 before the Royal Review of the Fleet. (FAA Museum)

they stopped. No 6 squadron, formed in January, was still not fully equipped, No 7 squadron was in the process of forming as was No 8 squadron. There was a motley collection of B.E.s, Avro biplanes, Blériots and Farmans lined up at Netheravon along with 700 officers and men, all proud to be serving in the RFC. It was no small achievement for the Corps to have progressed thus far, considering all the trials, tribulations and lamentable funding of its early years.

The Naval Wing was soon to be divorced from the RFC, finally recognising that the aerial needs of the two Services were quite different. Each could now develop and adopt methods, equipment and flying machines more suited to their operational requirements. On 1st July the Royal Naval Air Service was formed with Commodore Murray Sueter appointed as the first Director of the Air Department at the Admiralty. The Service had a Central Air Office, Flying School and a number of air stations along the coasts – Winston Churchill had prevailed. Early in the month many of the Service's airmen and aeroplanes gathered at Hilsea with its seaplanes at Calshot prior to their participation in the Royal review of the Fleet at Portsmouth. Several wags suggested that the initials 'RNAS' stood for 'Really Not A Sailor'! On the 28th there was a clear demonstration of the different requirements of the Service when a Squadron Commander flying a Short S.84 seaplane at Calshot became the first Naval airman to drop an aerial torpedo, the seaplane had been fitted with a quick release mechanism designed by Flt. Lt. D. H. Hyde-Thompson.

By the end of the month military preparations for hostilities had practically grounded all private flying. On the August Bank Holiday (3rd) Hendon held its last peacetime meeting before a very meagre crowd and needless to say Brock won the final peacetime handicap race. In the evening Grahame-White received an order from Reginald McKenna, the Home Secretary 'I prohibit the navigation of aircraft of every class and description over the whole area of the United Kingdom and the whole of the coastline and territorial waters adjacent thereto ...' Grahame-White thought at the time that 'the great war has come soon for aviation, almost too soon, but it may yet prove a blessing in disguise.' On 4th August the country was at war with Germany and many feared that 'the peaceful skies over England would be no more.'

6
'THE AERIAL BOMBARDMENT UPON ENGLAND'
(1914–1918)

By the end of the war the sight of aeroplanes and airships in the skies and on the ground had become commonplace such was the profusion of aerodromes, landing grounds, seaplane and airship stations that had mushroomed throughout the country. There were hundreds of companies, large and small, engaged in building aeroplanes under contract to the War Office and the Admiralty and employing nearly 350,000 workers. From 1915 the civilian population in many parts of the country found themselves under attack from the air, the first in history to suffer from 'an aerial bombardment' and aeroplanes and airships were revealed as 'instruments of death and destruction'; thus by 1918 the mystique of flying machines had long since vanished and with it much of the glamour and innocence of those peacetime days of flying.

At the outbreak of war the handful of private aerodromes were requisitioned under the Defence of the Realm Act; Hendon became a RNAS training depot and an Aircraft Acceptance Park for the receipt, assembly and testing of new aeroplanes. Brooklands remained on almost the same footing as pre-war but with its flying schools controlled by the RFC and amalgamated into a Military Training School; as the war progressed the military presence at Hendon and Brooklands was greatly extended.

The RFC comprised some one hundred and ninety assorted machines, of which only sixty-three were considered operational, whereas the RNAS possessed about ninety along with seven airships. These figures were well below the respective strengths of the French

BE.2c – the RFC's all-purpose aeroplane.

and German air forces. From 13th/15th August four RFC squadrons, Nos 2 to 5, left from Swingate Downs, Dover for Amiens in France, the first of thousands of airmen to cross the Channel to join the costly air war over the trenches, which is not part of this account. In one fell swoop virtually the whole of the RFC had departed to France under Brigadier-General Sir David Henderson with Sykes as his deputy. This left a handful of serviceable machines in the U.K. to be used for flying training, commanded by Major Trenchard, who was given a clear brief – to build up new squadrons for the RFC in France.

As for the public they waited in trepidation for the first appearance of a Zeppelin or 'Zepp', so convinced by propaganda that they posed a new and real potent threat from the hitherto 'peaceful skies'. Days passed and the Zepps did not come although there were ample rumours of sightings along the coasts and many false alarms. On 25th August a Zeppelin bombed Antwerp killing twelve civilians and was condemned as an atrocity; 'the writing was on the wall' for all those who cared to acknowledge it. Churchill certainly had no doubts that '... an aerial attack upon England must be a feature of the near future...'

In September Lord Kitchener, the new Secretary of State for War, decreed that the RNAS would be responsible for the country's Air Defence until such time as the RFC had trained sufficient pilots to take over. Although Churchill stated that the RNAS was in no fit state to undertake the task, his Air Service '... would do the best possible with the material available.' With characteristic verve and drive Churchill, assisted by Murray Sueter, devised a system of defence around London comprising a ring of anti-aircraft guns manned by Naval Volunteer Reservists, searchlights and volunteer observers to watch for hostile intruders. It was decided that a 'black out' would be imposed between the hours of 5 p.m and 7.30 a.m. and effective from the 1st October in London; street lamps were extinguished or shaded and householders were required to draw their blinds before lamps were lit. These measures were unpopular and many refused to conform claiming that they 'were not frightened of Zeppelins'! Nevertheless the imposition of the 'black out' only served to heighten public apprehension.

The few RNAS stations along the Kent and East Anglian coasts provided some aerial defence as would their machines based at Hendon. Indeed the first night-sortie of the war left from Hendon on 5th September, when Flt. Lts. Grahame-White and Gates took-off in response to an alarm, which proved to be false. Five days later Gates was killed when returning to Hendon late in the evening after another false alarm; the Air Defence of London had claimed its first victim, the first of many to be killed in night-flying accidents. Several new landing grounds in Essex and Kent were planned and emergency landing sites prepared in Regents, Battersea and Hyde Parks. Churchill also ordered 'vigorous and offensive attacks on the enemy's airships and aeroplanes before they reached these shores.' But his most contentious proposal

Bristol Scout about to take-off from RNAS Eastchurch. (FAA Museum)

German Navy Zeppelin – 1915 – the 'dreaded Zepp'.

was the pre-emptive bombing attacks on German airship sheds. Thus it was that the RNAS instigated the first strategic bombing raids and No 1 squadron crossed to Ostend to patrol the Channel.

The first attack was mounted on 22nd September when four Tabloids left Ostend for the airship sheds at Düsseldorf and Cologne; only Flt. Lt. Collet was able to locate his target but his two bombs failed to explode. The squadron moved to forward bases at Antwerp and Belfort, France and on 8th October two aeroplanes left for the same targets; this time Flt. Lt. Marix scored a direct hit on the shed at Düsseldorf and destroyed Zeppelin L9.(LZ.25). Sqn. Cdr. Spenser-Grey unable to locate his target, bombed the railway station at Cologne killing three civilians. But the most audacious attack was made on 21st November, directed at the Zeppelin sheds at Friedrichshafen on Lake Constance – the pride of the Zeppelin empire. Four Avro 504s despatched directly from Manchester were each loaded with four 20 lbs bombs. One machine failed to take-off and the other three led by Sqn. Cdr. Featherstone-Briggs flew from Belfort. A gas works was set on fire and Zeppelin L.7 (LZ.32) was damaged. Briggs wounded in the attack, was forced to land and he was taken prisoner but later escaped. Flt. Cdr. Babington and Flt. Lt. Sippe returned safely almost five hours later. This epic raid was considered one of the finest displays of courage and skill of the war. These operations ruffled the feathers of the War Office, who maintained that it was the duty of the RFC in

France to attack the German airship sheds. When the long anticipated air attack finally materialised it came not from Zeppelins but from a solitary FF.29 seaplane. On 21st December two bombs fell harmlessly into the sea near Admiralty Pier, Dover and four days later a bomb was dropped near Dover Castle. On Christmas Day a seaplane appeared over the Thames Estuary, it flew over Gravesend and Sheerness before dropping two bombs near Cliffe railway station. Although a RNAS Vickers Gunbus made contact and fired a couple of shots, the intruder escaped. Clearly if enemy aeroplanes could reach the coasts it would only be a matter of time before machines became available with the range to penetrate further inland.

1915 has been called 'the Year of the Zeppelin' with some justification as there were twenty raids in total causing considerable damage, the loss of 200 lives and over 550 injured. The 'Zepps' appeared to be indestructible, roaming the night skies over England with impunity, encountering scant opposition from the meagre force of Home Defence (H.D.) aeroplanes based around London. The distinctive roar of the engines could be clearly heard as they passed overhead and soon began 'to instil a special kind of fear'. The first raid was made on the evening of 19th January when twenty-three bombs were dropped in Norfolk killing four people and injuring another sixteen. There was outrage in the Press and whilst the country braced itself for the next attack, widespread rumours of German spies and reports of motor-car lights signalling to the dreaded 'Zepps' freely circulated and were firmly believed by most people.

From April to September Zeppelins bombed the Humberside, Tyneside, East Anglia, Kent and finally London. On 10th May the Commander of the Army Zeppelin LZ.38, *Hauptmann* Erich Linnartz, frustrated by anti-aircraft fire, left his 'calling card' over Southend-on-Sea, Essex; the message read 'You English. We have come and will come again. Kill or Cure. German.'! The final attack occurred on the night of 13/14th October and was the most severe; five Naval airships dropped 190 bombs on parts of London and the Home Counties killing seventy-one and injuring 128 people and causing damage estimated at £80,000. Second Lieutenant John Slessor in a B.E.2c from Suttons Farm, Essex actually sighted a Zeppelin, L.15, and gave chase but it escaped – the first interception by a H.D. pilot.

The problems facing these intrepid airmen were formidable. Taking-off and landing at night was extremely hazardous, without the

Airco DH.1 first flew in January 1915 and remained operational until 1917.

difficulty of sighting and giving chase to the well-armed Zeppelins. The H.D. aeroplanes (mostly B.E. 2cs) were too slow and did not have sufficient height to counter the Zeppelins, and their armament was woefully inadequate for the task. They were provided with bombs to drop onto the Zeppelins as their guns were thought to be of little use; incendiary bullets and rockets were introduced later. The celebrated Zeppelin commander, *Kapitan-Leutenant* Heinrich Mathy, remarked 'As to an aeroplane corps for the defence of London, it must be remembered that it takes some time for an aeroplane to screw itself as high as a Zeppelin, and by the time it gets there the airship would be gone.' Nevertheless one pilot, Flt. Sub-Lt. Warneford of No 1 RNAS squadron had, on 7th June, destroyed Zeppelin LZ.37 over Belgium by dropping six bombs onto the airship and was lucky to survive the blast. He was awarded the Victoria Cross but sadly was killed in a flying accident a few days later.

The October raid caused indignation in the country, the Government was attacked in Parliament and the Press for failing to protect London. Public meetings were held and there were strident demands for reprisal raids on German cities; newspapers dubbed the Zeppelin airmen 'women and baby killers'. Some action needed to be taken and it was decided to place the control of the Home Defence under the War Office and Lord French (who had recently been replaced as C-in-C France by General Sir Douglas Haig) assumed overall command. It was recognised that the RNAS was fully extended with its U-boat patrols but it was also clear that the RFC would not be in a position to take over the H.D. duties until early 1916; the formal handover was made on 10th February.

U-boats posed an even greater threat to the country than the air attacks and since the early days of the war they had taken a steady toll on shipping. At the end of 1914 the control of airships had passed to the Admiralty, and it favoured airships for the defence of the coasts and sea lanes rather than aeroplanes because of their greater endurance. Indeed the first coastal patrols had mounted as early as 10th August 1914 by H.M.A. Nos 3 and 4. The Naval Airship Service, which steadily increased from 1915, gave invaluable aerial cover and acted as escorts for convoys. The Admiralty established thirty airship stations/sub-stations along the coasts, their most prominent feature was the massive airship sheds some three hundred feet long and seventy feet high. From 1915 the Admiralty originally placed its faith in the small 'SS' (Sea or Submarine Scout) non-rigid airships, which were 'capable of being flown by young midshipmen with small boat training'. They were familiarly known as 'Blimps' and one airman wistfully recalled, 'To fly a ship on a nice day was a really delightful experience. One felt that the air was entirely one's own.' During 1916 they were mainly replaced by the larger 'Coastal' and 'Coastal*' airships, which became the 'work-horses' of the Service; fitted with wireless, they were able to patrol for ten/twelve hours and were armed with two machine guns as well as bombs and depth charges. Over the next few years many airships were built – 'SSZs' (Zero), SSPs (Pushers), SSE (Experimental), SSTs (Twin) along with the larger NS (North Sea) that appeared in April 1917.

The RNAS had over fifty aeroplane and seaplane bases along the coasts where a mixture of machines, many of them seaplanes, carried out coastal and North Sea patrols. One of the most lasting contributions made by the RNAS was the development and operational use of flying boats. In November 1914 John Porte, who had worked closely with the Curtiss Co. in America, persuaded the Admiralty to purchase two Curtiss flying boats. He was given the rank of Squadron Commander and he evaluated their performance at RNAS Felixstowe. There were problems with the seaworthiness of the hulls but Porte made certain modifications. As a result of his recommendation sixty-two were purchased and designated Curtiss H.4. In 1916 a larger and more powerful H.12 version was received, which became known as the large America and the H.4 the Small America. The former was crewed by two pilots and four gunners and carried two 230 lb bombs; it had a

Curtiss H.12. The Large America flying boat at Felixstowe. (Imperial War Museum)

maximum speed of 85 m.p.h and could patrol for up to six hours. Both became the mainstay of RNAS coastal squadrons and proved to be most reliable, although after the appearance of the H.12s, the Small America was largely used for training. These Curtiss machines led directly to the development of the Felixstowe F.2A flying boats, which entered the Service in the summer of 1918.

Zeppelins returned early in 1916; on the night of 31st January nine

roamed over the Midlands without any opposition, one managed to get as far west as Shrewsbury. Despite heavy ground mist at several landing grounds sixteen defence sorties were mounted but no sightings were made and sadly two experienced pilots were killed in landing accidents, one at Northolt and the other at Joyce Green. This raid resulted in Major T. Higgins of 19 squadron at Hounslow Heath being given overall command of all units at the airfields around London.

LIEUT. WILLIAM LEEFE ROBINSON, V.C.,
Worcester Regiment and R.F.C.,
Who brought down the Zeppelin at Cuffley, near Enfield.
ST. JAMES' PRESS, ROSOMAN ST., CLERKENWELL, E.C.

Extra B.E.2cs were provided for training squadrons around the country and it was also decided that ten of the seventy new squadrons planned for the RFC would be designated for H.D. However, the flying training programme was barely coping in providing replacements for RFC squadrons in France. Selected pilots were now being given two practice landings at night and that effectively qualified them as 'night-flying pilots'!

During April there were eight Zeppelin raids, five on consecutive nights, and although the number of night-sorties increased no contacts were made. Changes were made in the organisation of the Home Defence. Flying training was removed from the squadrons, six H.D. squadrons were allocated and a searchlight unit of six lights was attached to each. Nevertheless the misery for the civilian population continued through the summer but mercifully with few fatalities. The German High Command planned a major operation for the night of 2/3rd September – their largest so far and it became known as 'Zepp Sunday'. Fourteen Zeppelins and two Schütte-Lanz airships left to attack London, Lincolnshire and Nottingham; 463 bombs were dropped with four people killed and twelve injured. However, that night S.L.11 was famously brought down in flames over Cuffley in Hertfordshire by Lt. W. Leefe Robinson of 39 squadron at Sutton's Farm. The blazing airship was visible for miles, even as far as London, and it was reported that many thousands witnessed the destruction. Leefe Robinson became a hero overnight, within days he was awarded the Victoria Cross as well as receiving £4,250 in prize money as the first pilot to bring down a Zeppelin on British soil.

Quite undeterred the Zeppelins returned to London on 23/24th September. This time 2nd Lt. F. Sowrey, also of 39 squadron, destroyed L.32 – it came down in flames at Great Burstead, Essex. Another of the so-called 'super Zeppelins' – L.33 – crashed near Little Wigborough, Essex, after suffering damage from anti-aircraft fire and the attentions of Lt. Alfred Brandon; both airmen were awarded the Distinguished Service Order. As with the Cuffley airship, thousands of Londoners and local people flocked to the site to see the remains of an 'invincible Zepp', even special trains ran from Liverpool Street station to cope with the crowds. The squadron's reputation was enhanced eight nights later when Lt. W. Tempest from North Weald Bassett, Essex shot down L.31 near Potters Bar. The legendary Zeppelin commander, Mathy, was killed in L.31 and his death had a profound effect on the German Naval Airship Service. As a leader he was irreplaceable and his death really heralded the end of the Airship Service. Two more were lost on the final raid of 1916. On 27/28th November L.34, after bombing Hartlepool, was destroyed by 2nd Lt Pyott of 36 squadron at Cramlington. Further south another – L.21 – found a watery grave off Lowestoft after being attacked by Fl. Lt. E. Cadbury and Fl. Sub-Lt. E. Pulling of the RNAS. Of the ten Zeppelins that set out on that night, two turned back with engine trouble, six failed to reach their objectives and two were destroyed. The German High Command faced the grim reality that their grand design to bring Great Britain to its knees had apparently failed, and it seemed that at last the battle against the Zeppelins had been won.

There was precious little time to celebrate these victories because at around noon on 28th November an enemy L.V.G. biplane brazenly flew over central London and dropped six bombs on Knightsbridge and Victoria, slight damage was sustained and eleven people were injured. The intruder escaped unhindered although it crash-landed at Boulogne and the two airmen were captured. Most people considered this to be nothing more than a sporadic raid similar to those that had plagued the Kent coast on a number of occasions. However, the *Daily Mail* thought otherwise: 'It is wise to regard it as a prelude to further visits on an extended scale and to lay plans accordingly ...' *The Aeroplane* was convinced that it was a prelude of things to come: 'When the aeroplane raids start and prove more damaging than the airship raids, the authorities cannot say they have not had fair warning of what to expect.' An accurate assessment as the raid proved to be the curtain raiser to a new phase of the aerial bombardment of the country, only this time more frightening and more destructive.

The Government faced a constant problem of balancing the vociferous clamour for a strong and effective H.D. Force and the seemingly insatiable demand for airmen and aeroplanes by the RFC in France. From July to December 1916, 500 airmen had been killed or were missing with almost another 500 injured and although pilots were being trained at a rate of 300 per month, Field-Marshal Haig and Major-General Trenchard (Commander of the RFC in France) were continually demanding experienced H.D. pilots to be transferred to France. By the end of 1916 over 17,300 officers/men were serving in the anti-aircraft and searchlight batteries with some 110 aeroplanes and 200 airmen in ten H.D. squadrons, at a time when every trained man was needed on the Western Front.

In response to the rapid growth of the RFC and RNAS there had been a remarkable increase in aeroplane manufacture during the year with over 6,600 machines being delivered from some 1,700 firms now engaged in the industry or 'the trade', as it was rather disparagingly referred to by senior officials of the War Office! Several new companies had entered the industry and their names and the aircraft they subsequently produced would become well-known in the years ahead – Armstrong Whitworth, Beardmore, Boulton Paul, Fairey Aviation, Parnall, Supermarine and Westland. Unquestionably the technical design and performance of British aeroplanes had improved largely in response to the experiences of the RFC in France, which hitherto had been facing and fighting superior German machines. However, 1916 can be seen as the turning point when four famous fighters first appeared – Sopwith Pup and Camel, Bristol F2B Fighter (Brisfit) and the S.E.5 – all operated with H.D. squadrons and the RNAS, at least after winning their laurels in France.

The Sopwith Pup first flew in February and deliveries began in the late summer, originally to No 8 (RNAS) squadron. It had been designed by Herbert Smith in 1915 and was largely based on the successful Tabloid and 1½-Strutter. With a wing span of 26½ feet and 19 feet long it was a neat and compact single-seater biplane but also very rugged; it is reputed to have gained its name from when it was first seen beside a larger Sopwith machine with the remark '. . . it looks as though it had a pup . . .'! Pilots considered it 'a perfect flying machine . . . with no tricks or vices . . . by far the prettiest to look at and sweetest on the controls . . . it handled like a true thoroughbred . . .'. On 2nd August 1917 a Pup flown by Sqn. Cdr. Dunning made the first successful landing on HMS *Furious*; he was killed five days later when attempting his third landing. Over 1,840 Pups were produced but by 1918 they were taken out of the front-line units and relegated to training.

Its successor – the Camel – was Sopwith's most successful fighter, and immortalised by the famous *Biggles* stories of Captain W. E. Johns. The name, originally unofficial, derived from the humped appearance created by the fairing over the twin Vickers guns in the front of the pilot. It was also designed by Herbert Smith but had none of the Pup's docile handling qualities and was not easy to fly but once mastered it was highly manoeuvrable with an impressive performance. It proved to be the most successful WWI fighter credited with the destruction of more enemy machines than any other Allied fighter. The prototype first flew at Brooklands in December and Camels became operational in

Sopwith Pup hoisted from below decks aboard H.M.S. Furious. (FAA Museum)

July 1917, first with the RNAS. They were produced in prodigious quantities – over 5,800 – although not surviving long in the post-war RAF unlike the Bristol Brisfit. It was Frank Barnwell's most successful

Bristol Fighter – over 5,700 were produced and not retired until 1932. (via G. Weir)

SE.5A – a rugged and reliable fighter arrived in the spring of 1917.

German G.N. Gotha – '...mobile magazines of death...' (Imperial War Museum)

design for British & Colonial and first flew in September, was larger than the Camel, with a wing span of 39¼ feet and almost 26 feet long. The Brisfit had a top speed of 123 m.p.h and could operate up to 18,000 feet. It was a two-seater armed with a forward Lewis gun and Vickers in the rear cockpit. The first arrived with the RFC in March 1917 and quickly gained a fearsome reputation; over 5,700 were built and they were not 'retired' from the RAF until 1932.

The S.E.5A was the product of the Royal Aircraft Factory and first appeared in November. It was a rugged, reliable and steady machine armed with two Vickers guns, one sited on the top wing so that its fire was clear of the propeller. The first S.E.5As were issued to a new squadron, No 56, that was forming at London Colney in the spring of 1917. In action their performance was found to be equal to the German Albatros D.Vs but later in the year they were supplied with a more powerful engine, which made them a formidable fighter. Over 5,000 were produced and many were flying in private hands in the 1920s when they pioneered 'sky-writing'.

In early 1917 the Government, now a Coalition led by David Lloyd George, was under even greater pressure to release airmen from the H.D. Force for service in France. It was thought by many that they were 'idling their time away' whilst their colleagues in France were fighting for their lives almost daily. In February thirty-six H.D. pilots were sent

Sopwith NF Camel over Sutton's Farm, Essex. (via G. Weir)

to France mainly to form two new night-flying squadrons and it was also agreed that three squadrons would be sent to France on 'a temporary basis'. Thus the Home Defence comprised about seventy pilots described by one newspaper as 'a thin line of young men with their flimsy machines'.

As the memories of the Zeppelin raids slowly receded and RFC casualties in France escalated – 316 airmen were lost in what became known as 'Bloody April' – the H.D. Force was seen as an expensive luxury despite the fact that the Zeppelins had returned on 16/17th March when four crossed Kent and Sussex. These were the so-called 'height climbers', operating well out the reach of the defending fighters. Little damage was sustained and there were no casualties; one was shot down by anti-aircraft fire over France on return.

On 1st May the RNAS introduced a new patrol system code-named Spider's Web; four seaplane anti-U-boat and anti-Zeppelin patrols were set up to fly octagonal segments sixty miles across covering 4,000 square miles. Within two weeks the patrols were successful, a H.12, piloted by Flt. Lt. Galpin destroyed Zeppelin, L.22. and a month later another Large America flown by Flt. Lt. Hobbs destroyed Zeppelin, L.42. The H.12s were equally effective against U-boats, three were destroyed over a period of four months, without doubt a most successful time for the RNAS.

The country was unaware that the German High Command was assembling a fleet of G (large) bombers for a heavy bombing offensive on London and the South East – the project was known as *Turkenkreuz* (Turk's Cross) and the force as *Englandgeschwader* (England Squadron). The heavy bombers – G.IVs – were known as Gothas from the Gothaer Faggonfabrik Company that first designed them in 1915. They were twin-engined biplanes with a wing span of seventy-seven feet, manned by a crew of three and were armed with a forward gun as well as a dorsal gun, which could additionally be trained through a tunnel in the middle of the fuselage to fire downwards. Their cruising speed was about 80 m.p.h with a normal bomb load of 660 lbs and they were provided with a rudimentary Goertz bomb-sight. The England Squadron was led by *Kapitänleutant* Ernst Brandenburg, an infantry officer who had been wounded in 1914 and then qualified as an observer. By May *Kagohl* 3 with four Flights (*Staffeln*) of six G.IVs were ready at their four airfields in Belgium, their crews having undergone rigorous training; the squadron would operate in tight formations of aeroplanes to give added fire-power and greater protection and thus became the pioneers of heavy bomber formation flying – such a feature of WWII bombing operations.

On 25th May Brandenburg led twenty-one Gothas on their first mission, with London as the target. When they were sighted by a lightship the RNAS was informed and the first sorties were launched from Westgate. Heavy cloud over London frustrated Brandenburg so he turned south at Gravesend to seek military targets at Dover and Folkestone. The first bombs were dropped on Maidstone and the airfield at Lympne but it was Folkestone that sustained the heaviest damage and the greatest loss of life. The bombers flying at about 15,000 feet were described as 'bright silver insects' and '... beautiful with the sun on their wings ...' that is before the bombs began to fall. Despite all the valiant efforts of RFC and RNAS pilots they escaped, although Flt. Lt. Reginald Leslie of the RNAS at Dover was awarded the D.S.O. for his vain chase of the force over the English Channel in a Pup. Two were shot down by RNAS aeroplanes from Dunkirk and a third crashed in Belgium.

There was public anger in Folkestone when the full import of the damage and fatalities was known – '... The material damage, however is nothing compared with the casualty list, upwards of seventy having been killed at the time or succumbing since to their injuries ... an abominable attack in which women and children have been the main sufferers ...' In total 139 bombs were dropped, ninety-five people were killed and nearly two hundred injured. The Government suffered considerable opprobrium for its apparent complacency and lack of an air-raid warning system. Even the hastily convened high-level meeting at the War Office on 31st May was unable to propose anything more tangible than transferring extra training aeroplanes into the area, which were of no practical use to counter the Gothas. It was maintained that H.D. could not be allocated any more machines 'without prejudicing the requirements of other theatres ...'; perhaps more sobering was the opinion that '... no measures that could be taken would prevent bombs being dropped on towns ...'

On 5th June twenty-two Gothas were bound for London in broad daylight, several sightings were made in Essex, but London was once more saved by heavy cloud. The formation turned and bombed Shoeburyness on the Essex coast before attacking Sheerness. Although the raid lasted no more than fifteen minutes, thirteen people were killed and thirty-four injured. The anti-aircraft batteries claimed one, which was seen to crash into the sea; the officer in charge of the

Fine montage of aeroplanes from 1910 to 1918. Painted by G.H. Davis in 1935.

batteries reported 'I think the guns were well fought . . .' Sixty fighters were airborne but obviously their aircraft were quite inadequate for the task and also there were no accepted tactics for attacking a formation of strongly-armed bombers.

It was only a matter of time before the Gothas would reach London and the inevitable came on the 13th. One bombed Margate as a feint, whilst the squadron divided into two wings and carried on to London. The bombs fell in a random fashion – Barking, East Ham, the City, Islington and Liverpool Street station. It was almost perfect timing – lunchtime – and city workers were shocked to see and hear the explosions of bombs. Lt. Siegfried Sassoon, M.C., on leave from France, was at the station and later recalled 'This sort of danger seemed to me to demand a quality of courage dissimilar to front line fortitude. In a trench one was acclimatised to the notion of being exterminated and there was a sense of organised retaliation. But here one was helpless; an invisible enemy sent destruction spinning down from a fine weather sky' – the 'angry helplessness' felt by so many Londoners. But the worst disaster was caused by the bombs that fell on Upper North Street School at Poplar, where eighteen children (fifteen aged five or under) were killed and another eighteen injured. The raid cost the lives of 170 with another 432 injured, and brought insistent demands for Government action and a clamour for reprisal bombing raids. *The Times* wrote: 'It slew women and children as well as men . . . and increased the utter and most universal detestation with which the Hun is held by the people of this country . . .' The Government brought the successful 56 squadron back from France and also transferred 66 squadron to Calais to patrol the coasts, although Field Marshal Haig maintained this was merely a 'temporary measure' and their return to front-line action was guaranteed for 5th July. On 17th June two Naval Zeppelins crossed the Kent and Suffolk coasts. One, L-48, was brought down by the combined efforts of Captain Saundby, M.C. of the Experimental Station at Orfordness and 2nd Lt. Watkins of 37 squadron at Goldhanger, Essex. The airship crashed in flames near Theberton, Suffolk and was the last to be brought down on British soil.

The Gothas returned on 4th July, led by *Kapitän* Rudolf Klein; Brandenburg had been injured in a flying accident whilst returning from Mainz after receiving an award for his leadership of the England Squadron. Although extensive damage was sustained at Harwich and Felixstowe the casualties were relatively light, forty-seven, of which seventeen were fatal. Once again they escaped without hardly any

H.D. pilots sighting them. Three days later (7th July) they returned to London, two days after 56 squadron had returned to France. This raid caused heavy damage estimated at over £½ million with fifty-seven fatalities. One was shot down into the Thames estuary by Lt. Grace and his observer Lt. Murray of 50 squadron. This raid was likened to '... the time when the Dutch fleet sailed up the Medway in 1667'. *Flight* described the Gothas as '... mobile magazines of death ... we watched deeply humiliated that such a thing could be achieved in daylight over London'. The public, the Press and Parliament roundly castigated the Government for their lack of action in the face of this 'latest outrage'. There were also demands for an air-raid warning system and matters for the Government were not improved when Lord Derby, Secretary of State for War, insensitively commented that '... not a single soldier had been killed in the raid ...'

As a result of the furore Lloyd George asked Lieutenant-General Jan Smuts, a member of his War Cabinet, to head a small Committee to examine and report urgently on the defensive arrangements for the Home Defence, and secondly the existing aerial organisation for a higher direction of aerial operations. Smuts was selected because it was considered 'he would bring a fresh and able mind free from departmental prejudices'. His first report was speedy; on 19th July he recommended the creation of separate zones for fighters and anti-aircraft fire, a ring of gun sites twenty-five miles around London, the provision of speedier communication with the H.D. pilots at their airfields and the creation of an overall command to co-ordinate all aspects and plans of the London Air Defences. Two days later as a response to public demand, maroons (maritime distress rockets) were issued to eighty selected sites in and around London, to be used as a warning of an impending air-raid. At the end of the month the London Air Defence Area was formed and Brigadier-General Edward B. 'Splash' Ashmore was brought from France to command it. Three squadrons were designated specifically to deal with the bombers; No 44 at Hainault Farm, Essex and No 112 at Throwley, Kent were equipped with Camels, whereas No 61 at Rochford, Essex had Pups. The Gotha raids brought about another change: on the 17th a Royal Proclamation announced that the Royal family name of Saxe-Coburg-Gotha had been changed to that of Windsor for obvious reasons considering the universal anathema of Germany and its Gothas.

On 12th August Southend, Shoeburyness and Margate were bombed, a Gotha was shot down by Flt. Sub-Lt. Kerby from Walmer after chasing it to the Belgian coast, his perseverance earning him a D.S.O. The ordeal at Southend was brief but severe, thirty-four bombs had been dropped killing thirty-three people; several were day-trippers waiting for a train. On the 22nd ten bombed Margate and three were lost to anti-aircraft fire and RNAS pilots, this would be the last daylight raid by *Kagohl* 3. Nineteen Gothas had been lost or severely damaged and with strengthening anti-aircraft defences around London it was decided to change to night-operations. The first was mounted on 3/4th September and the Chatham Naval base was bombed with dire consequences – one hundred and thirty-two recruits were killed and over ninety injured. In the late evening of the 4th nine attacked the centre of London causing substantial damage – the City's ordeal by night had begun.

Early in September, Ashmore established a barrage balloon defence for London – comprising 'aprons', each of three tethered balloons arranged in a straight line some 2,000 yards in length and linked by horizontal wires from which were suspended wire streamers. The

Air raid damage in Southend-on-Sea, Essex in 1917. (via R. Palmer)

balloon defence could be raised to a height of 10,000 feet and stretched in lines to the east of London. This physical barrier was intended in theory to force the bombers to fly higher and thus reduce the accuracy of the bombing. The worst and most prolonged bombing experience of the war for Londoners came in the last week when the City was bombed on five out of six nights. The terrified population mostly sought refuge in basements, railway and underground stations, although some considered it safer to spend the night in the open spaces of the parks where they could also watch 'the Hun's Air Show'. Gothas had been joined by the massive Staaken R Type heavy bombers or Giants with a wing-span of one hundred and forty feet, powered with four engines and carrying up to 2,200 lbs of bombs. In what became known as 'the fateful week' sixty-nine people were killed and another two hundred and ninety injured.

During the next three months the H.D. pilots were faced with a most difficult task; night-flying was hardly known, although night-training was quickly established first at Throwley, Sutton's Farm and Rochford. The cockpits of their machines were not fitted with any instrument lighting and the airfields were only illuminated with lines of flares – basically paraffin-soaked cotton waste in buckets. Unlike the large Zeppelins, the bombers were difficult to locate in the night skies. Lt. Cecil Lewis, flying with 44 squadron at Hainault Farm, recalled that night-patrols were '... two hour stretches of utter frustration, all we could hope to locate was the glow of an exhaust ... and then at the end of the patrol, we hoped that by the grace of God we could land safely ...'. Perhaps it is not surprising that it was not until 18th December that the first Gotha was destroyed at night by a H.D. fighter. Captain G. Murliss Green, commander of 44 squadron, first attacked a Gotha over Essex but it eluded him. He returned to Hainault Farm to refuel and re-arm and finally engaged another over Kent; this one did not escape and it crashed into the sea off Folkestone. During the year there had been twenty-eight bombing raids killing over six hundred and ninety civilians with another one thousand, six hundred and ten injured.

Besides the continual debate on the effectiveness of the H.D. Force, the most contentious matter concerning politicians and military men was General Smuts' recommendations for the reorganisation of the whole of the country's aerial war effort. His second report was presented to the War Cabinet on 17th August and it acknowledged that the aeroplane had become a weapon of strategic importance. It

General Ashmore's Barrage Balloon Defence for London.

recommended the establishment of an independent Ministry for Air, the amalgamation of the RFC and RNAS and the formation of an 'independent' bomber force. Many senior military officers were strongly opposed to the amalgamation of the two air services *per se*. There were several, like Trenchard, opposed to the proposal solely on the grounds of timing, the RFC was beginning to gain a marked ascendancy in France. In mid-October after much debate a bill was presented to constitute the Air Ministry entitled 'The Air Force (Constitution) Act' and on 29th November it received the Royal Assent as 'The Air Force Act'. In December it was laid down that the new Air Ministry would come into being on 2nd January 1918 and the RFC and the RNAS would formally amalgamate on 1st April 1918 to be known as the Royal Air Force. Thus the Air Ministry was formed with Viscount Rothermere, the younger brother of Lord Northcliffe, as the first Air Minister. Major-General Trenchard was persuaded to leave France to take up the position of Chief of the Air Staff. Unfortunately the two men did not see eye to eye and within four months both had resigned, a not particularly auspicious start for the new Department and Service.

Hopes that the ordeal by night had ceased were dashed on 28/29th January when three Gothas and a Giant bombed London and others attacked Sheerness, Margate and Ramsgate. The largest bomb – a mighty 660 pounder – fell close to Odhams Printing Works in the City, killing thirty-eight people who were sheltering in the basement. There were also several tragic incidents at two stations where a number of people were crushed in the panic to seek shelter. Although the H.D. Force had been strengthened by two new squadrons – Nos 141 and 143 – only one Gotha was destroyed, shot down by Captain Hackwill of 44 squadron. By the middle of March, Giants had bombed on four nights causing sixty-six fatalities and several Zeppelins returned to Yorkshire, Hartlepool and the Midlands and all escaped scot-free.

The country's preoccupation with the latest raids and less than promising news from the Western Front meant that the amalgamation of the two air services was rather a muted affair. From 1st April the Royal Air Force comprised 168 squadrons, fifty of which were RNAS and renumbered in the 200 series; most were serving abroad, mainly in France. On the same day the various women's volunteer services became known as the Women's Royal Air Force – about 25,000 strong. Little really changed as far as operations were concerned: RNAS airmen were given the equivalent military ranks and the Navy retained its aircraft carriers. The new Service adopted a light-blue uniform in stark contrast to the dull khaki and this soon became nicknamed 'Gertie Millers' – a reference to the celebrated Edwardian music-hall star noted for her colourful costumes. Because of the date of the formation, RAF men were dubbed 'Royal April Fools' until the joke

The Royal Air Force was formed on 1st April 1918. (via J. Adams)

wore a trifle thin. On the occasion of King George V's fifty-third birthday – 3rd June – new air gallantry awards were introduced, the Distinguished Flying Cross/Medal and the Air Force Cross/Medal for officers and other ranks respectively.

Trenchard's resignation was accepted on 13th April and he was replaced by Major-General Sykes, who less than four years earlier had been considered too junior to command the RFC in France. When Viscount Rothermere resigned twelve days later Lord Weir, who had made a marked improvement in the supply of aeroplanes and aero-engines since becoming Controller of Aeronautical Supplies in 1917, was appointed Air Minister. Thus two new faces headed the infant Department of State and new Service at a most important time because of the critical stage of the war and just as the RAF was establishing itself as an independent Service.

In May, Trenchard was given command of the Independent Air Force, which had been expressly created to conduct a bombing offensive without being controlled by either the War Office or the Admiralty. It owed its origins to the 41st Wing set up in France in October 1917 to carry out reprisal raids on German targets. The Wing became the VIII Brigade in March and was planned to comprise one hundred squadrons, although only nine bomber squadrons actually went into action. From June to November the Force conducted some one hundred and forty raids, over fifty on targets in Germany. Most of its squadrons were equipped with the most famous 'strategic' heavy bomber of the war – Handley Page 0/400, an improved version of the 0/100. This large twin-engined biplane had been designed in 1915 in response to the Admiralty's requirement for a 'bloody paralyser of an aeroplane' and it entered service with the RNAS in the autumn of 1916. Some seven months later the 0/400 appeared, which was powered by two Rolls-Royce Eagle VIII engines giving it a maximum speed of 97 m.p.h. Variously armed with three to five Lewis guns, it could carry up to 2,000 lbs of bombs and was crewed by four airmen. Some 450 were built and although they remained in the RAF until 1920, being superseded by the Vickers *Vimy*, which did not see active service, over forty 0/400s were converted into civil transports.

Despite the failure of its bombing offensive the German High Command ordered a massive strike of London on 19/20th May. Thirty-eight Gothas and three Giants were detailed but only thirteen crossed the coast. Three Gothas were shot down by H.D. pilots from Nos 39, 112 and 141 squadrons and another three fell to anti-aircraft fire; it was their heaviest loss of the war and marked the end of London's ordeal and its 'first blitz'.

In July (17th) seven Camels left HMS *Furious* to attack the Zeppelin sheds at Tondern in Denmark and two airships L.54 and L.60 were destroyed – the first and last shipborne aeroplane operation of the war. Nevertheless five Zeppelins attempted to bomb Norfolk on 5/6th

Handley Page 0/400 operated with the Independent Air Force.

August, one – L.70 – was destroyed by Flt. Lt. Cadbury; this night marked the end of the 'aerial bombardment' of the country – the dreaded Zepps and Gothas had been finally vanquished. The total number of fatalities was over 1,410 with another 3,410 injured and although these figures may be considered infinitesimal compared with the truly horrendous losses on the Western Front, the full horrors of war had been visited on the civilian population in no uncertain manner, which many maintained was 'a sad consequence of man's desire to fly'. The 'first blitz' was an ordeal of courage and fortitude under extreme conditions, which was not easily erased from the collective memory and sadly it would be repeated a mere twenty-two years later at a far greater cost.

As the Great War came to an end on 11th November, the RAF was the largest air force in the world with almost 23,000 machines and 103 airships and a strength of over a quarter of a million officers and men. There were just over four hundred airfields in the country, the majority of which would disappear in the next few years. Perhaps the most enduring legacy of this first air war was the advent of the heavy bomber, although neither the German nor the British offensives could be considered successful, the *diktat* of 'strategic' bombing held sway with most politicians and Service chiefs during the inter-war wars and led to the awesome aerial bombardments of the Second World War.

In August 1914 aviation was really still in its infancy and yet four years later the aeroplane had developed into a potent fighting machine that had ensured that no future war could be waged without a strong air force. There had been considerable advancements in design, performance and safety and especially in aero-engines. It was now the time for such technical improvements to be progressed and harnessed for peaceful purposes. As Sir Sefton Brancker, a member of the Air Council, wrote in 'The Golden Peace' edition of the *Daily Mail* 'The War has bequeathed to us as a nation, a great heritage in the air. Our pilots are the best, our designs the most efficient and our industry the greatest in the world. Supremacy in the air is ours for the making.' Also it should be said that the vast number of people engaged in aviation during the war, either in construction, support services or flying itself, ensured that there was now a far greater awareness and regard for flying, and this largely accounted for the enthusiasm for aviation and the popularity of flying in the years ahead.

7
THE SCHNEIDER TROPHY AND IMPERIAL AIRWAYS
(1919–1924)

In the immediate postwar years aviation struggled to survive as the country came to terms with the crippling effects of the war. By late 1920 the RAF was reduced to a fraction of its wartime strength. The few pioneer airlines equipped with makeshift warplanes faced strong opposition from heavily subsidised foreign airlines. Although there was a surfeit of cheap ex-military machines available, the costs of maintaining a private aircraft had risen alarmingly. Aircraft and engine manufacturers found almost overnight that large military contracts were cancelled without compensation and there was not, as yet, a commercial market to take its place.

As 1919 dawned no peace agreement had been signed so the RAF remained virtually intact for the time being. Since December Nos 18 and 120 squadrons had operated airmail flights from Lympne and Hawkinge to Cologne for the Army of Occupation. In the same month No 1 (Communications) squadron was formed at Hendon, followed in March by a second squadron; their task was to convey politicians and VIPs to the Peace Conference at Versailles. They were equipped with DH.4As, modified to provide enclosed accommodation for two passengers and a few 0/400s carrying up to ten passengers in rather rudimentary surroundings. The flights commenced in January and by September well over seven hundred had been completed; at least the RAF had shown the way forward.

On 19th February a Department of Civil Aviation was formed, with Major-General Sir Frederick Sykes as its first Controller-General, and was placed within the Air Ministry where it remained for many years.

Churchill, now Secretary of State for War and Air, was aware that Lloyd George favoured returning the air services to the Army and Admiralty, a proposal he strongly opposed; thus he invited Sir Hugh Trenchard to return as Chief of the Air Staff as he held similar views. Sir Hugh began a tenure of ten years, during which time he stamped his personal mark on the Service, fully justifying his unofficial title – 'The Father of the RAF'.

Civil and private flying recommenced on 1st May with the introduction of the Air Navigation Regulations. The British Civil Register proper was established, under the control of the new Department, requiring civil aircraft to carry identification markings, originally K.100 onwards but changed in July to commence with 'G-EAAA'; aircraft were also compelled to have a Certificate of Airworthiness. The Department also regulated the issue of 'B' licences to commercial pilots. Several companies were ready to enter into commercial aviation – Handley Page Transport Ltd, A.V. Roe & Co, Aircraft Transport & Travel and North Sea Aerial & General Navigation Co.

Lt.-Col. W. F. Sholto Douglas piloting an 0/400 of Handley Page Transport made the first commercial flight on 1st May taking ten passengers from Cricklewood to Alexandra Park, Manchester. During the month passengers, along with newspapers, were conveyed to several towns and cities; in nine months over 1,500 passengers and forty tons of freight were carried. Ten days later Avro Civil Aviation Service started scheduled flights from Alexandra Park to Southport and Blackpool; when the service was withdrawn on 30th September, ninety-four flights had been made. Aircraft Transport & Travel was founded in October 1916 by George Holt Thomas, who was convinced that commercial aviation would have a bright future after the war. It was engaged in carrying food and clothing parcels to Belgium from Hawkinge using RAF pilots. North Sea Aerial & General Navigation (a subsidiary of Blackburn Aeroplane Co.) used Blackburn Kangaroos on a service from Hounslow Heath to Leeds. These large and ungainly aircraft had been used on anti-submarine patrols during 1918 and had been speedily adapted to take seven passengers. Thus it was that British civil aviation 'took to the skies', the next step would be international flights across the Channel.

The *Daily Mail*'s prize of £10,000 for the first non-stop trans-Atlantic flight now seemed possible and there were some intrepid airmen prepared to take up the challenge. The first attempt was made by

VICKERS-VIMY-ROLLS.

THE FIRST DIRECT FLIGHT ACROSS THE ATLANTIC
JUNE 14-15 1919
CAPT. SIR JOHN ALCOCK K.B.E. D.S.C-PILOT.
LIEUT. SIR ARTHUR WHITTEN BROWN K.B.E-NAVIGATOR.

Harry Hawker with Lt. Commander K. Mackenzie-Grieve as navigator in their Sopwith Atlantic. They left St John's, Newfoundland on 18th May and after about 1,050 miles the engine seized up. With great skill Hawker ditched about two miles ahead of a small Danish steamer *Mary* and they were safely rescued. Because the steamer did not have a radio, it was thought that the two airmen were lost. When they finally returned home it was to a remarkable welcome – over 100,000 greeted them at King's Cross station. The *Mail* gave them each £2,500 in acknowledgement of their brave attempt and both were awarded the Air Force Cross – a rare honour for civilians. Their aircraft was found floating ten days later, it was salvaged and subsequently exhibited at Selfridges in Oxford Street.

On 31st May an American Navy-Curtiss flying boat – NC-4 – under the command of Commander J. H. Towers – arrived at Plymouth from Lisbon and Spain, the sole survivor of three that had attempted the Atlantic crossing via the Azores. Fourteen days later Captain John 'Jack' Alcock, D.S.C. and Lt. Arthur Whitten-Brown left Newfoundland in a Vickers Vimy bomber. This aircraft had been produced towards the end of 1918, too late to become operational, but over forty were converted to Commercials by the provision of a more capacious fuselage for the carriage of passengers and freight. The two airmen, after almost sixteen hours in the air covering 1,890 miles, came down at Clifden, County Galway – completing the first non-stop crossing of the Atlantic. Their welcome was even more rapturous, the country had its first peacetime flying heroes. Both airmen were knighted; Sir John, Vickers' Chief test pilot, was killed in an air accident six months later. To add to this seeming flurry of trans-Atlantic flights, the Naval airship, R.34, arrived at Long Island, New York, after 4½ days in the air, and a week later arrived back in Britain; the first (and double) crossing by an airship and the first flight directly from Great Britain to the USA. Because of these successful flights the world suddenly seemed smaller and they paved the way for many epic long-distance flights in the years ahead.

The first post-war meeting at Hendon took place on 7/8th June and two weeks later the 'Victory' Aerial Derby was staged. There were sixteen entries and Captain G. Gatherwood won in DH.4R (Racer) at an average speed of 129 m.p.h; but the most interesting entry was an Avro 534 Baby which was the first light aircraft produced since the War. Although Hendon was still a military airfield, Grahame-White showed his confidence in the future of private flying by establishing a separate airfield to the south and building a lavish clubhouse with luxury facilities for the new London Flying Club. He also became engaged in a long and acrimonious dispute with the Air Ministry over the return of Hendon airfield; the Ministry was loath to relinquish its hold on this large airfield – the closest to London.

During the early summer Alan Cobham, recently demobbed from the RAF, went into partnership with Jack and Fred Holmes to form Berkshire Aviation Company. Equipped with a solitary Avro 504K, they proceeded to tour the country to introduce the 'miracle of flight' and 'joy-rides' to the public at large. By the end of the year it had taken up over 6,000 passengers and Cobham was advertised as 'the pilot who had carried more passengers than any other living airman'. In the years ahead 'joy-riding' in ubiquitous 504Ks was an essential feature of the summer scene and greatly helped to make the public 'air-minded' and popularise flying. *The Aeroplane* quickly recognised that '[it] might prove a great encouragement in recruiting future air passengers ...', the flaw in this reasoning was that the majority of 'joy-riders' were from low-income groups and because of the high cost of fares, air travel remained the preserve of the wealthier classes for many years.

Avro 504K of Berkshire Aviation Company with Alan Cobham as pilot. (via Colin Cruddas)

The highlight of 1919 should have been the Schneider seaplane competition, which took place off Bournemouth on 10th September. A heavy sea mist and poor organisation turned the competition into chaos and it was eventually declared null and void. The leading seaplane – SIAI (Savoia) S.13 – flown by Guido Janello was later declared the winner after an appeal by the Italian team. This decision was revoked by the FAI but a compromise was reached to the sorry affair when Italy was given the right to host the 1920 race. The Bournemouth race was of auspicious moment for British aviation with the entry of a Supermarine Sea Lion designed by Reginald J. Mitchell, who later designed the S.5 & 6s, Schneider Trophy winners, and, of course, the Spitfire.

In April, Hounslow Heath, a wartime airfield to the south-west of the present Heathrow Airport, was designated the first 'Customs-approved' aerodrome for foreign flights and the now familiar Customs controls of passengers and freight was introduced. Several other airfields were later approved – Hadleigh (Suffolk), Cricklewood, Lympne and Dover. In November (12th) Hounslow Heath was the departure point for two Australian brothers – Captains Ross and Keith Smith – making the first attempt to fly to Australia. They were

Fairey III flown by Vincent Nicholl in the Schneider Trophy Race – Bournemouth, September 1919. (via K. Harris)

supported by the Air Ministry and hoped to claim the £A10,000 prize offered by the Australian government. Accompanied by two mechanics, they left in a Vimy and finally arrived at Darwin on 10th December – a distance of 11,294 miles. Their flight via France, Italy, Egypt, Iran, India, and Malaya was widely reported in the press and readers were encouraged to follow their progress. They were closely followed by R.J. Parer and J.C. McIntosh, who left Hounslow on 8th January 1920 in a DH.9A and arrived in Darwin on 2nd August – the first single-engined aircraft to reach Australia. The press coverage of these many other long-distance flights that followed created immense public interest and helped appreciably to foster the popularity of flying.

The first scheduled passenger flight to Paris (Le Bourget Airport) was made on 25th August 1919 when a DH.16 of A.T.&T. with four passengers left Hounslow Heath and arrived 2½ hours later. Each passenger paid £21 for a single fare, including motor transport from London and to Paris. On the same day Handley Page Transport started its Paris service from Cricklewood (via Hounslow) with eleven journalists on board the 0/400. At the outset the prospect for civil aviation seemed bright, a rail strike in September offered opportunities for the delivery of mail and newspapers by air and the recently formed Daimler Air Hire became involved. At the end of the month Supermarine Aviation offered a flying boat service from Southampton to Le Havre, and in October Sir Samuel Instone, a successful shipowner and coal broker, moved into the business and founded Instone Air Line; its first foreign flight was made on 14th February when Captain F.L. Barnard flew a DH.4A to Le Bourget. However, North Sea Aerial & General Transport's entry into commercial aviation was a brief affair. In March 1920 the Company started a freight service from Leeds to Amsterdam via Lympne but the expected demand for cargo was too slow to sustain the service and it closed after a few months.

A DH.4, G-EAH, of A.T.& T. at Hounslow Heath in the summer of 1919. (via K. Brown)

In barely two months A.T.& T. completed 147 flights and Handley Page started a Brussels service as well as offering the first 'in-flight' meal – a basket of sandwiches, fruit and chocolate for 3s! But by the end of the year these companies were faced with stern opposition from French, Dutch and Belgian companies, which received hefty financial support from their governments. Sir Frederick Sykes reported at the end of 1919, 'It may be questioned whether civil aviation in England is to be regarded as one of those industries, which is unable to stand on its own feet, and is yet so essential to the National welfare that it must be kept alive at all costs.' He recommended that the airlines should receive some form of state subsidies but alas his words fell on deaf ears.

After the Peace Treaty was signed on 28th June, the RAF was dismantled with undue haste and by the end of the year over 160 squadrons had been disbanded. In December Trenchard produced his framework for the future RAF and it was modest in the extreme – twenty-three squadrons and seven flights. The main thrust of his long paper was 'the extreme importance of training'; it was clear that if he was prepared to accept a small Service, Trenchard wanted it to be highly trained and utterly professional. He recommended a Central Flying School for the training of flying instructors. Cranwell would become an Officers' College to rival Sandhurst and Dartmouth and he planned a Staff College for senior officers. Trenchard wanted to encourage youngsters into the Service, they would receive a sound grounding in the various trades at a Technical School. There was also a requirement for the RAF to be able to expand quickly in a state of emergency and he envisaged the formation of an 'Air Force Reserve' somewhat on the style of the Territorial Army. The Government approved his broad plans and £15 million was allocated as its budget, leaving precious little available for new aircraft, so the Service would have to soldier on with WWI machines, mainly DH.9As, Bristol Fighters and Snipes.

The DH.9A was a two-seater day bomber, which had served during the latter months of the war, and thirteen companies had built them besides Westland Aircraft, which had been responsible for the original redesign; over two thousand were finally produced. It was the 'workhorse' of the RAF, remaining on almost continuous active service overseas throughout the 1920s and then as a trainer until 1931. The Sopwith Snipe, designed in 1917 as the replacement for the Camel, served in France from September 1918 and equipped many RAF squadrons until 1926.

DH.9A – RAF's standard bomber from 1919 to 1931. (RAF Museum)

Bereft of long Service traditions Trenchard was keen to establish an *esprit de corps* for his new-look RAF, now comprising some 28,200 officers and men or 10% of its wartime strength – the WRAF had been disbanded. In August 1919 the Army ranks had disappeared to be replaced by the various senior 'Air' ranks along with Group Captain, Squadron Leader ... etc, the object was said '... to preserve and to emphasise the principle of independence and the integrity of the Royal Air Force ...' The unpopular light-blue uniform was changed in favour of a darker blue, which quickly became known as 'RAF blue'. He was also aware of the value of public relations. In 1919 he founded the RAF Memorial Fund, the war had left the Service with some 3,000 widows and 7,500 officers and men seriously wounded and he felt the Service needed its own charitable funds. A year later the Central Band was formed to further the Service's public image. The most important innovation was the introduction of the RAF Tournament, with the first mounted at Hendon on 3 July 1920 and the proceeds (£7,261) went to the Memorial Fund. A crowd of 60,000 attended and they were treated to a remarkable display of flying, aerobatics and mock bombing attacks; the event was highly praised even by those opposed to the idea of an independent Air Force. The Tournament was considered an outstanding success, the RAF announced that it would become an annual event. The Displays were always fully supported by the Royal Family, indeed Prince Albert (later the Duke of York) had gained his 'wings' in July 1919 and for a short period was a serving officer attaining the rank of Group Captain.

Hounslow Heath's existence as London's international aerodrome was brief; in March 1920 it was superseded by Croydon. Two adjacent WWI airfields at Beddington and Waddon were thought to be more suitable for commercial development. It was considered preferable to have an international airport south of London and the site was less prone to fog – a perennial hazard in those early days. Waddon had been the site of the large National Aircraft Factory No 1, and became the flying area, whereas Beddington, to the west, housed the military hangars and thus the aircraft were forced to taxi across a main road (Plough Lane) before take-off, whilst a man with a red flag held up the road traffic! The local Council did not want its name – Wallington – to be associated with the new venture and thus nearby Croydon was chosen as the name of London's new 'air terminus', under the control of the Ministry of Civil Aviation. Trust House Ltd established a hotel, the first to provide meals and accommodation for air travellers. In the early days Croydon aerodrome was far from a grandiose place, described as 'resembling ... a wild-west township of the early mining days ...'! However, it was greatly developed in the late 1920s and became the busiest international airport in Europe.

From mid-March Croydon was also the place to purchase an aircraft at a bargain price – the greatest aviation sale ever. The Aircraft Disposals Co. Ltd., with Handley Page Ltd. as technical adviser and sole selling agent, had purchased the entire stock of surplus WWI machines – some 10,000 aircraft and 35,000 aero-engines; large or small, fast or slow, prospective purchasers had a wide choice from Bristol

RAF Tournament at Hendon – 30th July 1920. (via J. Adams)

Fighters, Pups, Camels, SE.5As, 504Ks, DH.6s, DH.9As to Vimys, Kangaroos and even a few 0/400s. Somewhat ingenuously it was announced that a fixed rebate would be given to manufacturers who wanted to buy back any of their own designed machines! A Camel could be obtained for £25 and a DH.6 for as little as a fiver. However, the problem for private individuals was the cost of an air-worthiness certificate and registration, often more costly than the machine itself; nevertheless many were bought by ex-Service pilots for pleasure flying as well as joy-riding.

Although motor-racing returned to Brooklands during Easter 1920, private flying would take much longer to re-establish itself there. The airfield was largely dominated by Vickers' large aircraft works and saw the first flights of its various post-war aircraft – Vimy Commercial, Vernon, Viking, Vulture and Virginia. On 24th January it was the departure point for a Vimy Commercial, contracted by *The Times*, attempting the first flight to South Africa. Two Vickers pilots, Captains Stan Cockerell and Tommy Bruce, along with Dr Mitchell, a representative of the newspaper, left on the pioneering flight. However, tropical weather defeated them, they crashed in Africa over a month later, although the aircraft was destroyed all the airmen survived. Two South African airmen, Lt. Col. Pierre van Rynevald and Major Christopher Q. Brand, with two mechanics, set off for South Africa in a Vimy on 4th February; Brand was a celebrated fighter pilot who had claimed a Gotha in 1918. After various mishaps and two changes of aircraft they finally arrived at Cape Town on 20th March to claim the £5,000 prize. On their return both were knighted and Brand had a distinguished RAF career.

The problems facing aircraft manufacturers were grave, considering the glut of surplus aircraft now available. In 1919 Airco had been bought out by Birmingham Small Arms (BSA), who were not really interested in its aviation activities. Holt Thomas resigned as Chairman in March and it was just a matter of time before Airco departed from the scene. In December A.T.&T. flew its last passenger service and Daimler Hire took over its assets. Perhaps a greater shock to the aviation world was the winding-up of Sopwith Aviation in September. The Company had built only fifteen aircraft since the war but it was a massive tax claim for excess war profits that proved the final straw. But from the ashes two famous aircraft companies arose.

On 25th September Geoffrey de Havilland, partly financed by Holt Thomas, founded the de Havilland Aircraft Co. Ltd. at Stag Lane,

Edgware – a small wartime training airfield; as he later ruefully admitted '... it was with an unwarranted degree of optimism.' At least the new company took over the production of Airco's DH.14 and DH.18A, the latter was the first speculative airliner for A.T. & T., accommodating up to eight passengers, and three were operated by Instone Air Line. Two months later the directors of the defunct Sopwith Aviation formed H.G. Hawker Engineering Co. Ltd at Kingston with Fred Sigrist as Managing Director along with Sopwith and Hawker as directors. Initially cars and motor-cycles were constructed and the first successful Hawker aircraft did not appear for a few years.

The pioneer airlines were also finding it difficult to compete with foreign airlines without any Government help. Churchill had made it clear that 'civil aviation must fly by itself. The Government cannot possibly hold it up in the air ... taxes cannot be used to fund the travel of wealthy members of society ...' Matters were not helped by the first fatal crash of a 0/400 on 14th December near Cricklewood, two crew and two passengers were killed. During the winter Handley Page and Instone suspended their services, so Croydon – funded by taxpayers – was solely used by foreign airlines. Despite this dismal prospect, early in 1921 de Havilland set up a Hire Service, advertising 'an aeroplane to take you anywhere for 2d a mile'. His 'taxis' were scarlet DH.9Cs, which carried three passengers and a 'driver', the term was then invariably used instead of 'pilot'! He engaged Alan Cobham as his first 'driver' and later in the year he made the longest charter flight, flying a wealthy American around Europe and the Middle East; he also tested several early de Havilland aircraft.

Despite Churchill's trenchant views, the Government felt compelled to take some action to revive the air services. A Cross-Channel Committee was formed and on 19th March a trial scheme of subsidies was introduced, with the proviso that they would not exceed £88,200 in a year, at a time when the French government was underwriting its two airlines to the tune of £1.3 million! However inadequate, the subsidy was better than nothing, although the whole thorny question of government assistance bedevilled British airlines for the next two years. On 19th March Handley Page resumed its Paris service from Cricklewood and moved to Croydon in May. Instone Air Line, boasting itself as 'Britain's Premier Air Line', was back on 21st March when its Vimy Commercial, *City of London*, left Croydon for Paris. Instone was the first to introduce uniform for its pilots – a dark-blue naval-type. During the year airliners were supplied with Marconi wireless equipment with a range of fifty miles and Brussels and Amsterdam were added to the services schedule. However, another foreign competitor emerged, the Dutch airline K.L.M, their Fokker F.IIIs were initially flown by British pilots.

Many people in aviation were convinced that airships offered a brighter future for long-distance air travel. Such devotees suffered a setback in January (27th) when R.34 was wrecked in a storm whilst moored at Howden, Yorkshire. Nevertheless R.36 made its maiden flight on 1st April but was heavily damaged in June. A couple of nights later, 23/24th, R.38 first flew from the Royal Airship Works at Cardington, Bedfordshire and in July the famous R.33 made an appearance at the RAF Pageant as well as Croydon. The airship lobby received a severe and almost fatal blow on 23rd August when R.38 broke up and exploded in flames to the south of Hull; only five of the forty-nine persons on board survived. With this disaster all military development of airships ceased and R.33 and R.36 remained shedded for several years.

The second RAF Show – now called a 'Pageant' – was held at Hendon on 2nd July, and was again well attended. Three new flying stars entertained the large crowds with their aerobatic skills – Flt. Lt. W. H. 'Scruffie' Longton, Flg. Offr. P.W.S. Bulman and Flt. Lt. J. 'Oojie'

Handley Page W.8a, G-EBBI, Prince Henry.

Noakes. There was a fine display of formation flying by five Snipes of the Central Flying School led by Major C. Draper; they were the RAF's first formation team – a tradition perpetuated today by the Red Arrows. The King, who attended the Pageant, had approved the design of the RAF's ensign – a fly of sky blue with the wartime roundel of Royal blue, white and red in the centre with the Union flag inset in the top quarter.

Despite the popularity of the Hendon displays private flying was at a low ebb, it had still not recovered from the effects of the war. Although the public viewed WWI pilots as heroes, they clung to the belief that aviation was a dangerous affair. The Royal Aero Club tried to engender some interest, offering four aircraft for hire to members at £3 per hour including oil and petrol, and on 16th July it mounted the first Oxford versus Cambridge air race. There was an ample number of ex-Service pilots studying at the universities to form the two teams; Cambridge won with ease. Because of a lack of public interest the event was not repeated. The Aerial Derby was clouded by the fact that Harry Hawker was killed on 12th July whilst practising for the Derby. *Flight* commented '... the name of Hawker deserves to live in the history of aviation, not for the performances popularly associated with his name but for his contributions to the increase of aeronautical knowledge ...' How prophetic those words were with so many fine and memorable military aircraft carrying his name.

On 21st October Handley Page's first purpose-built airliner, W.8a, went into service on the Paris route. It had first flown in December 1919 and had won the Air Ministry's prize in the large aeroplane contest; its subsequent tardy development was due to the Company's lack of funds. The W.8a was a twin-engined biplane that carried twelve passengers in relative comfort and in November the Air Council ordered three, later named *Princess Mary*, *Prince George* and *Prince Henry*, which operated successfully with Handley Page Transport and later Imperial Airways. One also flew with the Belgian airline Sabena and another three were built there under licence.

By the end of 1922 the RAF was developing into the Service that Trenchard had envisaged. Cranwell College's first intake of cadets entered in February 1920 for a rigorous two-year course leading to a permanent commission. In the following year the first boy entrants (15 to 16½ years) joined No 1 School of Technical Training, Halton; known as 'aircraft apprentices' but later were dubbed 'Trenchard brats'! Nevertheless they formed the backbone of the RAF. Adult recruits were

Air Marshal Sir Hugh Trenchard, the Chief of the Air Staff, inspects the first aircraft apprentices to pass out of Halton – 17th December 1924. (RAF Museum)

trained at Uxbridge and the feature of these training establishments was a strict regime of discipline almost to a point of harshness. In April the RAF Staff College opened at Andover to groom officers for senior posts and later the Officers' Engineering School moved to Henlow, where it produced many fine aeronautical engineers. There were also a number of Specialist Schools along with four Experimental Establishments. Thus the basic format of the RAF was in place and although numerically small, its officers and men were highly trained and thoroughly disciplined. Trenchard recalled that he had '... laid the foundations of a castle, and if nobody wanted to build anything bigger on it than a cottage it would at any rate be a very good cottage.'! Moreover he had successfully maintained the RAF's independence, fending off all the many attempts to decree otherwise.

The third RAF Pageant held at the end of June attracted large crowds despite poor weather; it was now an essential part of the summer scene. A novelty event in this year's programme was a demonstration of 'sky-writing'; the previous August Major J. C. Savage had formed the Savage Skywriting Company with a number of SE.5As adopted with his patented smoke system. He, along with his chief pilot Cyril Turner, had devised a system of 'writing' letters – fifty feet high by using coloured smoke. Sky-writing became a feature in the coming years as commercial companies readily saw the advantage of so advertising their names and products.

The Aerial Derby, about a month later, now seemed a mere shadow of its former glory, it failed to attract the crowds or indeed create much interest. According to reports, '... it was even duller than last year ... there was a lack of atmosphere, almost one of indifference ...' For the second year running J. H. 'Jimmie' James won in a Gloucestershire Mars I Bamel racer at a remarkable speed of 177 m.p.h. It had been designed by Henry P. Folland, the Company's Chief Engineer – the first of several fast aircraft designed by the Company. There was an almost universal quest for speed, as flying vied with motor-racing as a spectator sport. There was some encouraging news from the Continent; on 12th August at Naples Captain Henri Biard, Supermarine's test pilot, won the Schneider Trophy in a Sea Lion II at an average speed of 145 m.p.h; Reg Mitchell's first successful aircraft. It was an important victory because should the Italians (placed 2nd and 3rd) have won for a third time, the Trophy would have become their property outright. The victory also ensured that the country would stage the competition in 1923.

Gloucestershire Mars 1 Bamel won the Aerial Derby in 1922 for the second time. (Imperial War Museum)

Alexis Maneyrol with his Peyret Tandem sailplane – Itford October 1922.

In September a new competition was inaugurated, the 'Circuit of Britain Race' for a cup presented by King George V. It was contested annually, becoming THE flying competition of the inter-war years known as the 'King's Cup Air Race'. Croydon was the venue for the handicap race held on the 8/9th. The 'circuit' covered about 810 miles, with compulsory stops at Birmingham and Newcastle, an overnight stay at Glasgow and then stops at Manchester and Filton before returning to Croydon. Twenty-two entries were accepted and the Air Ministry arranged for full radio coverage, which greatly added to the interest in the race enabling the public to follow closely the progress of the competitors. The weather over the two days was poor and only eleven aircraft finished the course. Franklyn. L. Barnard, the Commodore of Instone Air Line, was declared the winner in his Company's DH.4A – *City of Cardiff* – averaging 123 m.p.h; all agreed that the race was an outstanding success.

Although the sport of flying was slowing recapturing the public's interest, it was far beyond the means of 'the man in the street'. But in October there emerged a cheaper method to experience all the joys of flight – 'sailplaning' or gliding – which had already taken a firm hold on the Continent especially in Germany. Encouraged by successful European gliding competitions, the *Daily Mail* offered a prize of £1,000 to any airman making the longest duration flight in England during October providing it was more than thirty minutes. The Royal Aero

Club selected Itford Hill on the Sussex Downs for the first British gliding competition and thirty-five entries were received, including leading German and French exponents as well as a number of British 'home-made' machines. The meeting was held from 16th/21st October and was well attended, one spectator recalled 'The fun was tremendous but the weather did not encourage much gliding. But it was just like returning to the earliest days of flying' with many pioneer airmen (Handley Page, Roe, Fairey, de Havilland, Howard Wright ...) attending. A Frenchman, Alexis Maneyrol, won the *Mail*'s prize in his Peyret Tandem Monoplane with a splendid duration record of 3 hours and 21 minutes; but perhaps the 'star' of the meeting was Sqn. Ldr. Alexander Gray with a glider built from a Bristol fuselage and Fokker wing for 18s 6d – aptly named *Brokker*. He managed to remain airborne for $1^{1}/_{2}$ hours, gaining him the Club's £50 prize. The successful meeting led *Flight* to offer a prize for the best British glider design and the *Daily Telegraph* came forward with £1,000 for the longest flight in 1923. Gordon Selfridge topped that with £1,005 for the first flight of fifty miles made by a British pilot in a British glider – shades of 1909 and Cody, Roe and Moore-Brabazon! It was generally agreed that gliding was here to stay and Itford is the accredited birthplace of British gliding. However, the usually perceptive Charles Grey commented, 'As a sport one has no great opinion of the future of gliding and soaring ...', and one newspaper rather disparagingly called it 'the poor man's flying'!

British airlines experienced another difficult year. The method of subsidies changed twice and neither scheme was particularly satisfactory. In April (7th) a DH.18 of Daimler Airways crashed head-on with a French Goliath airliner in thick fog over France killing all seven occupants. There was over-capacity on the Paris route – five airlines competing for passengers – and it seemed more sensible rather than fight amongst themselves that the British airlines should specialise. Daimler agreed to start a service from Manchester-London-Amsterdam with a planned extension to Berlin, whereas Instone retained its Brussels service with possible expansion to Cologne and Prague. Handley Page retained the prestigious Paris service because it had the largest airliners. All three tried to stimulate national interest ('Fly British'?), as well as arranging press trips, tours of Croydon, 5s joyrides 'around the aerodrome' and 'honeymoon flights'. Instone claimed 'No other Company has Such a Record for Safety' and Handley Page proclaimed 'Once you have flown to Paris, you will never go by boat again.' On 31st December the first German aircraft to land in Britain since the war arrived at Lympne – Junkers Komet; carrying a four-man delegation to discuss a passenger service from Berlin – yet another foreign competitor to contend with in 1923.

Despite the so-called 'Geddes Axe' of the previous year when all defence spending had been drastically reduced, there was mounting concern in early 1923 about the paucity of the RAF's Home Defence Force. Lord Salisbury was delegated to chair a sub-Committee to examine the problem, which made its report in June. The new Prime Minister, Stanley Baldwin, announced that in addition to the RAF's commitment overseas, the Home Defence would be strengthened '... to protect against an air attack by the strongest air force within striking distance of this country ...' It was recommended that it should comprise thirty-two squadrons within five years and Sir Stanley Hoare was instructed to take the preliminary steps to implement the decision. Nevertheless it took many years before fighter squadrons reached this strength. The over-riding tenet of the inter-war years was that propounded by Lloyd George and Trenchard back in 1919 that the threat of another European war would be detected within ten years giving ample time to achieve a strong force, which effectively precluded any expenditure on new aircraft that would be obsolete in ten years. This 'ten-year rule' restricted the growth of the RAF in the years ahead.

A Parliamentary Bill authorising the formation of RAF Reserve units had been passed in 1922 but did not become law until two years later.

Armstrong Whitworth Siskin III first flew in May 1923.

Grebes entered No 111 squadron in October 1923.

However, in February 1923 the Air Ministry invited ex-Service pilots to volunteer for reserve service, as well as 'gentlemen qualified as civilian pilots but had not previously held a commission in the RFC, RNAS or RAF'. They would be subject to regular training as well as attending an annual summer school, all for a retainer of £30. The Ministry was concerned about the lack of flying schools, especially with future pilot requirements in mind, and tenders were invited for the establishment of new schools. Five were accepted: Bristol School at Filton, Armstrong Siddeley Motors at Whitley near Coventry, William Beardmore & Co. at Renfrew, de Havilland at Stag Lane and Blackburn Aeroplane Co. at Brough. They only provided refresher training, there were no plans as yet to introduce initial flying training.

The RAF Pageant was held at the end of June and there was a fine display of formation and aerobatic flying – *The Aeroplane* described it as 'a monumental day of flying ... with Hendon well and truly conferred with the seal of approbation, like that of Ascot or Henley ...' It also boasted the largest collection of prototype and experimental aircraft yet seen; not only could they be examined in the static park but they taxied past the spectators and many gave a fly-past. The 'New Types Park' became an integral part of all future displays. Two fighters in particular created great interest – Armstrong Whitworth Siskin III and Gloucestershire Grebe. The latter was considered the most advanced fighter yet

165

developed with a maximum speed of 162 m.p.h. and entered the RAF with No 111 squadron in October – the first new fighter since WWI. Such was the state of the aviation industry that Gloucestershire Aircraft Co. (formed in June 1917) was compelled by the Air Ministry to contract the manufacture of wings and tail units to de Havilland, Avro and Hawker. The Company, which used 'Gloster' for marketing from 1926, produced over one hundred and thirty Grebes. The Siskin had been developed in 1919 as a replacement for the SE.5a and Mark IIIs first appeared in May 1923; although inferior in speed and range to the Grebe they were considered safer. When they equipped No 41 squadron a year later, they were the RAF's first all-metal aircraft and the first to introduce 'vee' interplane struts.

In July Hendon was the starting point for the second King's Cup, which compared with the Pageant was 'a most tame affair barely a couple of hundred turned up to witness the start despite the presence of many celebrated airmen ...' The Schneider Trophy competition held at Cowes on 28th September was also a disappointment, certainly as far as the result was concerned. The United States took first and second places with Naval Curtiss CR-3s seaplanes and last year's winner, Captain H. Baird in a Sea Lion III, came third. The event that captured the greatest public interest was the 'Motor-Glider' competition held at Lympne during the first weekend of October. There were prizes on offer from the *Daily Mail* and the Abdulla Tobacco Co., as well as the Duke of Sutherland's £500 for the longest flight on a gallon of petrol by a machine powered by a 750 cc engine or less! There were twenty-three entries and it was obvious that 'light aeroplanes' offered the way forward for private flying. The meeting had '... rekindled the cheerful unselfish spirit of the early days of aviation ... the aeroplane, so recently a weapon of war, has now become a vehicle for the use and enjoyment of sport and pleasure for the "ordinary man"...'. One small aircraft that caught the eye was the English Electric Wren, an ultra-light aeroplane powered by a 398 cc ABC motor-cycle engine. In the hands of 'Scruffie' Longton it managed to fly 87½ miles on a gallon of petrol and shared the £500 prize with W.S. Shackleton's ANEC flown by Jimmie James. The Wren was an exceptional little machine but even at a cost of £350 it failed to attract demand and only three were built.

Although air travel was on the increase, British airlines carried under five hundred passengers a week. British Marine Air Navigation Company had started a flying boat service from Woolston, South-ampton to the Channel Islands and Cherbourg, using Supermarine Sea

Imperial Airways had six DH.34s on its formation; this one, City of New York, *was scrapped in 1926.* (via B. Mann)

Eagles – amphibians – which could carry six passengers along with a pilot and wireless operator in an open cockpit. Sir Herbert Hambling, with two businessmen, had been asked to look into the subsidy scheme and to propose one '… with the greatest benefit to the airlines at the least cost to the taxpayer.'! They recommended that the four airlines should amalgamate into one Company, and after much discussion agreement was reached in December. Early in 1924 the proposal was unveiled to the public, the Company with a capital of £1 million, would be known as the Imperial Air Transport Co. Ltd or according to the Press 'the Million Pound Monopoly Company'. The assets of the existing airlines would be purchased by this Company, who would run an airline with a government subsidy of £1 million spread over ten years. The proposed name of British Air Transport Service was quickly changed when it was pointed out that the initials spelt 'BATS', hence Imperial Airways came into being.

When Imperial Airways was formed on 31st March 1924, each airline had a representative on the Board along with two government directors, with Sir Eric Geddes of Dunlop Rubber Company as the Chairman. Imperial started with a mixed fleet of aircraft – six DH.34s, three W.8bs, two Sea Eagles, a Vimy and Vulcan along with a couple of DH.50s on charter. Since April 1919 over 34,600 passengers had been carried, only five passengers and six crewmen had been killed. Passenger comfort had certainly improved with the provision of wicker seats and toilets on some aircraft, but little in-flight services – lunch boxes could be purchased from the airport canteen. Furthermore the cabins were not heated or indeed insulated from engine noise; although Imperial assured its passengers that '... there is no need for special clothing than there is on a railway journey.' It should have started services from 1st April but the management were suddenly faced with a pilots' strike due to the unsatisfactory salary that had been offered them. Ultimately the sixteen pilots agreed to £880 per year and life assurance cover of £1,000. On 26th April Imperial's first scheduled flight left for Paris, followed on 3rd May by the Brussels and Cologne service and then on 2nd June the Berlin service via Amsterdam and Hanover. Pilots were expected to fly any of the aircraft types and they became celebrated names in the world of aviation especially as Imperial produced signed postcards of their leading Captains.

In January there was a new departure for the RAF when the Air Ministry announced that four hundred Short Service commissions were available for young men (18/22 years) to be trained for flying duties. It was recognised that military flying was basically a young man's job and the Short Service system would obviate burdening the Service with a build-up of officers for higher ranks. The Air Ministry was surprised by the flood of applications from young men who were quite prepared to serve for five years, receive a small gratuity and spend time in the reserve, all in order to learn to fly. As one military historian remarked '... The Air Force was essentially a short service force. Its flyers were birds of passage.'

The Naval element of the RAF had always been the 'poor relation' and its control had long been a bone of contention between the Air Ministry and Admiralty; this was somewhat resolved when the Fleet Air Arm was formed on 1st April. Although it was still administered by the RAF, its operational control was largely exercised by the Admiralty. The FAA mainly operated with the aircraft carriers *Argus* and *Eagle* and Trenchard conceded that 70% of its pilots would be drawn from Naval officers, although there were never enough Naval volunteers to maintain this proportion. Nevertheless over the coming years the control of the FAA would remain a contentious and, at times, acrimonious issue.

The Air Ministry was aware that in order to retain public support for the RAF as well as creating a reservoir of civilian pilots for its Reserve, private flying had to be resuscitated and encouraged. As a result of the successful Lympne meeting, in January the Ministry announced a competition for the best two-seat light aircraft powered by an engine not exceeding 1,100 c.c., with a prize of £3,000. Later in the year further encouragement to private flying was given by offering financial assistance to ten approved light aeroplane clubs over an initial two-year period; an annual grant to buy light aircraft, with additional payments for each club member qualifying for a private flying licence on a club aircraft. The clubs would be inspected periodically by the Ministry and the Royal Aero Club was delegated to operate the scheme. This Government incentive greatly stimulated the growth of private flying over the next few years.

During the summer interest was centred on the attempts of British and American airmen endeavouring to fly around the world. It seemed quite inconceivable that less than twenty years had passed since the Wrights' historic flight, such was the progress of aviation. Four Douglas World Cruisers of the US Army Air Service left Seattle on 6th April flying west over Alaska. Three arrived on 16th July at Croydon to a grand reception from distinguished members of the RAF, the Air Ministry and the Royal Aero Club; they left from Kirkwall on 2nd August bound for Iceland. Only *Chicago* and *New Orleans* made it back to Seattle after six months and 26,345 miles – a remarkable achievement. The British team, led by Sqn. Ldr. A. S. MacLaren as navigator, Flg. Off. J. Plenderleith piloting and Sgt. Andrews as engineer, left from Calshot in March in a Vickers Vulture amphibian. They headed east and by July had arrived off North Japan, but there their brave attempt ended when their aircraft was damaged beyond repair and forced to land on the open sea. MacLaren said, '... We would not have missed the adventure for worlds, we did our best, but failed ...'

At home the summer aviation scene progressed along what had become a normal and accepted pattern, except for the absence of the Aerial Derby; only Gloucestershire Aircraft had submitted a competitor, thus the country's oldest speed air-race disappeared from the aviation calendar, although there were a number of other Challenge Cups on offer, notably one sponsored by the Air League in 1921, and the Grosvenor Handicap Cup for aeroplanes powered with engines less than 150 h.p., introduced by Lord Edward Grosvenor in June 1923. The second race was won in mid-October by H. J. L. 'Bert' Hinkler, another fine Australian airman and Avro's test pilot. His Avro 652 Avis achieved a speed of 65 m.p.h. to win the Cup and prize money of £700.

On 28th June the fifth RAF Pageant was staged at Hendon with over

82,000 attending. The event was described as '... perfect weather, perfect organisation and perfect flying ...' The highlight was a display by eighteen DH.9As – '... both spectacular and technically brilliant with the aeroplanes passing headlong through each other in a manner never seen before ... it was truly heart stopping. ...' The Pageant closed with a realistic attack by fighters on two replica steamships erected in the centre of the airfield. These set-piece battles became a feature of future displays.

The King's Cup race was held at Martlesham Heath in August; this was the home of the Aeroplane & Armament Experimental Establishment where all new aeroplanes built for the RAF underwent a series of rigorous tests by RAF 'test' pilots. Such was its reputation that many manufacturers sent their private and civil prototypes for assessment by the Service experts. Alan Cobham won the King's Cup at his third attempt in a de Havilland DH.50, completing the 950 miles at an average speed of 106 m.p.h. The DH.50 was designed to replace the DH.9Cs of the Company's Hire Service and had first flown in July 1923. Over thirty were produced and many were used extensively in Australia, where it was the first aircraft to be flown on the famed 'Flying Doctor' Service. The aeroplane became almost synonymous with Cobham, he used one for two celebrated long-distance flights. On 24th November, accompanied by Sir Sefton Brancker, a most dedicated Director of Civil Aviation, he left in a DH.50 on a survey flight to India and Burma.

At the end of September the light aircraft trials took place at Lympne. Nineteen aeroplanes had been entered but only eight managed to pass the eliminating trials. By the end of the second day another two failed, the problem seemed to be the engines, clearly it took far longer to develop a reliable aero-engine than a new aeroplane. The winner was a Beardmore Wee Bee I, designed by W. S. Shackleton (another Australian!) and flown by Maurice Pearcey. It was powered by a 32 h.p. Bristol Cherub engine but other than gaining the prize no orders were received; the solitary Wee Bee I was still flying in Australia in 1950!

Air travel was beginning to catch on, by the end of the year Imperial Airways had flown in excess of $\frac{1}{2}$ million miles, but it must be said that air fares were still prohibitive; although it was reported that '... many women now travel to the Continent by aeroplane, they go to the French capital in the morning for shopping and return to town by the evening service.'! However, on Christmas Eve air travel suffered a set-back when a DH.34 carrying seven passengers crashed shortly after take-off from Croydon and all were killed. Despite this tragedy the prospects for private and civil aviation at the close of 1924 seemed promising, and that was the view of de Havilland Aircraft Company: '... we firmly believe there is an immense field for civil aviation. We are therefore devoting considerable time and energy to furthering this branch of our enterprise. ...' The Company would, in fact, revolutionise private and club flying with its remarkable Moth series of aircraft.

8

A PLETHORA
OF MOTHS
(1925–1928)

From 1925 private flying expanded at a singular rate due to the proliferation of Aero clubs around the country. The exploits of the various long-distance flyers created immense public interest and inspired countless young men and women to join the swelling band of private pilots. Air travel began to be accepted as a fashionable, if expensive, alternative to train and boat journeys and the larger, more comfortable and reliable airliners stretched their wings beyond the narrow confines of Europe. Although the RAF had mainly a 'decorative' role in the United Kingdom with its spectacular displays and pioneering flights, its squadrons abroad always seemed to be engaged in some minor insurrection and thus the Service was rarely out of the news. Indeed aviation, in all its facets, appeared to match the mood of the times – 'the Roaring Twenties'.

The aviation event of the year was the appearance of the DH.60 Moth, the first really *practicable* dual-control light aircraft. On 22nd February Geoffrey de Havilland flew the prototype – G-EBKT – for the first time from Stag Lane aerodrome and a legend was born. He later maintained '… it was intended, above all, for the amateur, for the week-end flyer, and for instruction.' The Moth was powered by a 60 h.p. Cirrus engine designed by Major Frank Halford of the Aircraft Disposals Company, later enhanced up to 105 h.p.; it gained its name in deference to de Havilland's reputation as an enthusiastic lepidopterist.

Hubert Broad, the Company's test pilot, unveiled the Moth to the Press on 2nd March and it was immediately recognised as an outright winner with so many features to attract club and private owners – sturdy construction, good cruising speed and range (80 m.p.h and 320 miles), low landing speed and short take-off, extremely easy to handle,

DH.60 Moth, G-EBKT, the prototype first flew on 22nd February 1925.

space for two persons and luggage and dual-control. The wings could
be folded to facilitate storage, it was easily towed by a family car and
could also be fitted with floats. The price started at £795 but was
ultimately reduced to £650. The Press were almost ecstatic in their
praise of the delightful little aircraft. On 29th May it made headline
news when Cobham flew G-EBKT from Croydon to Zurich (1,000
miles) and back in a day, and success was ensured when eight of the
twenty-five produced in 1925 were supplied to the five subsidised
flying clubs. As production steadily increased and several versions
with different engines appeared Moths virtually dominated club and
private flying; by 1929 85% of all privately-owned aircraft were Moths
including those owned by two Royal princes, which merely sealed its
social acceptance.

In January the RAF comprised forty-three squadrons and was
beginning to resemble a modern Air Force with most squadrons
equipped with current aircraft. It was quite an occasion when the
Service received its first Hawker fighter – Woodcock II – supplied to
No 3 squadron in May. A wooden and fabric-covered biplane, which
truthfully was not too dissimilar in appearance, but not in performance, to the Snipe it replaced. The most famous RAF aircraft of the
year was the Supermarine Southampton, a long-range flying boat that
had been ordered by the Air Ministry direct from the drawing board –
a unique occurrence then. In August Southamptons equipped No 480
Flight at Calshot and were almost immediately in the news when

Hawker Woodcock of No 17 squadron with early squadron markings. (RAF Museum)

during the autumn two made a long cruise around the British Isles stopping off at many places – an early demonstration of their worth. They became famous for such flights, 'showing the flag' in many parts of the world and gaining a fine reputation for reliability. Southamptons remained in service until December 1936 – a record only surpassed by the legendary Short Sunderland of WWII fame.

The Service also modernised its organisation. A new Command – Air Defence of Great Britain (A.D.G.B.) – came into being as an unified force with Air Marshal Sir John Salmond appointed as its first Air Officer Commanding-in-Chief; later divided into the Wessex Bombing Area and a Fighting Area with the regular bomber and fighter squadrons concentrated at airfields within these areas. The existing 'Coastal Area' was retained to control the flying boat units, and the 'Inland Area' was responsible for training, maintenance and the Army Co-operation squadrons. As support for the regular squadrons, the first Special Reserve and Auxiliary Air Force units were formed during the year. No 502 (Ulster) was the first to be founded on 15th May at Aldergrove and four Auxiliary Air Force squadrons formed during September and October – 602 (City of Glasgow) at Renfrew, 600 (City of London) and 601 (County of London) at Northolt and 603 (City of Edinburgh) at Turnhouse; all four were equipped with D.H.9As.

The Reserve squadrons comprised a mixture of regular and reserve airmen with the Commanding Officer being a regular officer. They were directly administered by the RAF, whereas the AAF squadrons had more local recruits including the Commanding Officer, and were administered by the County Territorial Association. All the officers had to hold private pilot licences and were compelled to attend courses, summer camps and flying tuition to qualify for RAF wings. The AAF squadrons especially gained the reputation for being very select 'social clubs', indeed 601 squadron acquired the nickname the 'Millionaires Mob'. They were famously dubbed by Churchill – 'Weekend flyers' – but twenty Reserve and AAF squadrons were operating by 1939. In October Oxford and Cambridge Universities formed Air Squadrons operating from Abingdon and Duxford respectively, free flying training by RAF instructors was given during term time and they were required to attend a summer school. These and other University Air Squadrons produced many Reserve and AAF pilots in the years ahead.

Another major change during the year was the decision to issue a type of 'free-fall' parachute into the Service. The RAF had been experimenting with various types of parachutes for several years and now opted for an American parachute designed by Leslie Irvin. Two officers, Flt. Lt. F. O. Soden and Flg. Off. Lacey, underwent parachute training in the States and returned to tour squadrons demonstrating the new parachute. In September a Parachute Test Section was formed at Henlow and a Training Unit moved in twelve months later. The Parachute Centre used Vickers Virginia or 'Ginnies' for parachute testing and training. It had been developed from the Vimy and remained a front-line bomber until 1937. Although wing-walking was strictly forbidden in the RAF, the trainee parachutists walked from the cabin along the wing to the jumping-off position beside the outer struts; they had already been instructed on packing their own parachutes. By 1927 seat-pack Irvin parachutes were in general use in the RAF.

A display of parachuting was one of the features of the RAF Display on 27th June. It was the first time that the RAF had completely organised the Display right down to the catering and car parking. Hendon was due to be taken over by the Air Ministry, a financial settlement (reputed to be in the region of £500,000) had finally been agreed with Grahame-White. His luxurious flying club had closed and this was the last Display he attended. The celebrated airman had finished with aviation and went abroad to live. When Grahame-White died in August 1959 aged seventy-nine, he was the only pioneer airman not to have been honoured; his long battle with the Treasury and Air

Parachute training from a Vickers Virginia over RAF Henlow. (Bedfordshire & Luton Archi
Record Services)

Ministry may not have been forgiven. The Display attracted even
greater crowds perhaps due to the opening of the nearby Colindale
underground station providing easier access to Hendon. It was also the
first time that the British Broadcasting Company (founded in 1922 and
not a Corporation until 1927) broadcast the event. Additionally a
formation display by Grebes of 25 squadron were given instructions by
King George V from the ground by means of radio/telephony – a
unique occurrence. The Display was intentionally less spectacular than
of late because Trenchard had ordered that it should show 'the average
work of the RAF rather than aerobatic displays by individual officers';
although in truth it was these displays that attracted and thrilled the
crowds.

The King's Cup was held at Croydon at the beginning of July. It was
claimed that this competition was 'to encourage flying as a recreational

activity but also as a stimulus to navigational skills and an incentive to improve the reliability of civil aircraft.' Heavy fog caused havoc with the race and two Moths flown by de Havilland and Cobham were forced to withdraw as were many other entrants. Captain Barnard won for the second time in a Siskin IV although there was a sparse crowd at Croydon to witness the finish.

In July the first Air Ministry subsidised Aero Club, Lancashire, opened and inevitably Cobham was in attendance to give joy-rides in the prototype Moth. The Club's new Moth looked resplendent in its blue livery, each Club would sport different colours – silver for London, red for Newcastle, green for Midland and red and orange for Yorkshire. On 19th August, London Aero Club at Stag Lane was formally opened by Sir Philip Sassoon, the Under-Secretary of State for Air; he remarked that the Royal Aero Club '... had won for London

Supermarine Southampton. A remarkable flying boat that remained in service from 1925 to 1936.

and rightly for London the first Light Aeroplane Club in the country' – these comments were not greatly appreciated in Lancashire! The operating costs for Moths were £2 15s an hour, but with the subsidy Clubs were able to charge 30s per hour dual and £1 for solo flying. Thus for about £20 a member could learn to fly; this covered membership fee, flying tuition, the mandatory three hours solo and the charge for the 'A' pilot's licence. One of the first to receive training at London Aero Club was Mrs Mary Elliott-Lynn (later Lady Heath), a well-known sportswoman and soon a celebrated pilot.

Of the many flying meetings held during the summer, none was more successful than that held at Lympne over the August Bank Holiday weekend. The large crowds were treated to a feast of races, exhibition flying, parachute descents, joy-riding, sky writing and there were several new aeroplanes to admire. All the famous airmen of the day attended and it was said that the meeting '...showed the fine sporting spirit of the early days of flying is still alive and well... completely banishing all thoughts of dreaded war machines...' Unfortunately the Light Aeroplane Competition due to be held there in the autumn had to be postponed because the competition rules were published too late for the aircraft and engines to be prepared in time. The *Daily Mail*'s total prize fund of £5,000 was held over.

Since Cobham had returned from Rangoon in March, he had been heavily engaged in promoting the Moth. By November he had planned his next long-range flight – to Africa; a survey flight on behalf of Imperial Airways. He was sponsored by Castrol Oils, B.P. and Imperial Airways. On the 15th, along with his trusty engineer Arthur Elliott and B. W. Emmott, a Gaumont cine-cameraman to take photographs of suitable landing sites, Cobham left Croydon in the faithful DH.50J. Although only close family and friends braved the foggy conditions to see them off it would be a completely different matter when they returned in triumph four months later.

Now 1926 is best remembered as the year of the General Strike but in aviation terms it could rightly be considered 'Cobham's Year'. He arrived at Cape Town on 17th February and his progress had been followed by his many reports sent back to the Press in Britain. The flight was a diligent survey of twenty-five landing sites that might be used by Imperial Airways, proving that a scheduled service to South Africa was a viable proposition. One newspaper described him as '. . . a latter-day Welsey preaching the Gospel of Aviation wherever he landed.'! The return flight was tinged with some drama, Cobham had wagered a bet with the Master of the S.S. *Windsor Castle*, that he would arrive back before the liner docked at Southampton. Both aircraft and liner left Cape Town on 26th February and Cobham landed at Croydon on 13th March, winning his wager by two days. His arrival proved to be a gala occasion, a welcome normally reserved for Hollywood film stars. A convoy of aircraft escorted him in and the public enclosure was crammed with people; as the aircraft came to a halt the crowds broke through the barriers and Cobham was carried shoulder high to the Customs. He was summoned to Buckingham Palace to meet the King, his aircraft was placed on display at Selfridges in Oxford Street and he was awarded the AFC. Within a week Cobham announced his intention of flying to Australia in the same aircraft but this time fitted with floats. He was inundated with requests for public appearances and speaking engagements and without doubt was the most celebrated airman of the day.

The year also saw the first of many long-distance flights by RAF aircraft. On 1st March Wing Commander C. W. H. Pulford led four Fairey IIIDs to Cairo *en route* to Cape Town, arriving there on 12th April. The Fairey IIID was a development of the IIIC seaplanes that had entered the RAF in late 1918, IIIDs served until July 1930. The four Faireys returned to Lee-on-Solent in late May having accomplished over 13,000 miles without any mechanical faults. Later in the summer two Southamptons flew from Felixstowe to Egypt and back, another

Sir Alan Cobham, KBE, AFC – the most celebrated airman of the day. (Flight Refuelling Ltd via Colin Cruddas)

fault-free flight of some 7,000 miles and demonstrating their capability to operate from unprepared bases.

It was also quite a vintage year for new military aircraft. The Gloster Gamecock first flown in February 1925, entered the RAF with No 43 squadron at Henlow, hence the squadron nickname the 'Fighting

Fairey Fox – an advanced day bomber that outpaced all contemporary fighters.

Cocks'; a replacement for the Grebe, with the dubious honour of being the last wooden fighter to serve with the RAF. The Hawker Horsley, a day/torpedo bomber, came into service in August; another wooden biplane originally named Kingston but changed to Horsley after Thomas Sopwith's estate in Surrey – 'Horsley Towers'. But the most advanced aircraft to see service in 1926 was the Fox, which had been produced by Richard Fairey as a private venture. When Trenchard watched a demonstration flight in the previous August he immediately ordered a full squadron. It was a day bomber some 50 m.p.h. faster than its predecessors and furthermore it out-paced all contemporary fighters – unique in those days. No 12 squadron gave many spectacular displays with their Foxes proudly boasting the motto it 'Leads the Field'. However, due to financial constraints only twenty-eight were produced. More profitable for Fairey Aviation were its IIIFs, the prototype flew in March and proved to be one of the stalwarts of the RAF for many years, operating from land bases, as seaplanes, catapulted from Naval vessels and for transporting VIPs; over 600 were produced and they survived until August 1935.

Imperial Airways recognised that to achieve greater reliability and improved safety it required more multi-engined aircraft. In 1924 Handley Page developed a three-engined version of its W.8 for the Belgian airline SABENA, which led directly to their solitary W.9

Argosy II – G-AACI City of Liverpool *– at Croydon. It crashed in Belgium in 1933.*

Hampstead delivered to Imperial in November 1925 as *City of New York*. The Company was planning an improved twin-engined version in response to Imperial's urgent demand. To save time they grafted a W.8 nose section onto the airframe of their Hyderabad heavy bomber to produce a W.10 airliner; four were delivered to Imperial by 31st March – *City of Melbourne . . . of Pretoria . . . of Ottawa* and *City of London* – the latter ditched in the English Channel in October but with no loss of life.

Two famous British airliners of the period both appeared in 1926. Armstrong Whitworth's Argosy first flew at Coventry on 16th March, powered by three Jaguar III engines – the largest airliner yet produced. It carried twenty passengers, each had a window which could be opened! The Argosy was the first to provide near to 'Pullman' luxury, carrying a steward and on-board buffet, enabling Imperial to introduce a special lunchtime 'Silver Wings' service on the London-Paris route. It cruised at 90 m.p.h, had a range of over 400 miles and was far cheaper to operate. Three were originally ordered, again named after cities – *Glasgow, Birmingham* and *Wellington* (later *Arundel*) – followed by four improved models in 1928.

The other classic airliner was the de Havilland DH.66, Hercules, making its first appearance on 30th September. Another three-engined airliner with a cruising speed of 110 m.p.h., it had been specifically designed for Imperial's Cairo to Karachi passenger/mail service, and could carry fourteen passengers. On 18th December *City of Baghdad* left Croydon for Egypt to inaugurate the desert airmail service, with the tireless Sir Sefton Brancker and Air Commodore James Weir as passengers. On Boxing Day *City of Delhi* left on the first stage of a flight to India carrying Sir Samuel and Lady Hoare – the first Empire air route had opened at last justifying Imperial Airways' name. Nine of the eleven DH.66s operated with Imperial until 1935. Like earlier airliners both these originally had open cockpits; the pilots (all WWI airmen) disliked cabins because they '... needed the wind on their faces better to assess the wind drift on landing approach', despite the intense cold conditions experienced during the winter months – they were a hardy bunch!

The General Strike lasted from 3rd to 12th May and gave an opportunity to show what aviation could achieve in a national emergency. The *Daily Mail*, always in the forefront of aviation matters, arranged with the Royal Aero Club to send their newspaper by air to various airfields acting as distribution centres – Avro 504Ks, Moths, and DH.9s were used. With the railway system brought to a standstill Imperial was inundated with a demand for seats to the Continent. For the first time every airliner left Croydon full and even after the Strike ended, business continued to be brisk, obviously many converts had been made.

The Strike delayed Cobham's proposed flight to Australia but he and Arthur Elliott finally left from Rochester (where Shorts had fitted the

DH.66 Hercules of Imperial Airways.

floats) on 30th June. Whilst flying low over the desert south of Baghdad Elliott was shot in most bizarre circumstances, a stray bullet from a local tribesman had penetrated the cabin and struck Elliott in the chest. Tragically he died the following day at Basra hospital and was buried locally with full military honours. Cobham was devastated and wanted to end the flight. However, he received so many messages of support that he realised he owed it to his late friend to complete the flight. On 13th July he continued his journey, with Sergeant A.H. Ward as replacement engineer, and finally landed at Darwin on 5th August.

The RAF Display was held on 3rd July at what was now RAF Hendon. A Gamecock was put through its paces by Fg. Off. R. 'Batchy' Atcherley of the Central Flying School and acknowledged as the finest display of aerobatic flying ever seen at Hendon. Viriginia and Hyderabad bombers circled the airfield throughout the afternoon and the four Fairey IIID crews recently returned from South Africa were presented to the King. Several new aircraft made their first public appearance but for most it was also their last, their strange names – Sprat, Vendace, Hyena, Gorcock etc. – now long forgotten! But by far and above the most startling demonstrations were by two new and revolutionary aircraft – the Cierva C.6D Autogiro and the Hill Pterodactyl.

The Autogiro was the brainchild of Juan de la Cierva who had first conceived the idea of a rotor-driven machine that could take-off and land almost vertically. He had brought his latest model C.5 from his native Spain in order to gain financial support for its further development. A. V. Roe had shown great interest and a C.6D (a two-seater) was constructed from a '504K fuselage and fitted with a four-bladed revolving engine. It had been flown by Captain Frank Courtney at Royal Aircraft Establishment (RAE) at Farnborough the previous October and Major Wimperis, the Air Ministry's Director of Research, considered it 'the most important aeronautical invention of recent years' and two were purchased by the Ministry. In March 1926 the Cierva Autogiro Company was formed with the financial backing of Air Commodore Weir and it grew steadily over the years as a variety of small Autogiros were developed; the Company even offered flying tuition courses to 'A' licence for £35. Several aircraft companies were licensed to construct the aircraft, notably A. V. Roe and in 1934, their C.30A entered the RAF, known as a Rota I. Unfortunately Captain Geoffrey Hill's Pterodactyl was not blessed with the same success. This tail-less aircraft, redolent of Dunne's experiments at Farnborough in the

Cierva's Autogiro – C.19 Mk.II, G-AALA, dating from August 1929.

The amazing Avro 504K – production ceased in November 1926. (RAF Museum)

pioneering days, was flown at Hendon by Flt. Lt. J. S. Chirk of the RAE; although Westland Aircraft became involved in its subsequent development, the aircraft became nothing more than an exciting and radical oddity that had scant commercial or military application.

A week later Hendon hosted the King's Cup and was won by Hubert Broad in a Moth at 90.4 m.p.h. – the first of three successive Moth victories. The aeroplane was in great demand, over a hundred had been ordered during the year; glossy magazines featured photographs of celebrated airmen in their flying gear clustered around their Moths. In November Neville Stack, Chief Instructor of Lancashire Aero Club, and B. S. Leete, another Club member, flew two Moths from London to Karachi and arrived on 8th January to a tremendous welcome, acknowledged as 'the world's longest light aeroplane flight'. These flights brought fresh laurels, demonstrating to the owners of Moths that the world was their oyster.

The only other light aeroplane to come even close to competing with Moths for the club/private market was the Avro 581 Avian, which was first flown by Bert Hinkler on 7th July. It was a most successful and highly respected light aircraft, which, like the Moth appeared in various versions and remained in production until 1933 with many sold abroad. Its popularity owed much to Hinkler, who bought the prototype, G-EBOV, and with several modifications to it won a number of races as well as using it for his celebrated long-distance flights.

With the appearance of the Avian, the production of the amazing Avro 504K ceased in November with the last ten aircraft being delivered in the following January. It was one of the most successful designs of all time with in the region of 4-5,000 being manufactured in this country and abroad. In 1927 it was replaced by the 504N, which was used by the RAF as an elementary flying trainer until 1933.

The Avian had been designed with the Lympne Light Aeroplane Competition in mind, held in September. Although the Air Ministry no longer supported the event, the *Daily Mail*'s prizes remained on offer. Sixteen entries had been accepted but few were new aircraft, mostly re-designs or re-engined; only thirteen were present on the opening day and four of these were eliminated. First and second places went to the ultra-light Hawker Cygnets, designed by Sydney Camm in 1924, and the Company's only real attempt at the private market; although it was an elegant little machine, the Cygnet was not really practicable for private owners. The Lympne event was the last Light Aeroplane competition, which is perhaps not really surprising considering the

Sir Alan Cobham's DH.50J lands on the Thames – 1st October 1926. (via Colin Cruddas)

competition had failed to recognise the obvious merits of the most commercially successful light aircraft – Moth, Avian and Blackburn Bluebird.

On 1st October Cobham arrived back from Australia in some style, the return flight had taken twenty-five days. He flew the DH.50J low over the Thames to land alongside the Houses of Parliament, thousands of spectators thronged the embankments and bridges. He was officially welcomed home by the Secretary of State for Air and in due course was knighted for his epic flights. In December the FAI unanimously voted to award him their Gold Medal for 1926, but by this time he and Lady Cobham were on their way to the USA where Sir Alan undertook a six-week lecture tour as well as publicising the Moth; one was carried on board the S.S. *Homeric*.

As the year closed Imperial Airways reviewed its progress, over 16,650 passengers had been carried, the last of its bomber-converted airliners had been withdrawn and it now had eleven multi-engined aircraft. Croydon was in the throes of a major rebuilding programme. However, there was no cause for complacency because the German airline *Deutsche Luft Hansa*, formed by an amalgamation of two airlines in January, had carried over 56,000 passengers and would dominate European air travel in the years ahead. Nevertheless the Government and Imperial saw that its future lay with the development of passenger/mail routes to Empire countries.

The new year opened on a dismal note for the RAF when it was revealed that in the previous twelve months there had been fifty-one fatal accidents. Although half had occurred in WWI machines – Bristol Fighters and DH.9As – there was deep concern expressed about the Service's flying training programme, especially as 58% of the fatalities were Flying Officers, the most inexperienced pilots. There was also a call to reduce the number of RAF aircraft and pilots giving displays at the numerous air meetings now burgeoning throughout the country; Trenchard especially felt that as the public were paying for the Service's expansion, it was only right and fitting that their aircraft and pilots should appear at such events, helping to make the country 'more air-minded'. These tragic fatalities only strengthened the public's perception that flying was still a dangerous activity, which was reinforced later in the year with the loss of three very experienced civilian pilots.

Nevertheless there was no shortage of people eager to learn to fly; seventy-six had gained their 'A' licences at London Aero Club alone since it had opened and there were long waiting lists at all the clubs. Many new clubs opened around the country – Brooklands, Filton, Lympne, Hadleigh, Hamble, Glasgow, Shoreham, Liverpool, and Norwich – and light aircraft sales were buoyant with Moths well in front. In April the first production Avian became available at a cost of

The prototype Avro 581 Avian – G-EBOV – and Bert Hinkler.

£695. But perhaps the feature of private/club aviation during the year was the number of ladies involved in flying, appearing at the meetings and entering competitions for the first time; Sicole O'Brien, Winifred Spooner, Mrs Elliott-Lynn, Lady Mary Bailey and Mary du Caurroy, the Duchess of Bedford became familiar names in the near future. The Duchess had taken her first flight in June 1926 in a Moth at the age of sixty-one and 'enjoyed the experience immensely'. In April 1927 she hired a Moth and engaged Charles Barnard as her private pilot. They then completed a flight of some 4,500 miles covering France, Spain and North Africa arriving back at Croydon on 12th May, where their arrival was greeted by hordes of photographers. This flight was wonderful publicity for the aircraft, especially as de Havilland's proudly proclaimed 'the tool box was not opened on a single occasion.'! From now onwards the Duchess flew everywhere as a passenger in her own Moth, known as 'The Flying Duchess'. In October *Flight* commented '... British aviation in general owes the Duchess of Bedford a great deal for her practical encouragement of flying. By her constant use of her aeroplane she is setting an example which undoubtedly in the years to come will be followed by many ...' At the age of sixty-two she received her first flying lesson!

May proved quite an auspicious month for aviation. The RAF announced its intention to make an attempt on the world record for the longest non-stop flight – 3,345 miles – set by two French airmen in 1925. Thus on 20th May Flt. Lt. C. Roderick Carr and Flt. Lt. L. E. M. Gillman, in a Horsley loaded with 1,100 gallons of petrol, left Cranwell for India only to ditch in the Persian Gulf after 3,420 miles. They had achieved a new record but were not destined to hold it for very long. On the same day, Charles Lindbergh in his Ryan NYP monoplane, *Spirit of St Louis*, left New York attempting to win the $25,000 for the first non-stop flight to Paris; it would become one of the most famous flights in aviation history. By the afternoon of the 21st the BBC broadcast hourly bulletins of his progress – at 5.20 p.m. he crossed the Irish coast, by 7.20 p.m. he was over Cornwall, 8.30 p.m. over Cherbourg and finally landing at Le Bourget at 10.22 p.m. after $33\frac{1}{2}$ hours in the air and a flight of 3,610 miles – a new world record – the unknown American airman had become a worldwide hero.

Such was the press coverage of this epic flight that the arrival of four RAF Fairey IIIFs seaplanes at Cairo on the 22nd passed hardly noted, except for complaints at the cost of £3,000 to recondition landing grounds for the RAF! The crews led by the pioneer airman C.R. Samson

Charles Lindbergh arrived at Croydon on 29th May 1927.

(now Air Commodore) had left Cairo on 30th March for Cape Town and returned in less than two months. In direct contrast the welcome Lindbergh received when he arrived in *Spirit of St Louis* at Croydon from Paris (via Brussels) on Sunday 29th May was almost beyond belief. It was estimated that over 120,000 people were present and as his aircraft taxied in the crowds overwhelmed the policemen and burst through the barriers to get close to the aircraft and Lindbergh. It was described as '... scenes of wild enthusiasm, the like of which have never been known in the history of aviation ...' Lindbergh was finally rescued and taken to the control tower where he thanked the crowds saying 'this is a little worse than Le Bourget or I should say better ...' He was whisked away to the American Embassy along streets lined by cheering people. Charles Grey wrote in *The Aeroplane* about the poor security and his distaste of the crowd's 'unseemly' behaviour '... They behaved just like a lot of foreigners ...'! The next few days were a dizzy round of receptions, visits and meetings. Lindbergh was cheered wherever he went and women tried to kiss him. He met many important people and was presented with the AFC by the King; no airman had received such adulation. One newspaper commented '... Never has a flying exploit so stirred the public's imagination. This young man has raised the esteem for flyers and flying in this country and for that we cannot thank him enough ...' Lindbergh left for Paris on 2nd June from Kenley in a RAF Woodcock of No 23 squadron and his *Spirit of St Louis* was crated at Gosport for transport back to the States.

With his departure the aviation world returned to some normality and the Whitsun weekend meeting at Ensbury Park racecourse at Bournemouth attracted large crowds to see and support British flying aces. Mrs Elliott-Lynn won the Ladies Race, which showed the growing band of lady pilots. She was flying a Westland Widgeon III, the Company's first attempt to break into the club/private market. It was a delightful parasol monoplane, the earliest version had been around since 1924, and was advertised as 'the fastest two-seat light aircraft in the world with the ability to fly twenty miles on one gallon of petrol.' Sadly it was not commercially successful, perhaps it was a trifle expensive at £730. Hinkler won the Private Owners Handicap race in his Avian and another Avian was successful in a different event. The final day was sadly marred by a tragic accident; Laurence Openshaw, Westland's test pilot, in a Widgeon III collided in mid-air with a Bluebird flown by 'Scruffie' Longton and both airmen were killed. The King's Cup Race, which was due to be held at Ensbury Park on the August Bank Holiday, was hastily transferred to another venue – Hucknall near Nottingham. The accident brought about a tighter control of aircraft competing in such racing events, it was decreed that no more than four machines should fly in any heat, there had been no less than eleven rounding the aerodrome's turning point when the collision occurred.

Over 90,000 people braved the elements – wind and rain – to attend the RAF Display at Hendon on 2nd July. The new grandstand with a capacity of 3,000 was packed. Five scarlet-painted Moths of the C.F.S., led by Flt. Lt. D'Arcy Greig, gave what was described as 'a breath-taking display of co-ordinated flying ... their precision almost beggared belief marking a peak of flying perfection ...' However, the Display made headline news for another reason, fourteen German military officers attended as guests of the Air Ministry and at least six were known to have flown with the German Flying Corps during WWI including a certain Captain Hermann Göring. The French press vociferously complained that this was against the terms of the Versailles Treaty, whereby Germany was banned from any military aviation and forbidden to send any military mission abroad. The British government claimed, somewhat disingenuously, that it was not an official delegation, the officers were merely spectators the same as any others that had paid for their tickets!

Within days of the Hendon Display Lady Mary Bailey, the wife of Sir Abe Bailey, a South African millionaire, took up Mrs de Havilland in a DH.60X Moth with a new 85 h.p. Cirrus engine and they reached a height of 17,283 feet, a new world record for a light aircraft. Not to be upstaged, in October, Mrs Elliott-Lynn, flying an Avian II, completed a flight of over 1,300 miles in a day including seventy-nine landings and reaching a height of 19,200 feet. The two ladies entered the King's Cup Race at the end of July but both failed to finish. There was a tragic prelude to the Race when days earlier Captain Frank Barnard of Imperial Airways was killed near Filton whilst testing a Bristol Badminton. Wally Hope of Air Taxis Ltd won in a Moth, but all interest was centred on de Havilland's latest creation – DH.71 Tiger Moth. A small streamlined monoplane primarily designed for high speed research, only two were produced, one with a Cirrus II engine and the other with the newly developed 135 h.p. Gipsy engine, designed by Major Halford and built by de Havilland's. Both were entered but only one actually competed, it was retired after reaching Spittalgate. The Gipsy powered Tiger Moth achieved a speed of 186.47 m.p.h. on 24th August – a world record for its category. Subsequently one crashed in Australia in 1930 and the other was destroyed by enemy bombing in October 1940. It is interesting to note a *Daily Mail* report in May 2002 that an American couple had built a replica DH.71 in their second floor Manhattan apartment – 'all the parts were taken up by elevator ... and when finished we detached the wings and eased the fuselage out of the window and on to the back of a truck.'! It was exhibited at an air meet in Connecticut in June.

In April the RAF announced its intention of competing for the Schneider Trophy Race to be held at Venice in late September. Its High Speed Flight, based at Felixstowe under Wing Commander Maycock, had been training for the event. The Air Ministry had ordered three Supermarine-Napier S.5s, designed, of course, by that doyen of seaplanes – Reginald J. Mitchell; they also had three Gloster IV seaplanes and a Short Crusader for practising. It proved to be a most comprehensive victory, Sqn. Ldr. S. N. Webster came first in S.5 (N.220) at an average speed of over 281 m.p.h., with Flt. Lt. O. E. Worsley placed second in S.5 (N.219). No other competitors completed the course and during the race Sqn. Ldr. Webster set a new world speed record of 283 m.p.h. Five years had elapsed since Britain last won this prestigious Trophy, and it was now agreed that because of the large costs involved in developing high-speed seaplanes, the Race would be held every two years.

Flying boats were in the news as the year drew to a close. Four Southamptons left Felixstowe for Singapore via the Mediterranean and India and from thence to Hong Kong, Australia and New Zealand, returning to Singapore in December 1928 – a majestic cruise of over 27,000 miles. In November Sir Alan Cobham was again on his travels in a Short Singapore I flying boat, loaned by the Air Ministry. It had first appeared the previous August but did not enter the RAF until 1934 as Mark IIIs. Sir Alan had ambitious plans to journey around the whole of Africa with the thoughts of establishing his own airline. Once again Lord Wakefield of Castrol Oils sponsored the provision of oil and petrol, and the crew comprised Captain H. V. Worrall as co-pilot, two engineers, a Gaumont cameraman and Lady Cobham for 'secretarial duties ... a kind of ship's purser so to speak ...' They completed over 22,000 miles and returned to Plymouth at the end of May to yet another warm welcome.

A dominating feature of aviation during 1928 was the number of long-distance flights made in light aircraft; they became almost commonplace. It was also when Lady Bailey and Lady Heath, inevitably called the 'Flying Aristocrats', became known to a far wider audience than the enclosed world of aviation. They completed their long-distance flights with a certain style and the minimum of fuss and given their glamour, wealth and undoubted courage they provided 'heaven-sent' copy for the Press; indeed Lady Heath sedulously courted publicity.

However, it was Bert Hinkler who first made the headlines in February when he flew to Australia in 15$\frac{1}{2}$ days. He left Croydon on the 7th in his modified Avian and arrived at Darwin on the 22nd, despite being arrested in Italy for landing at a military airfield in error. 'Hustling Hinkler', as one newspaper called him, arrived to a tremendous welcome, the Australian public lionised their returning hero. He had completed the first solo flight to Australia – 11,005 miles – and established six major records. Hinkler was awarded the Air Force Cross although the Australian public felt he should have been knighted; indeed this became quite a political battle between the two countries but Hinkler, ever the quiet and unassuming man, managed to remain aloof from the debate.

Lady Heath, a rather extrovert and colourful Irishwoman, left

Johannesburg for Cairo in her Avian on 24th February accompanied by Lt. R. R. Bentley of the SAAF, who in the previous September had completed the first solo flight to South Africa. They arrived at Cairo and Lady Heath continued on alone to Paris, where it was said she '... stepped from her tiny airplane looking as fresh as a daisy ...' She is reported to have commented, 'It is so safe that a woman can fly across Africa wearing a Parisian frock and keeping her nose powdered all the way.'. Meanwhile Lady Bailey, a reserved and modest mother of five children, was making her way south to Cape Town in a Moth. She left Croydon on 9th March and finally arrived in Cape Town on 30th April; she reputedly apologised to her husband for being '... a bit late, but I got muddled up in the mountains.'! After spending about five months flying around Africa Lady Bailey flew back to Britain, arriving at Croydon on 16th January 1929. Her 'excursion' of some 11,000 miles was described '... not only by far the most remarkable feat ever achieved by a woman, but the greatest solo flight ever made by any pilot of either sex!'; it gained her the Brittania Trophy for 1929.

On 1st April the RAF was ten years old and Lord Weir, who had been involved at its inception, sent a message to Trenchard, 'I regard it as incomparably the most efficient Air Force in existence. ...' Certainly under Trenchard's close guidance and direction it had developed into a most efficient and effective Service. Perhaps 'its finest hour' so far came in December, when eight Vickers Victorias of No 70 squadron assisted by other aircraft evacuated 586 people (including the Afghan Royal family) from Kabul right from under the rebel guns. In two months the squadron flew more than 28,000 miles over mountains and in some atrocious weather conditions. It was the world's first major airlift of civilians and baggage.

Lady Mary Hoare formally opened the new and imposing terminal buildings and the reconstructed airfield at Croydon on 2nd May. The spacious domed booking hall with its arrival/departure indicators, weather information board and clocks displaying the times around the world became a famous meeting place. But it was dwarfed by the impressive control tower, which would feature in many photographs in the years ahead. It was the first specially-constructed modern air terminal, replicated by several European cities. One travel guide claimed that Croydon demonstrated '... Civil Aviation in England has been established on a sound basis ... it is a reality and not a toy played with by enthusiasts ...' Nevertheless several years passed before the volume of air traffic justified such splendid buildings. The new

Fine aerial photograph of the new terminal and control tower at Croydon. Argosy, G-AAEJ City of Coventry *and a KLM Fokker.*

Aerodrome Hotel close by had a flat roof enabling spectators to watch the arrival and loading of the airliners; it also became the social centre of the airport not only for travellers and their friends but also for airline crews.

The only aerodrome to compete with Croydon in the late Thirties was formally opened on 5th July – Heston in Middlesex. Owned by Air Work Ltd. it became 'socially accepted' when the Household Brigade Flying Club moved in from Brooklands. It was one of three airfields sited in a relatively small area. Some miles due south was Hanworth Park, also opened during the year by National Flying Services Ltd; originally known as London Air Park, it hosted the King's Cup in 1930. The other new airfield in the vicinity was Fairey Aviation's 'Great West Aerodrome'. The Company operated from Hayes and was growing in importance with its fine military aircraft. Hitherto Northolt had been used for test flying but the Air Ministry wanted to develop Northolt into a permanent station and the Company were given notice to leave. Fairey's were forced to find suitable land not too far from their factory and in early 1929 some 180 acres of land near to the village of Heathrow was purchased; the new aerodrome was called Harmondsworth later acquiring its more familiar name.

Two women aviators stole the headlines in June. The redoubtable

'Flying Duchess' left Lympne on the 10th in her newly acquired Fokker VIIa – *Princess Xenia* later renamed the *Spider* – bound for Karachi. It was flown by Charles Barnard with Alliott as co-pilot; they were attempting to fly to India and back in eight days. However, engine problems were encountered at Bushire, Persia and they had to wait eight weeks for a replacement engine. Just eight days after the Duchess had left Lympne, America's most celebrated woman flyer, Amelia Earhart, landed at Burry Port, Carmarthenshire in a Fokker triplane – *Friendship* – along with the pilot Wilmer Stultz and mechanic, Lon Graham. They had left Newfoundland the previous day and their flight took twenty hours and forty minutes, thus Amelia became the first woman to cross the Atlantic by air albeit as a passenger. She bore an uncanny resemblance to Lindbergh and the Press on both sides of the Atlantic quickly named her 'Lady Lindy'! About three months later Britain's own celebrated woman pilot, Amy Johnson, took her first flying lesson at the London Aero Club. Her flying instructor advised her '... to save your money, you are unlikely to make a pilot'; in less than two years she was flying solo to Australia.

At the end of June the ninth RAF Display was the most successful so far, with a record crowd of nearly 100,000 and over £10,000 collected for the RAF Benevolent Fund. Hendon was now the home of 600 and 601 AAF squadrons and also used for official military demonstrations for visiting foreign delegates and heads of State. *Flight* considered '... the whole standard of flying at the Display was more finished, neater and cleaner than any previous occasions. That means we may pride ourselves on being streets in front of everybody for we have undoubtedly got the finest Air Force and the best built aeroplanes and engines in the world.'

The following month the seventh King's Cup was held there and no less than fourteen Moths entered including three DH.60Gs, Gipsy Moths. They were powered by the Company's new Gipsy engine and one flown by Wally Hope won at an average speed of 105 m.p.h. The Gipsy Moth became the best known light aircraft the world over, immortalised by Amy Johnson's *Jason* and Francis Chichester's *Madame Elijah*. By 1929 the Company were producing almost three a day and licences were granted to companies in France, Australia and America. Production continued until 1934; the majority were British registered but they were successfully flown in most countries. Geoffrey de Havilland's personal Gipsy Moth was given the first new civil registration letters – G-AAAA – when the system changed in July.

Short Calcutta flying boat – City of Athens.

During August the A.D.G.B. held its second Air Exercises or 'Air War', as the Press liked to call them. They were intended to test the strength and effectiveness of the units engaged on the defence of London. For three days simulated day and night bombing attacks were made by DH.9As, Fawns, Foxes and Victorias opposed by Siskins and Woodcocks. According to the Air Ministry the exercises had been 'remarkably successful', over ¼ million miles flown with only one minor accident. No official comment was made about the 'night-raids' by Victorias, several journalists considered that most had managed 'to attack their targets' without being intercepted and the general consensus was that the Air Ministry was loath to admit just how successful they had been.

In September Sir Eric Geddes, Imperial Airways' Chairman, reported a profit for the second year running, passenger traffic had increased by 55% to 26,479. He also announced a new government subsidy amounting to £2½ million over ten years. In August Imperial had taken delivery of its first large flying boat, Short Calcutta; essentially a commercial version of the military Singapore but with three engines instead of two. The accommodation for its fifteen passengers was comfortable, well-appointed and quite luxurious by the standards of the time. The first Calcutta, *City of Alexandria*, operated on the service from Southampton to the Channel Islands but by the following year all five were engaged on the airline's new Mediterranean service from Genoa.

As the number of Aero Clubs grew and provincial airfields opened, air meetings played an increasing part in the summer scene. There were numerous joy-riding companies plying their trade not only from airfields but also from any level field that could be rented from farmers. The air meetings had become more elaborate affairs, vying with each other to attract the public and increasingly billed as 'Air Pageants'. Typical of these was the Pageant held at Sywell aerodrome, the new home of Northamptonshire Aero Club. On 29th September Sir Sefton Brancker, the tireless Director of Civil Aviation, arrived in his Moth to formally open the new facilities and watch the subsequent flying displays; seventy-five years later Sywell aerodrome is still thriving. Brooklands was beginning to regain some of its pre-war eminence. Captain Duncan Davis, who as a schoolboy had helped Cody at Farnborough, had taken over Henderson's Flying School and renamed it 'Brooklands'; although two years would elapse before Brooklands hosted its first post-war meeting.

The *Daily Mail* set an example to other newspapers in October, when it bought a DH.61 Giant Moth, *Geraldine*, and equipped it as the first flying newspaper office. It had typing facilities, a dark room to develop photographs and also carried a motor-cycle to enable the reporter or photographer to reach a scene of news interest without delay. The aircraft remained with the newspaper for about eighteen months. The Giant Moth had first flown the previous December intended as a replacement for the DH.50J and mainly for use in Australia. Of the ten that were produced, only two were registered in Britain, the other was purchased by Sir Alan Cobham and famously named *Youth of Britain*.

In four years British aviation had made immense strides. The aircraft industry had prospered largely as a result of military contracts. As the sales of Moths burgeoned de Havilland's could be considered the most successful aircraft company not reliant on Air Ministry orders; it was these aeroplanes that had almost solely brought about the rapid growth of club and private flying. Imperial Airways had struggled to compete with European airlines but was now at the gateway of the routes to India and Africa, which it hoped to develop with new airliners. The RAF had remained independent and achieved a slow but steady expansion during a period of economic restraint. The Service had captured the public's support largely through its spectacular displays. Thus at the end of 1928 there were grounds for considerable optimism for the future of British aviation in all its aspects.

9
AIR CIRCUSES AND PETTICOAT PILOTS
(1929–1932)

Just as the prospects for British aviation seemed so promising the country was plunged into severe recession with soaring unemployment, mounting inflation and a deep decline in business activity. Nevertheless British manufacturers produced an increasing number of admirable light aircraft though regretfully for a diminishing market. However, it was not quite all doom and gloom. Private and club flying not only survived but managed to slowly grow, there appeared to be sufficient wealthy flying enthusiasts, seemingly untouched by the grim economic conditions of the times. During these years many clubs and private airfields were established and the first municipal aerodromes opened. Solo long-distance flights came to the fore, continuing to stimulate public interest and the air races and meetings still attracted large crowds. The RAF memorably secured for the country the coveted Schneider Trophy outright and the world speed record.

Croydon was in the news on March 30th when Imperial Airways inaugurated the commercial air service to India. The total journey time was seven days and cost £130 single including hotel accommodation. In April, Sqn. Ldr. A. G. Jones-Williams and Flt. Lt. N. H. Jenkins left Cranwell in a Fairey Long-range monoplane and arrived in Karachi on 26th having completed the first non-stop flight to India – 4,100 miles in $50\frac{1}{2}$ hours – but were prevented from attempting a new world record because of adverse headwinds. The monoplane had been designed for the Air Ministry expressly to capture the world record; it crashed in Tunisia in December *en route* to South Africa in another record attempt and both airmen were killed.

In May the first Bristol Bulldogs entered the Service with No 3 squadron at Upavon; this single-seat fighter was a replacement for the

Bristol Bulldog: probably epitomised the RAF of the early Thirties.

Siskin and probably more than any other single aircraft epitomised the RAF of the early Thirties. They regularly performed at Hendon, where their displays were great favourites with the crowds. Although significantly slower (top speed 174 m.p.h.) than contemporary light bombers, they equipped ten squadrons remaining in service until July 1937 when they seemed very out-dated!

During May Sir Alan Cobham started his long flying tour of the country in an attempt to persuade local authorities to establish their own airfields – his 'Municipal Aerodromes Scheme'. Starting from Mousehold near Norwich on the 16th Sir Alan visited over one hundred cities and towns in his *Youth of Britain*, and during his tour, which lasted until October, he carried 10,000 schoolchildren (sponsored by Lord Wakefield) and over 40,000 other passengers. Hull gained the distinction of opening the first municipal aerodrome in the country, at Hedon about six miles out of the City. On 10th October H.R.H. Prince George arrived in the Royal Westland Wapiti piloted by Sqn. Ldr. D. S. Don, to formally open the aerodrome. He was greeted by a crowd of over 35,000 and was the fourth Royal prince to learn to fly. Hull would soon be able to boast of its own celebrated airwoman, Amy Johnson; she was born there in 1903. In the summer she gained her 'A' licence and was now at de Havilland's working towards a Ground Engineer's certificate.

The progress of private flying in the last few years can perhaps be

Sir Alan Cobham's DH.61 Giant Moth, G-AAEV, Youth of Britain. (via Colin Cruddas)

gauged by the number of candidates using aeroplanes in their campaign during the May General Election; the majority were Moths. The Labour party won the election and Lord Thomson was appointed Secretary of State for Air, a post he had previously held in 1924 and since then he had zealously supported British aviation. According to Charles Grey he was '... like most converts more fervent than those brought up to the faith.'! Lord Thomson soon faced a serious blow to Imperial Airways' prestige; on 17th June its W.10 airliner, *City of Ottawa,* ditched in the Channel about three miles from Dungeness after one engine failed and tragically seven passengers drowned. The Press led the campaign for a formal investigation demanding that no more twin-engined airliners be used on the cross-Channel service; Imperial stressed that since 1925 over 100,000 passengers had been carried safely. The Inquiry revealed that metal fatigue caused the accident rather than pilot error as many had assumed. In September a DH.66, *City of Jerusalem,* crashed whilst landing at night at Jask, Persia, killing two crew and a passenger; this accident *was* attributed to pilot error. Despite these setbacks Imperial had a favourable year, profits increased to £140,000 and over 35,500 passengers had been carried; there were now signs that a scheduled South African service was coming closer to reality.

Early in the year there was a heated debate concerning the pioneer days of flying when the Royal Aero Club, for whatever reason, set up a Committee to examine which British airman had been the first to fly in Britain. Maxim and Cody were eliminated as being foreigners at the time of their first flights. The claims of Phillips and Roe were also dismissed, although de Havilland strongly supported Roe's cause but he was in a minority; Moore-Brabazon's flights at Leysdown during 30th April/2nd May 1909 were declared the first flights by a British airman. Needless to say Charles Grey had something to say on the matter, '... nevertheless in a general way the position seems to be that S. F. Cody made the first flight in the British Isles.' Roe, himself, was not too perturbed by the whole affair, he had founded a great aircraft company and in 1928 was the first pioneer airman to be knighted. He had also sold his interest in Avro to John Siddeley of Armstrong Whitworth and had obtained control of S. E. Saunders Ltd to form Saunders-Roe Ltd, which produced many fine flying boats over the next thirty years.

Over 132,000 spectators attended Hendon on 13th July to witness the RAF Display but for the first time King George V was not present, he was recovering from a serious illness. Although known as 'the Sailor King' he had loyally supported these events and aviation generally despite his rumoured dislike of aeroplanes, which he had originally considered 'noisy and dangerous machines.'! In the following week the King's Cup was won in convincing style by Flg. Off. 'Batchy' Atcherley in a Grebe II averaging 150 m.p.h. – rather pedestrian compared with his speeds at Calshot in August and September! It was the last time Hendon staged the race; other airfields such as Heston, Fairey's at Hounslow and London Air Park were coming to the fore. On 6th July Heston was formally opened by Lord Thomson and two weeks later the first 'Aerial Garden Party' was staged there, over sixty aircraft were engaged in the proceedings and 1,000s attended. By January it had been approved as a Customs aerodrome and was increasingly used by private pilots leaving on foreign flights. London Air Park was formally opened in August (29th) by the Duchess of Bedford, who had recently returned from her flight to India, which was described as '... a trip of physical endurance that many young men might have shirked ... she proved to be an active, useful and efficient member of the crew ...'

Press attention was centred on Calshot and the RAF's preparations

Heston Aerodrome was formally opened on 6th July 1929.

for the defence of the Schneider Trophy. The team, led by Sqn. Ldr. A. H. Orlebar, comprised Flt. Lt. D. D'Arcy Greig and Flying Officers Atcherley and Richard Waghorn. Their seaplanes were perhaps the most elegant and spectacular group of British speed machines ever produced. There was a Supermarine S.5/25 previously entered in the 1927 competition and two new Supermarine S.6s, which Reginald Mitchell had developed from the S.5 but slightly larger and powered by a new 1,900 h.p Rolls-Royce racing engine. Besides these superb racing machines there were two Gloster VIs designed by Henry Folland, considered by many to be the most elegant monoplanes yet produced – 'the Golden Arrows of the Air'. They had cost £25,000 each; this type of speed racing was without doubt a very expensive business. However, technical problems resulted in both Gloster VIs being withdrawn. The competition was staged at Spithead on 7th September – seven laps, each about thirty-one miles – and there was strong competition from the Italian team. The event was won by a S.6, N.247, flown by Flg. Off. Richard Waghorn at an average speed of over 328 m.p.h. The Italian Macchi M.25 piloted by Thomaso Dal Molin was placed second and Flt. Lt. Greig in a S.5 was third. It was a magnificent victory for British aviation and the RAF's team.

In direct contrast to these speedsters, two massive and lumbering airships captured attention during the autumn. It was fitting that Lord Thomson should be on board the R101, when it made its second flight from the Royal Airship Works at Cardington on 18th October. In 1924 he had been instrumental in the Government's decision to initiate an airship research programme costing £1.35 million, with the aim of building two airships capable of carrying up to a hundred passengers on services to India and Canada. On 1st November R101 flew over Sandringham in order that King George V could view it and eight days later it flew with eighty-two persons on board. The other airship, R100, was the result of private enterprise; constructed by the Airship Guarantee Company (a subsidiary of Vickers Ltd.). It made its maiden flight from Howden to Cardington on 16th December; the Chief Designer was Barnes Wallis, later famous for the Wellington bomber and the 'bouncing bomb', also involved was Nevil S. Norway (the novelist Nevil Shute). Another smaller non-rigid airship – AD-1 (Advertising Airship) – made its appearance in September and a month later it flew over an air meeting at Cramlington, Newcastle boldly proclaiming on its side 'This Space to Let'.

In December Marshal of the Royal Air Force, Sir Hugh Trenchard, retired at the age of fifty-six. He had long advocated that five years should be the maximum term of tenure for the top post in his beloved Service and he had served for ten years. Sir Hugh could look back on that time with considerable satisfaction, having accomplished all the objectives he had set down in 1919. It had been a singular achievement, if he had not quite built 'a castle', his legacy to the Service might well be described as 'a rather fine mansion'! The RAF comprised fifty-six regular and nine Reserve/AAF squadrons and most regular squadrons were equipped with modern aircraft. All his Colleges and Technical Schools were firmly established and highly regarded and the RAF was recognised as the world's leading Air Force. Baron Trenchard of Wolfeton, so honoured in the New Year, remained a powerful influence on the Service and when it faced its sternest test just ten years later, it still bore all the hallmarks of his visionary zeal. He was succeeded by Air Chief Marshal Sir John Salmond, who had taken command of the RFC in France when Trenchard had first been appointed Chief of the Air Staff.

Francis Chichester, an unassuming young man, captured the

attention in January with his solo flight to Australia. He had emigrated to New Zealand at the age of eighteen but returned with the intention of learning to fly, which he did at Brooklands during 1929. Just four months after completing his first solo flight he calmly decided to fly back to New Zealand. With the minimum of fuss Chichester left Croydon on 20th December in his Gipsy Moth, *Madame Elijah*, finally arriving at Port Darwin on 27th January, thus completing 12,050 miles in 180½ flying hours. When he arrived at Sydney he said 'The fame I ran into hit me like a shock ...' His remarkable feats of aerial navigation across the Tasman Sea in 1931 added to his renown but it was thirty-six years later that he gained worldwide fame with his solo round-the-world voyage in his yacht, *Gipsy Moth*, for which he was knighted.

The first Hawker Harts entered No 33 squadron at Eastchurch in January. These classic aircraft, designed by Sydney Camm, were perhaps the RAF's most remarkable and adaptable biplanes. The Hart was a fast and highly maneouvrable two-seat light bomber constructed of metal but fabric covered, which first flew in June 1928. With a maximum speed of 184 m.p.h. it outpaced contemporary fighters, even making the Bulldog technically obsolete after barely six months' service. Harts equipped eighteen squadrons up to 1936 and were still operating with the AAF two years later. They were also used as trainers and several variants – Demon (fighter), Audax (Army-Co-operation) and Hind (light bomber) – saw service over the next six years.

Despite the deepening recession that was gripping the country, private/club flying was flourishing. There were over twenty aero clubs, six flying schools and some one thousand aspiring pilots receiving flying tuition. In the spring de Havilland's RAF Reserve Flying School moved from Stag Lane to 'a large green field site' at Hatfield, Hertfordshire, and in May Brooklands Aero Club reformed and became one of **the** clubs, especially as H.R.H. Prince George was one of its earliest members. During the year a number of private and public airfields opened – notably Barton (Manchester), Desford (Leicester), Ipswich, Tollerton (Nottingham), Whitchurch (Bristol), and Gatwick. In the following year another dozen would open for flying, although several proposed developments were postponed until the economy improved.

Most clubs favoured Moths with a few Bluebirds and Avians for good measure, whereas the flying schools used Avro 504Ks and 548s, Bristol Fighters and DH.9Js besides, of course, Moths. Prospective

Hawker Hart: a classic aeroplane designed by Sydney Camm.

private owners were almost spoilt for choice providing they had the necessary finance. As flights became longer there was a growing demand for improved flying comfort eliminating the need for heavy 'flying gear'. Needless to say de Havilland's quickly responded by producing their DH.80A Puss Moth, a high-wing monoplane with a comfortable cabin for two passengers. There was also available the Desoutter II, modified from the Dutch FK.41 monoplane by the pioneer airman Marcel Desoutter, which set new standards of cabin luxury; both cost £1,000. Much cheaper were the Spartan Arrow and Three-Seater biplanes, elegant and successful aircraft that retained open cockpits and sold for £720/750. The latter was one of the mainstays of the numerous small joy-riding companies plying their trade during the summer seasons. One highly acclaimed small machine was the Comper CLA.7 Swift, a single-seat racing monoplane with a cruising speed of 100 m.p.h. Designed by an ex-RAF officer, Nicholas Comper, with the sportsman racer in mind, it was a rather luxurious aircraft for such harsh financial conditions and was not as commercially successful as it deserved.

The economic recession was perhaps just one reason why a far less expensive type of flying – gliding – was increasing in popularity. The British Gliding Association had recently formed and there were now six gliding clubs, the most active being the London Club at Tring, Buckinghamshire and the Kent Club at Lenham. The Royal Aero Club awarded the first gliding certificate in May – No 1 to Jimmy Lowe-Wylde. One problem was a lack of British 'sailpanes', most were of German manufacture where gliding reigned supreme due mainly to strong official support and financial backing for clubs. One of the first to design, build and fly her own glider was Constance Leathart, a well-known pilot now operating her own company – Cramlington Aircraft. Gliding competitions and displays attracted the young and old alike, from pioneer airmen remembering their early flying days to such celebrated pilots as Sir Alan Cobham, 'Batchy' Atcherley, Frank Barnard and Lady Bailey.

A glorious and successful summer for women pilots was ushered in by the Duchess of Bedford; she arrived back at Croydon on 30th April in her Spider to a splendid welcome, besieged by photographers and well-wishers. She, along with Charles Barnard and co-pilot Bob Little, had completed a round trip to Cape Town (19,000 miles) in twenty days. But it was Amy Johnson that captured the headlines in May.

Although she had only ninety hours solo flying in her log and had not yet crossed the Channel, Amy Johnson was determined to emulate Hinkler's solo flight to Australia. She estimated that the flight would cost £1,500 so she sought sponsorship. Her proposal interested Sir Sefton Brancker, who persuaded Lord Wakefield to finance her. He provided half the cost of the aircraft (Amy's father paid the rest), all the oil and negotiated with petrol companies for a supply along her route. Amy purchased a Gipsy Moth from Wally Hope for £600, painted it dark green with silvered wings and tailplane and christened it *Jason*. Early on 5th May there was only a handful of people at Croydon to watch her leave for Vienna, her first stop; her parents were a little relieved to know that she was wearing an Irvin parachute. By the time she arrived at Karachi five days later she had become famous, the U.K. record to India had been broken and she was two days ahead of Hinkler's time. After several mishaps Amy finally landed safely at Port Darwin on the 24th, 19½ days after leaving Croydon; the first woman to fly solo to Australia. She was deluged with telegrams and letters from celebrated airmen, as well as from the British public. Newspapers called her the 'Queen of the Air' and even songs were written about

Amy Johnson: the celebrated airwoman first captured the headlines in May 1930.

her, one with the famous refrain 'Amy, Wonderful Amy'. Her fame almost surpassed that of Lindbergh, life would never be the same for the 'little typist from Hull' though few realised that she held an Economics degree from Sheffield University.

Hanworth Air Park was the venue of the King's Cup on 5th July and there was an unexpected result, the Cup was won by a woman pilot. There were no less than one hundred and one entrants, the largest number ever; the preceding year there had been just thirty-seven. Over eighty actually started, including seven ladies and over half of the aircraft were *Moths*. The course covered some 750 miles with stops at Whitchurch, Barton, Cramlington, and Hedon and at each aerodrome thousands turned out to cheer the competitors. Sixty managed to finish and the winner was Winifred Brown, an international hockey player and member of Lancashire Aero Club, in her Avian III at an average speed of 102 m.p.h. It would be another fifty years before the Cup was claimed by another woman pilot.

Two weeks later seven British pilots gathered at Templehof airport in Berlin for the gruelling International Tour of Europe covering some 4,680 miles in seven days. The highest placed British pilot was Winifred Spooner in her Gipsy Moth, she came in fourth but was judged overall first in her aircraft category and won prize money of 16,500 francs. According to Charles Grey she was 'a truly professional pilot ... without doubt our leading woman aviator ...' Within days her success was eclipsed by the arrival of Amy Johnson at Croydon on 4th August as a passenger on board the *City of Glasgow*. Amy was 'officially welcomed' by Lord Thomson, Sir Sefton Brancker, Lord Wakefield and thousands of spectators. There was a formal reception at the Savoy attended by leading figures in the aviation world and Amy was presented with the *Mail*'s £10,000 and a gold cup. A week later she attended Buckingham Palace to receive the C.B.E. This was followed by a flight to Hendon aerodrome in *Jason* for a civic reception from her hometown. From then on it was a long whirlwind publicity tour for 'Our Amy' organised by the *Daily Mail*. She was given a new Puss Moth by de Havilland's, William Morris (later Lord Nuffield) presented her with a MG saloon car and *Daily Sketch* readers subscribed to buy her a new Gipsy Moth. It was a real-life 'rags to riches' story.

All this Press attention had overshadowed the successful crossing of the North Atlantic by the airship R100. It left Cardington on 20th July under the command of Major G. H. Scott, who had been in charge of R34 for its successful crossing in July 1919, and arrived safely at

R101 at its masthead at Cardington.

Montreal on 1st August; after touring around Canada the airship arrived back at Cardington on 16th August. The Royal Airship Works had to prove the worth of their airship, R101. It had been lengthened by fifty feet and Lord Thomson wanted R101 to make its proving flight to India by the last week of September in order that he might return in time for the Imperial Conference in London on 20th October. A hurried trial of the lengthened airship was made on 1st October and only Sir Sefton Brancker expressed his misgivings on the proposed flight without further tests. Nevertheless on the evening of 4th October R101 left Cardington for India with several distinguished passengers on board including Lord Thomson and Sir Sefton Brancker.

On the following morning *The Times* reported 'The airship R101 struck the ground and was wrecked and totally destroyed by fire near Beauvais, in the north of France, early on Sunday morning. Of the fifty-four persons on board, only eight were saved. The rest must be presumed to have lost their lives. Among them Lord Thomson and Sir Sefton Brancker ...' This dreadful disaster deeply shocked and saddened the whole nation. Sir Stanley Hoare wrote '... [it] is so overwhelming in the suffering it imposed upon many families and the injury it inflicted on aeronautical society … The names Lord Thomson and Sir Sefton Brancker will rightly hold high place in the history of British aeronautics. …' A Memorial Service was held at St Paul's Cathedral on 10th October and the following day the officers and men were buried in the local churchyard at Cardington, where there is now an impressive tomb memorial.

In the aftermath of the tragedy British aviation was bereft of its two most important and influential officials and they would be difficult to replace. Within days Lord Amulree, a distinguished lawyer, was appointed Secretary of State for Air; he was hardly known in aviation circles and had shown no interest in the subject. However, it was thought that this might 'not be too disastrous perhaps better than an enthusiastic amateur'! It was January before a new Director of Civil Aviation was appointed, Lt.-Col. Francis Shelmerdine, an ex-RFC/RAF pilot, who had been in charge of civil aviation in India. The R101 disaster sounded the death knell of British rigid airships, R100 was broken up and by the end of the year its design team had left Howden.

During the autumn there were several long-distance solo flights, perhaps the most impressive was by the celebrated Wing Commodore Charles Kingsford-Smith, he flew to Australia in just nine days and twenty-two hours in an Avian Sports – *Southern Cross Junior*. He was the first airman to fly across *both* the Pacific and Atlantic oceans and Lindbergh considered 'Smithy' to be 'the World's greatest airman.' Unhappily during that time there were many fatal accidents – private, military and civil – almost one a week and they mainly occurred in heavy fog. On 30th October Imperial's *City of Washington* crashed at Nechchâtel, France, three of the four passengers were killed and the two crewmen seriously injured. In Britain, as in other countries, the techniques of blind landings were being urgently investigated and as one American pilot engaged in testing a radio beacon system commented '… The terrors of darkness are still too great and in fog they are paralysing.'

In July, Handley Page Ltd left its Cricklewood premises and airfield and moved to a new site at Colney Street near Radlett, Hertfordshire. The new aerodrome was formally opened on 7th July by Prince George and there was a grand party to celebrate the Company's twenty-first anniversary. The distinguished guests were able to inspect the latest heavy bomber – HP.38 Heyford – which entered the RAF in April 1934 as the last of its biplane bombers. Handley Page's versatility to design and produce large military and fine civil aircraft was plain to see in the

HP.42, G-AAGX, Hannibal, *under inspection by the AA – July 1931.*

prototype of its new airliner – the HP.42E. Eight were ordered, four
European or Western types and four Eastern types for the India service.
By the end of October the prototype had completed its taxiing trials
and had already been named *Hannibal*; Charles Grey quipped
'probably to encourage it to cross the Alps.'! On 14th November the
Press returned to Radlett to witness its first flight. It was an elegant and
graceful airliner becoming a legend during the 1930s, although some
critics said that it epitomised Imperial Airways – 'very safe, very
reliable and very slow'! It was the first British four-engined airliner and
the first to be designed with an enclosed cabin for the crew. Emphasis
had been placed on passenger comfort, the engines had been so located
to minimise noise and vibration. The Western version carried forty-
eight passengers in two cabins, whereas the Eastern type accommodated eighteen/twenty-four with provision for extra fuel tanks and
larger baggage space. Two stewards provided refreshments but
passengers had to pay extra for this service, as indeed had the crew!
Hannibal made its first scheduled flight to Paris on 11th June 1931 and
by the end of the year all eight had been received by Imperial and other
than *Hengist*, which burnt out in 1937, all were still operating eight
years later.

During January the aviation world received some shocking news.
The Air Ministry declared that because of 'the present financial

situation' it could not authorise the expenditure of over £80,000 for the RAF to defend the Schneider Trophy in September. The Press were outraged at this decision, questions were asked in the House of Commons, the Royal Aero Club became involved in the heated debate as did senior figures in the aviation world. Just as it appeared that the matter would remain unresolved, a 'fairy godmother' emerged in the shape of Lady Fanny Houston, a 74-year-old wealthy widow; she most generously offered to guarantee the full amount of £100,000 to the Government. Her stated reason was '. . . to give England the chance of winning and retaining for ever the Schneider Trophy. I live for England and I want to see England always on top.'!

It was difficult to keep the ladies out of the headlines. On 21st February the Hon. Lady Victor Bruce (neé Mildred Petre) arrived back at Croydon in her Bluebird IV, escorted in by Winifred Spooner in another Bluebird and Amy Johnson in her Puss Moth at the conclusion of a 20,000 mile journey by air and sea virtually around the world. She had left Heston on 25th September on what she described as 'a long flight' and her subsequent 'odyssey' was considered a flight of 'epic proportions under extreme conditions . . .'. It was also excellent publicity for Blackburn Aircraft, making a welcome change from Gipsy Moths continually claiming the headlines. Nevertheless in early April Flg. Off. Charles W. A. Scott, in a Gipsy Moth, reduced 'Smithy's' record to Australia by nineteen hours. Scott had famously referred to Amy Johnson as 'a petticoat pilot.'! Most male pilots felt that airwomen were accorded far too much publicity.

'Petticoat pilots' or not, they were a fast growing band of dedicated enthusiasts; in May (16th) they competed for their own Challenge Cup donated by Lord Northesk. Many gathered at Woodley aerodrome, Reading and Grace Aitken of the Cinque Ports Club won the Cup with Pauline Gower and Amy Johnson placed second and third. Pauline Gower, a friend of Amy, was at twenty-one years the youngest woman to attain a 'B' licence; she and Dorothy Spicer would form a joy-riding and air-taxi company. Later in the summer over forty women pilots gathered at Sywell aerodrome to attend the first all-women's flying meeting, which was opened by the Duchess of Bedford. Sadly one pioneer pilot was missing, Sicele O'Brien, whom in 1927 had been the second woman to achieve a 'B' licence, was killed in June in a flying accident. The women were certainly making their mark in the world of aviation but they would always have to live down the quip 'The hand that rocks the cradle wrecked the kite'!

'Petticoat pilots' at Sywell – 16th September 1931. From left Dorothy Spicer, Pauline Gower, Mrs Victor Bruce, Molly Olney and the Duchess of Bedford.

The first 'Air Circus' made its appearance in April – Barnard Air Tours Ltd – it was owned and operated by Charles Barnard, hitherto the Duchess of Bedford's pilot. He had bought her Fokker, *The Spider*, which he used for giving 'joy-rides'. Barnard was heavily sponsored by the *Daily Mail* and during the summer his 'Air Circus' visited about 118 towns throughout the country, with a variety of aeroplanes including a couple of Avians, Spartan three-seaters and an Autogiro. Over the coming years such travelling air displays became a major summer attraction.

Perhaps the main feature of the RAF Display at Hendon on 27th June was the polished aerobatic display by three Hawker Furies of No 43 squadron. This elegant biplane was light and easy to control, it had an excellent rate of climb and was the first RAF fighter to exceed 200 m.p.h. It was quite unsurpassed for aerobatics and Furies became the star attractions in future displays. They were also used in Flying Training Schools and many famous WWII fighter pilots began their careers in this classic fighter. Few of the record crowd of 170,000 realised that they were watching displays by two airmen later to gain lasting fame; Flt. Lt. Basil Embry (later Air Chief Marshal) led a flight of inverted Gipsy Moths of the C.F.S., while Pilot Officer Douglas Bader performed 'synchronised aerobatics' with Flt. Lt. Harry Day in two Gamecocks of 23 squadron; tragically, in December (14th), Bader crashed in his Bulldog at Woodley aerodrome, the accident in which he lost both legs.

The King's Cup, held at Heston on 25th July, was won by Flg. Off. E. C. T. Edwards in a Bluebird IV at a speed of 117 m.p.h. Yet more publicity for this excellent light aircraft, which probably never sold in the numbers that its styling, performance or indeed its price – £595 – warranted. The Bluebird dated back to June 1926 and in the intervening years it had been much developed and improved. The Mark IV was the first all-metal light aircraft and when side-by-side seating was introduced sales did improve, but only fifty-eight were produced virtually all under licence by Saunders-Roe Ltd.

Three days later Amy Johnson, accompanied by C. S. Humphreys previously ground engineer at London Aero Club, left Lympne in *Jason II* for Tokyo. They arrived there on 6th August, completing 7,000 miles

Blackburn Bluebird IV – an excellent light aircraft. (via B. Lane)

215

in nine days with a total of seventy-nine flying hours. By coincidence on the day she landed at Tokyo, a certain young Scotsman James Mollison, landed at Lympne from Australia in his scarlet Gipsy Moth after a flight of eight days and twenty-one hours, reducing the record by more than two days. He had also been sponsored by Lord Wakefield and would quickly become well-known due to publicity tours, sponsored advertising and talks. When Amy Johnson returned to Croydon on 9th September, her arrival passed almost unnoticed; according to one newspaper '... the public had become rather *blasé* of all these long-distance flights, which are now rather commonplace ... and in any case Miss Johnson is now an experienced pilot and therefore about to be forgotten by the British public which loves a helpless amateur'.

There were now over forty aero clubs with over six thousand members and some three hundred and eighty private aircraft on the British Register. Heston and Brooklands were firmly established as the centres of flying for 'London Society' whilst Hanworth was favoured by the less wealthy enthusiasts. It was estimated that 2,000 persons held 'A' licences with another 300 with 'B' licences enabling them to carry passengers and fly commercially. The *Country Life* magazine in May provided some idea of the costs involved in maintaining a private aircraft. The cheapest light aircraft on the market was the Comper Swift at £550 as compared with 'the comfortable Puss Moth' at £1,000, although it was stressed that 'a decent second-hand aircraft' could be obtained for about £500. The cost of petrol was considered to be 'a minor expense at 1s 4d a gallon'. Taking into consideration hangarage, insurance, maintenance and the annual airworthiness certficate, the overall cost was estimated at £250-300 per year. This figure should be set against the prevailing economic conditions when unemployment exceeded 2.75 million and the pay of public servants, the armed forces and unemployment benefit had been reduced by 15%. It would be fair to say that the flying fraternity were a small and rather privileged minority.

As the summer progressed it seemed doubtful that the Schneider Trophy competition, planned for September 12th, would actually take place. For various reasons the Italian and French teams requested a postponement for twelve months otherwise they would be forced to withdraw. The Government made it clear that the British team was quite prepared to compete and as a consequence Italy and France withdrew their teams. Nevertheless it was announced that 'the British

Supermarine S6B won the Schneider Trophy outright – September 1931.

team will carry out its programme as arranged and endeavour to beat the world speed record set up in 1929.' The RAF team had several officers new to the competition. One of these Lt. (RN) G. L. Brinton was a late replacement and on 18th August, whilst trying out the Supermarine S.6A he crashed on take-off and was drowned. Despite the tragic accident the team continued their test flying with Mitchell's two improved seaplanes – the S.6Bs – now provided with larger floats and more powerful 2,300 h.p. Rolls-Royce R engines. Just one member of the team needed to complete the course without mishap to capture the Trophy outright. Despite the 'no contest' large crowds gathered at every vantage point overlooking Spithead. Flt. Lt. John Bootham was selected to make the first attempt in the blue and silver S.6B, S1595; he completed the course at an average speed of 340.08 m.p.h. Seventeen days later Flt. Lt. G. H. Stainforth in S1595 completed four runs at an average speed of 407.5 m.p.h. to gain the world speed record; it was the first aircraft to exceed 400 m.p.h.

Despite this splendid victory and, with the benefit of hindsight, the highlight of the year was surely the first flight, on 26th October, of the DH.82 Tiger Moth, which became one of the most famous trainers in the world. It had been developed from the Gipsy Moth at the request of the Air Ministry to improve the egress of an instructor wearing a parachute from the front cockpit; thus the Tiger Moth had staggered and swept-back wings as well as an improved forward view. The Tiger Moth was powered by a 120 h.p. Gipsy III engine, providing a top speed of 109 m.p.h and cruising comfortably at 85 m.p.h. Once the aircraft had passed its certification trials and been cleared for aerobatic flying it was adopted as the standard RAF trainer, entering the Service in February 1932. They were not completely replaced in the RAF until 1955 by which time over 8,800 had been produced.

Bert Hinkler, whom some newspapers called 'The Quiet Hero', completed an outstanding solo flight in late 1931. He arrived at Hanworth Air Park on 8th December in a Puss Moth having accomplished a flight of 10,500 miles. Hinkler had left New York on October 27th flying down to Brazil before making a twenty-two hour crossing of the South Atlantic on 25th November in atrocious weather conditions and yet landing within ten miles of his planned destination, Bathurst. This alone was considered an amazing navigational feat and in addition he had made the first light aircraft crossing of the South Atlantic. Thousands turned out to welcome him back and the Prime Minister, Ramsey MacDonald, sent a telegram 'I have followed every stage of your flight and am convinced that it will rank as one of the

DH.82 Tiger Moth: one of the most famous trainers in the world. (RAF Museum)

218

most remarkable achievements in the history of aviation.' But perhaps even more gratifying for Hinkler was the full acknowledgement of his peers in the aviation world that his latest feat of courage and endurance was technically most significant.

1932 opened on a far brighter note for Imperial Airways. On 20th January an HP.42 *Helena* left Croydon to initiate the new airmail service to Cape Town; the whole 8,000 mile journey was planned to take 10½ days and passenger bookings were accepted in April for a return fare of £234. When the service was finally established the Cairo to Cape Town section was flown by HP.42s until 1937. Imperial had experienced a difficult twelve months, passenger traffic had fallen sharply as had its profits (by 60%); it also lagged far behind other European airlines in the number of operational aircraft (thirty-two) and the weekly air mileage (38,000) flown. Perhaps the best that could be said for Imperial was its reputation for reliability and safety, but undoubtedly it was also known for the ponderous speed of its airliners!

Most aircraft companies had suffered from the economic recession, and even a company as successful as de Havilland's was not immune from the harsh financial times, recording far lower profits. But on 29th January the Company produced yet another winner, when its DH.83 Fox Moth flew for the first time. It accommodated four passengers in a comfortable cabin and was designed for joy-riding, air taxiing and executive touring. Powered originally by a 120 h.p. Gipsy III engine, it cruised at 91 m.p.h. and cost just under £1,000, which made it according to *Flight* 'a most economical method of flying', and *The Aeroplane* reckoned that it was 'the first British aircraft to support itself financially in the air ...'. Ninety-eight were ultimately produced and they were used by several new air companies establishing internal air services and one was bought by the Prince of Wales. Early in July Wally Hope flew a racing Fox Moth to victory in the King's Cup at an average speed of 124 m.p.h. It was the first time that Brooklands had hosted this event and Hope became the first airman to win this prestigious Cup for a third time.

In fact in 1932 the future of the RAF seemed anything but encouraging. There was an increasing debate and discussion on disarmament and really in such times of financial restraint there were precious little resources available for new aircraft let alone even any modest expansion. It comprised sixty-five squadrons and was still ten short of the fifty-two Home Defence squadrons promised back in 1924 and it had fallen to fifth place in the world rankings of air power; with

DH.83 Fox Moth, G-ABUT, winner of the 1932 King's Cup Race. (via B. Lane)

a cut of 10% in defence expenditure the situation was unlikely to improve. In July, Stanley Baldwin, Lord President of the Council, made his famous remark 'I think it is well for the man in the street to realize that no power on earth can prevent him from being bombed. *The bomber will always get through* [my italics.]. I just mention that so that people may realize what is waiting for them when the next war comes ...' A precept readily subscribed to within the Service but nevertheless a chilling prediction!

Sir Alan Cobham's boundless enthusiasm for aviation had led him to set up a touring airshow formally registered as 'National Aviation Day [later Display] Ltd' but more popularly called 'Cobham's Flying Circus'. Like Charles Barnard, it was his intention to bring the thrills of flying to hundreds of cities and towns throughout the land in an attempt to make the public more 'air minded'. He gathered a small fleet of aircraft and a number of aerobatic pilots, wing-walkers and parachutists to provide the paying customers with an expert and exciting display of aviation. The pride of his fleet were the two Airspeed Ferries – ten-seater small airliners, which had been built by a new company – Airspeed Ltd of York; the company had been formed in March 1931 by two members of the redundant R100 design team, Neville S. Norway and Alfred H. Tiltman. They operated alongside Tiger and Fox Moths, an Avro 504N, Desoutter II, C.19 Autogiro and a

Sir Alan Cobham's 'Flying Circus' comes to town! (via Colin Cruddas)

Handley Page W.10 ; all were based at Ford aerodrome in Sussex. The tour commenced at Hanworth Air Park on 12th April but sadly heavy rain kept most of the public away. The following day Luton was the venue and the show was on the road. When the long tour ended at Chingford, Essex on 16th October, 168 places had been visited throughout the country and over 200,000 passengers carried. It had been a most successful venture, long remembered by those spectators, many of whom gladly accepted the opportunity to take to the air for the first time.

For the previous thirteen years *The Aeroplane* and *Flight* had become the authorative voices on aviation matters. From April they faced competition from a new magazine *Popular Flying*, founded by John Hamilton and edited by Captain William Earl Johns. Johns had served as a pilot in the RFC, was shot down and taken prisoner, making three escape attempts. Johns served in the RAF from 1920 to 1927 and then turned his hand to aviation painting. For the next seven years *Popular*

Flying, as its name suggests, reflected the changing aviation scene as flying became more readily accessible to the general public. It was Captain Johns' *Biggles* stories that brought him lasting fame and greatly encouraged the spirit of flying in young people as many WWII airmen freely attested. The first James Biggleworth stories appeared in *Popular Flying* between April and October 1932 and were then published in book form, *The Camels are Coming,* later in the year – the first of ninety-six books. In 1983 the RAF Museum staged a centenary exhibition entitled 'The Man Who Was Biggles'.

Jim Mollison arrived back by sea from South Africa on 18th April after making the fastest solo flight to Cape Town in March; he had completed the journey in four days and seventeen hours, and such was his fame that the BBC asked him to broadcast to the nation. On the following day Charles Scott left in his Gipsy Moth for Australia, he too beat the existing record by over five hours averaging 1,000 miles a day. But it was the arrival of 'Lady Lindy' that really captured the public's imagination when she landed at Londonderry, Northern Ireland in her red Lockheed Vega monoplane on 21st May after flying solo from Newfoundland in 13¼ hours. Amelia (now Mrs Putnam) was the first woman to fly solo across the Atlantic and she received a tremendous welcome in England, the public were entranced by this slim young woman that had flown such a powerful aircraft across the Atlantic.

During the summer hardly a day passed without the steady drone of aircraft passing overhead, there were over four hundred registered private aircraft, a 125% increase in four years; their owners were now using them like their motor-cars, to attend air events and races, to visit friends or just for the sheer joy of flying. Cobham's 'Flying Circus' was slowly wending its way around the country and at each venue it attracted large crowds. Several other smaller companies had also got in on the act, notably the Crimson Air Fleet operating from Shoreham. Edward Hillman, owner of a large fleet of coaches in Essex, had turned his attention to aviation and Hillman Airways Ltd was operating a regular air service from Maylands (Romford) to Clacton and Ramsgate. Most seaside resorts offered holiday makers the opportunity of joy-riding and despite the severe recession it became a popular pastime, the public was fast becoming 'air minded'. Although one newspaper correspondent wrote about '... those favoured few in their expensive flying machines peering down like gods upon those less fortunate beings patiently queueing for their 'dole' money ...'!

Many of 'those favoured few' and their guests attended the Royal

The RAF Display at Hendon – 27th June 1932 – with its New Types Park. (via Colin Cruddas)

Aero Society's Aerial Garden Party at Hanworth on 19th June. The cost of admission was five shillings which included tea and a ten-minute flight and throughout the afternoon there were long queues of people eager to avail themselves of a free flight! In a completely new departure the Society of British Aircraft Constructors (SBAC), which had been formed in April 1916, held its first Air Show at Hendon on the Monday following the RAF Display (27th June) – the precursor of the now internationally renowned Farnborough Show. The Air Ministry had left many of the military aircraft in the New Types Park but another nineteen aircraft had been added. Attendance was by invitation only, the general public were not allowed in and cameras were prohibited. Thirteen companies were represented and each was allowed an eight-minute trial flight to demonstrate the performances of their aircraft. Perhaps the two most interesting exhibits were Armstrong Whitworth's AW.15 airliner, *Atalanta*, and Fairey's Night Bomber, later appropriately called the *Hendon*.

The *Atalanta* was a sleek four-engined high-wing monoplane, its design owing much to the fashionable 'art deco' of the time. John

223

AW.15 Atalanta – first flew on 6th June 1932.

Lloyd, Armstrong Whitworth's designer, had been asked by Imperial Airways to produce a nine passenger/mail airliner. It had first flown on 6th June and entered Imperial in September, making its first scheduled service to Brussels and Cologne on 26th September. Eight were produced, later operating on the South African service. Three were lost in accidents but four were still with the RAF in 1941. The Fairey Night Bomber was an advanced design, the first all-metal low-wing monoplane to enter the RAF in November 1936 with No 38 squadron at Mildenhall. Its large wing (over 101 feet span) and its streamlined undercarriage gave it an unique appearance, although only fourteen were ultimately built they remained in the Service until January 1939.

The major news story of the summer was the marriage of Amy Johnson and Jim Mollison on 29th July. They had met briefly in Australia back in 1930 and earlier in the year Amy had been present at the welcoming party when Jim Mollison completed his solo flight to South Africa, although they returned to Britain in different liners. The wedding of the country's most celebrated flyers took place in the fashionable St George's Church in Hanover Square with the reception held at the Grosvenor House Hotel, and large crowds gathered outside to celebrate what was described as the 'aerial wedding of the year'. Within weeks Jim was back flying, on 18th August he left Portmarnock Sound, Dublin in his Puss Moth, *The Heart's Content*, bound for

DH.84 Dragon of Jersey Airways Ltd. (via B. Lane)

America. The successful flight was completed in 31 hours and 20 minutes, making him the first British pilot to fly across the North Atlantic from east to west.

For the rest of the year 'the Mollisons' were in great demand, their celebrity and popularity could hardly have been higher. To maintain their expensive life-style they needed to continue flying. On 18th November Amy left Lympne in *her* silver-grey Puss Moth, *The Desert Cloud*, bound for Cape Town; according to her this flight was '... for fresh experience in navigation ... not to beat Jim's record.' Actually she did beat his record by ten hours and when she returned to Croydon a month later, it was to a tumultuous welcome. She had become the first woman to fly solo across the trans-Sahara route in both directions. A reception was held in her honour at the Park Lane Hotel hosted by the Royal Aero Club, Royal Aero Society and the SBAC – a unique occasion for a woman pilot. In just two years not only had she become the most celebrated pilot in the land but had become an icon for women, proving that a woman could compete and even excel in what was still considered a man's world.

Shortly after her return Amy was at Maylands aerodrome, Romford to name formally Hillman Airways' latest small airliner *Gidea Park*. She would briefly fly as a pilot with Hillmans during August/September 1934. Edward Hillman, buoyed by the success of his Fox Moths, had suggested to de Havilland's that they design a twin-engined version capable of carrying six passengers. The result was the DH.84 Dragon and Hillman was so impressed with the original drawings that he ordered four (later increased to six) before the prototype had been built. As Geoffrey de Havilland later wrote '... the success of the Dragon design was largely due to Hillman's far-sighted and courageous action in ordering a small fleet of them "off the drawing board".' The Dragon first flew at Stag Lane on 24th November and was delivered to Hillman's a week or so later. This well-proportioned little airliner, which could be adapted to take eight passengers, was used extensively on British internal routes. Over one hundred were built in this country besides another eighty or so by de Havilland's Company in Australia. Thus it may be said that a trying year for British aviation had at least ended on a high note, a positive augury for the future and maybe a prelude to even greater achievements.

10
THE GOLDEN AGE
OF FLYING
(1933–1935)

As the economic situation gradually improved aviation entered a period often described as 'the golden days'. Each summer many thousands of people thronged air displays, meetings and pageants held throughout the length and breadth of the country. Private and club flying thrived as never before and flying instruction became far more readily available. Many new and exciting aircraft were unveiled and there were greater opportunities for air travel around the country. The RAF began its slow expansion and Empire Air Days were introduced, allowing the public to view the Service in a relaxed and 'At Home' atmosphere. The only cloud to darken such peaceful skies was the resurgence of a strong German Air Force.

On 7th January 1933 Bert Hinkler left the Great West Aerodrome in his Puss Moth, *Karohi*, bound once again for Australia and nothing more was heard of him. It was not until 28th April that the wreckage of his aircraft was found in mountains near Florence, his log showed that he had encountered severe weather, only 750 miles completed in eleven hours. The aviation world mourned his loss. Hinkler had been somewhat of an enigma in an age of dashing and colourful aviation heroes; dressed in a business suit and tie he crossed continents and oceans with the minimum of fuss but without doubt ' "the quiet hero" had achieved a place in aviation history on merit and courage ...'

Two long-distance flights left the shores on 6th February. A Fairey monoplane, K1991, piloted by Sqn. Ldr. O. R. Gaylord with Flt. Lt. G. E. Nicholetts as navigator, took-off from Cranwell and 57½ hours later landed at Walvis Bay, South Africa having completed 5,310 miles – a new world record. To explain this apparent predilection for long-distance flights, the Air Ministry commented, 'Our Empire is large but

This greetings card captures the 'Golden Age of Flying' – Gipsy Moth & Dragon Rapide alongside a vintage Rolls-Royce and Austin Seven.

the Air Force is small and therefore must compensate with greater mobility.' Meanwhile Jim Mollison departed from Lympne in *The Heart's Content* for Port Natal, Brazil, where he arrived three days later, thus accomplishing the first solo flight to South America, as well as becoming the first pilot to fly across the North and South Atlantic. Another milestone was passed in April when two Westland biplanes, PV.3 and PV.6, became the first to fly over Mount Everest. The object of these flights was to demonstrate the feasibility of mapping mountainous terrain by air; the project had been largely financed by none other than Lady Houston. The PV.6 was better known as the Wallace, which entered the Service in 1933 and survived for another ten years.

A feature of private flying during the thirties was the assistance offered by the Automobile Association, although this is perhaps not too surprising as since the pioneer days aeroplanes and motor-cars had been closely linked. Ernest Cooke, the Association's Secretary since 1905, was instrumental in developing its close connection with flying and its Air Department was managed by the enthusiastic Ivor McClure. The A.A. provided British and European touring maps as navigational aids and since 1931 had offered a weather information service at Heston. A.A. men attended air meetings and airfields and in 1933 the Association produced its *Register of Approved Landing Grounds* listing seventy-four landing grounds with information on surfaces, obstructions, hangarage, nearest telephone, railway station and hotel (all A.A. registered of course!). The grounds, frequently farm land, were inspected monthly and several were subsequently developed during WWII. Additionally there were now seventy-five local authority and private airfields besides Croydon.

Miles and Percival were names that became virtually synonymous with light aircraft during these pre-war years; they designed and produced a number of successful aeroplanes, which almost dominated the private, club and racing scene in these halcyon days. Frederick G. Miles designed his first aeroplane Southern Martlet in August 1929 but the first to bear his name was M.1 Satyr, a single-seat biplane bought by Mrs Victor Bruce in 1933. He became a director of Phillips & Powis Aircraft Ltd which was formed to produce his designs; the parent company (a wood-working firm) had established Woodley (Reading) aerodrome a few years earlier. It was from Woodley that the successful Hawk series of aircraft were first flown. The first M.2 Hawk appeared on 29th March, an open-cockpit two-seater monoplane which cruised at 100 m.p.h. and cost £395. It was an obvious winner from the outset and over sixty were produced. Miles, along with his wife Maxine (usually known as 'Blossom') and younger brother, George, were leading figures in the aviation world.

Captain Edgar Percival was yet another Australian airman to make a valuable contribution to British aviation in the inter-War years. He had served in the R.F.C. and returned to England in 1928; five years later he formed Percival Aircraft Company. However, his first Gull D.1 was built by BAC (British Aircraft Co.) at Maidstone. It was a cantilever (low-wing) three-seat cabin monoplane with a cruising speed of 125 m.p.h., and set new standards of speed and comfort for others to emulate. Production of Gulls began in early 1933 at George Parnall's works at Yate, Gloucestershire until Percival established his own factory at Gravesend in 1934. Although a trifle expensive at £1,275 (including compass!) it was advertised as 'the last word in flying luxury for it combines speed and beauty of line with comfort and safe flying qualities.'. Percival usually flew his aircraft in a lounge suit and wearing a trilby hat, which became his 'trademark'; he was really proving that to fly his aircraft there was no need for special flying gear.

Percival Mew Gull, G-ACND, prototype flown by Captain Edgar Percival in a lounge suit and trilby hat.

His various Gulls were always leading contenders in air races as well as being used on several celebrated long-distance flights, and as such were rarely out of the news.

In May, de Havilland's produced their 'luxury' three-seater, DH.85 Leopard Moth, as a successor to the Puss Moth. It had a similar performance to the Gull and competed at the same price. Geoffrey de Havilland had the satisfaction of winning the 1933 King's Cup for the first time in his own Leopard Moth; a popular victory, which showed that despite his fifty years he was still one of the best pilots in the country. The success provided spectacular publicity for the new aircraft and in three years over one hundred and thirty were sold.

Cobham's 'Flying Circus' trundled off on 14th April starting another long round of displays – almost three hundred; this year two separate tours operated simultaneously. Sir Alan now employed twenty-two pilots and over one hundred ground staff, it had mushroomed into quite a business. Also in April the British Hospitals' Air Pageant began touring the country, successfully appearing at over one hundred and eighty venues. The Pageant was organised by Jimmy King and Harry Barker with the object of raising £100,000 for hospitals in five years. Each hospital on the itinerary received 10% of the day's takings and a third of the programme sales. King had assembled three parachutists and fifteen pilots including Charles W. Scott, Mrs Victor Bruce, Pauline

Avro 504N, G-EBVY, of the British Hospitals' Air Pageant. (via G. Harris)

Gower and Captain Percival Phillips of Cornwall Aviation, who had been engaged in joy-riding and sky advertising since the early 1920s. Thus for six months of the year the public had ample opportunities to attend one of these displays and countless thousands did just that, fondly remembering the experience many years later when such displays had become a thing of the past.

Brooklands hosted the second GAPAN air display on 20th May. The Guild of Air Pilots & Navigators had been formed in 1929 with Sir Sefton Brancker as its first Master and had developed into a rather 'exclusive and elitist club', nevertheless both Amy Johnson and the Duchess of Bedford had been elected as honorary members. Indeed the Duchess flew in from Woburn Abbey in her Moth to formally open the

231

*Brooklands had become one of **the** flying clubs.*

display; she had obtained her 'A' licence at the age of sixty-seven! H.R.H. the Prince of Wales arrived in his new Vickers Viastra, piloted by Flt. Lt. Fielden. He was '... suitably attired in a light-grey suit and wearing a straw boater ... the spectators at Brooklands were dressed very much like an Ascot crowd, obviously showing that flying was "the done thing" ...'

Heston was another 'place to be seen' certainly when the Household Brigade Club held one of its flying displays. It had been designated the diversion airfield for Croydon and in April Spartan Airways started a summer service to Cowes (where else!) for £2 return. Hillman Airways was prospering, its cheap fares introduced the joys of air travel to a wider clientèle. It would soon move to a new 'Essex Airport' at Stapleford Tawney such was its increased traffic. Hillman's was just one of the growing number of airlines operating around the country. The four major railway companies, G.W.R., L.M.S., L.N.E.R. and Scottish, were given permission to operate air services. Imperial Airways were relieved to announce a profitable year of operation,

some two million miles had been flown. 'Be up to date and aviate' was the slogan of the day. Unfortunately Imperial suffered two fatal accidents during the year. In March *City of Liverpool* crashed in flames at Dixmunde, Belgium killing the three-man crew and twelve passengers. Then on 30th December an Avro Ten, *Apollo*, on the Cologne service, crashed in fog near Brussels killing Captain J. M. Gittens and nine Belgian passengers.

The RAF had a new Chief of Air Staff, Sir Edward Ellington; he had first flown in 1912, then served as a Staff Officer in WWI and later held command posts in India and the Middle East. It was considered that '... with his all-round modern experience none could be more fitted for the highly responsible post he held.' Ellington was in charge of the RAF during the early stages of its unprecedented expansion and when he retired in September 1937 it was a transformed Service. Perhaps a more crucial appointment was that of Air Vice-Marshal Hugh Dowding as Air Minister for Supply and Research. Under his direction the Spitfire, Hurricane, Blenheim and Wellington were ordered and he strongly

Avro Tutors of the Central Flying School. (via J. Adams)

supported the development of Radio Direction Finding (later known as Radar), a critical factor during the Battle of Britain.

The RAF Display was held on 24th June and despite pouring rain it was still well-attended; one of the most impressive displays was a demonstration on inverted formation flying by six Avro Tutors of the C.F.S.; the pilots, all instructors at the School, spent weeks of practice to refine such skills. *Flight* considered it 'a most polished and technically brilliant exhibition of inverted flying'. The Tutor, which had first flown in November 1932, followed in the long tradition of RAF Avro trainers and replaced 504Ns as the standard elementary trainers. Pilots found them 'a delight to fly', and they were ideal for aerobatics, some flew with Cobham's 'Flying Circus' as well as being used by many 'joy-riding' operators.

Jim and Amy Mollison captured the headlines in July, although in truth they were rarely out of the news. They planned to undertake a three-stage flight from Britain to New York then to Baghdad and finally back to Croydon – some 12,000 miles. On the 22nd the couple left Pendine Sands, Wales in their black Dragon, *Seafarer*, but when within fifty-five miles of New York and low on fuel they attempted to land at Bridgeport, Connecticut they crashed and wrecked the aircraft. Nevertheless they were still the first to fly directly from Britain to the U.S.A. When they finally arrived at New York on 1st August over 200,000 people turned out to greet them with a 'ticker-tape' welcome redolent of Lindbergh's back in 1927. Whilst Jim returned to London to arrange for a replacement aircraft, Amy was 'lionised' in the States, she even flew as co-pilot with T.W.A. (Transcontinental & Western Airways). Early in October they attempted the second stage to Baghdad from Canada in their new *Seafarer II* but after sustaining damage to the undercarriage, and with the weather deteriorating, they called off the flight.

On 13th May the gliding world suffered the loss of one of its pioneer pilots and most dedicated supporters, Charles Lowe-Wylde. He was killed on 13th May at Maidstone, not whilst gliding but at the controls of his BAC VII two-seat glider that he had converted for powered flight by installing a Douglas motor-cycle engine. Following his death his company, British Aircraft Company, was acquired by Colonel W. F. Forbes-Sempill and moved to Hanworth, where under the management of Robert Kronfeld, the celebrated Austrian glider pilot, it produced over thirty low-powered BAC VII Drones. They were simple to fly, cost only £275, and although slow and noisy, they were, in fact, the first *serious* attempt to provide a safe and cheap introduction to flying.

In January *Popular Flying* posed the question – 'Where Stands Germany?'. It reported '... Germany is a nation of flyers. Flying has become a national sport. Aviation meetings are attended by vast crowds. Even a gliding meeting is attended by everyone, young and old ...'. Winston Churchill had for some time been cautioning the Government that Germany, in violation of the Treaty of Versailles, was creating an Air Force under the guise of flying clubs, police units and commercial ventures. Later, during a radio broadcast he claimed that Britain was less well defended than for hundreds of years and the least the country needed was an Air Force equal to that of its potential enemies. In March Stanley Baldwin, the Prime Minister felt constrained to reassure the country that 'should disarmament fail, the RAF would be brought up to the strength of any Force within striking distance'. Less than two months later Germany walked out of the International Disarmarment Conference, it was in total disarray and adjourned indefinitely; now 'rearmament' became the watchword and the expansion of the RAF was set to begin in earnest. In July it was announced that Home squadrons would be increased to seventy-five bringing the total strength to one hundred and twenty-eight. Known as Expansion Scheme 'A', it was the first of eight such Schemes over the next four years, which were abandoned and amended with bewildering regularity! Nevertheless Churchill still maintained that within three years the German Air Force would be twice the size of Britain's. He was almost 'a lone voice crying in the wilderness', but soon his warnings were proved to be correct.

1934 was an auspicious year for de Havilland's. It had sold its Stag Lane aerodrome and was in the process of moving 'lock, stock and barrel' to Hatfield, where the airfield was being greatly extended. The year saw the production of four successful aircraft. The first appeared on 14th January – DH.86; the smallest four-engined airliner yet produced and frequently referred to as the 'Express'. It had been designed and built in just four months to an Australian requirement to operate between Australia and Singapore on the proposed Empire Air Route. It carried ten passengers in relative comfort with mail in a rear compartment and cruised at 145 m.p.h. Sixty-two were built, operating successfully with Imperial, Qantas Empire, Jersey and Hillman Airways, and Railway Air Services. But the Company's most successful pre-war aircraft was the classic DH.89 Dragon Rapide, which first flew from Hatfield on 17th April. Designed as a faster and more comfortable Dragon, originally called the Dragon Six because of its twin Gipsy Six engines, they became known everywhere simply as Rapides. This classic aircraft was the mainstay of British commercial aviation well into the 1950s; 728 were produced operating first with Hillmans Airways as well as over a dozen other British airlines besides serving air-charter and air-taxi companies world-wide. The Prince of Wales owned a Rapide, as did the Air Council. Over 500 were built for the RAF operating as VIP transports and trainers and known as Dominies. The Rapide was an exceptional aircraft accommodating six/eight passengers with a range of 578 miles and a cruising speed of 132 m.p.h.; it rightly deserved to be called 'The Queen of the Airways'. In 1979 Sir Geoffrey de Havilland proudly claimed '... there are today hundreds of Rapides still flying all over the world. It shares with the D.C.3, the distinction of being the most reliable, useful and easily maintained aeroplane ever made ...'

In May the DH.87 Hornet Moth made its maiden flight. A cabin biplane because the Company considered that 'open cockpits were becoming a thing of the past ...'; it was also equipped, for the first time, with side-by-side seating and dual controls. This delightful little aircraft originally cost £875 and was advertised as 'Everyman's Aeroplane'. When production ceased in 1938 over 160 had been built and they withstood the test of time, a Hornet Moth won the 1968 King's Cup thirty-four years after its first appearance!

Hillman Airways' DH.86 being named Drake *by Lady Cunliffe-Lister at Stapleford Tawney, Essex – 20th June 1935.* (via D. Brown)

Back in March the wealthy Australian philanthropist, Sir MacPherson Robertson, offered a Gold Cup and £15,000 in prize money for an International Air Race from England to Australia to commemorate the centenary of the State of Victoria. Geoffrey de Havilland was concerned that '. . . an American aircraft might be the easy winner unless something out of the ordinary was designed . . .' He therefore took a large financial risk on producing a fast racing monoplane specifically for the 'MacRobertson Race', as it became known. Under the greatest secrecy the legendary DH.88 Comet was designed and produced; indeed the prototype did not make its first flight until 8th September, about six weeks before the start of the race. The all-wood finely engineered and streamlined cantilever monoplane with retractable undercarriage was powered by twin Gipsy Six 'R' engines, giving a maximum speed of 237 m.p.h and a range of 2,200 miles. The price was nominally set at £5,000, which was heavily subsidised by the Company, and three were ordered; by the Mollisons, A. O. Edwards, the Chairman of Grosvenor House Hotel and Bernard Rubin, a millionaire motor racing-driver.

Although 1934 could be considered the year of the Comet, Captain

Percival stole some of de Havilland's thunder when, in March, he flew his new racing machine – E.1 Mew Gull. The small cabin low-wing monoplane became one of the fastest on the racing scene. Percival entered it in the King's Cup held at Hatfield on 18/19th July and although he averaged 191 m.p.h., the highest speed in any King's Cup to date, he was placed fifth on handicap. Only six Mew Gulls were produced, the last – E.3H – in 1937, had a top speed of 235 m.p.h just fractionally slower than the much vaunted Comet.

Another aircraft company was also making its mark – Airspeed; it had been rescued from financial difficulties by the shipbuilders Swan Hunter and a new public company was formed – Airspeed (1934) Ltd. It moved from York to the recently opened Portsmouth Airport in March 1932 and had produced a most advanced aircraft at the behest of Sir Alan Cobham – AS.5 Courier. Cobham was proposing to make a non-stop refuelling flight to India and required a suitably adapted machine. The Courier had first flown in April 1933, an all-wood cabin single-engined monoplane capable of accommodating five passengers. It was the first aircraft produced in any quantity with a retractable undercarriage. Sixteen were ultimately built, operating with several small airlines and ten were requisitioned by the Air Ministry during WWII.

Sir Alan's Courier, the prototype G-ABXN, had refuelling equipment fitted in the rear of the cabin. On 22nd September he and Sqn. Ldr. Bill Helmore left from Portsmouth bound for Karachi on what was expected to be almost a two-day flight. The Courier was successfully refuelled twice by the National Air Display's Handley Page W.10, *Youth of New Zealand*; but over the Mediterranean the Courier suffered an engine problem and Sir Alan had to make a forced-landing at Malta, where news reached him that the W.10 had crashed on its return flight to England killing all four crewmen. Sir Alan was determined to continue his pioneering work on aerial refuelling and in October he formed Flight Refuelling Ltd.

Perhaps Airspeed's most successful civil aircraft appeared for the first time on 26th June – the AS.6 Envoy. It was essentially a twin-engined development of the Courier but larger and designed to carry six/eight passengers. Almost fifty Envoys were produced in three Marks and with a bewildering number of different engines. They operated with several small British airlines as well as with a number of foreign airlines. The Envoy led directly to the famous RAF advanced trainer – the Oxford.

AS.5 Courier first flew in April 1933. (via Colin Cruddas)

Largely because of THE Race, Australia was the focus of attention in the aviation world during the year, and it seemed appropriate that a young woman would come forward to try to improve on Amy Johnson's 1930 solo record. Jean Batten, a New Zealander, had accompanied her mother on a visit to Britain in 1929, and she decided to stay and learn to fly. She gained her licence in September 1930 and was determined to make a solo flight to Australia. On 8th May, 1934 'Try-Again Jean', as the newspapers had dubbed her because her two earlier attempts had failed, left Lympne in a Gipsy Moth sponsored by the generous Lord Wakefield. This time she was successful and arrived at Darwin on the 23rd having taken 14 days and 23 hours, beating Amy's record by more than four days. Much more would be heard of this plucky young lady.

On Saturday 24th May the first Empire Air Day was celebrated when thirty-nine RAF/FAA stations opened to the public, along with many civil and private aerodromes. It was the inspiration of Air Commodore J. A. Chamier, the Secretary-General of the Air League of the British Empire since 1932. Chamier was determined to make the country, and especially young people, more 'air-minded'. The concept was a resounding success, over 77,000 visited the Service airfields and of the other aerodromes, Croydon attracted the largest crowd – 8,000. The King and Queen on holiday at Sandringham visited RAF Bircham Newton in Norfolk to set the Royal seal of approval on this new event. Over the next five years these Air Days became increasingly popular with attendance figures rising markedly as new RAF stations opened, giving the majority of the public their only opportunity to view the Service's many new aircraft.

The summer provided the usual rash of air meetings, displays and races, although *Flight* remarked '... "Garden Parties" rather than spectacular flying meetings were becoming more prevalent and this trend should be applauded ...'! Nevertheless from April to October Cobham's 'National Aviation Display' was again touring the country from northern Scotland to south-west England, these highly professional displays attracted even larger crowds. Private flying was on the increase; over 3,000 licensed pilots and of some 470 privately registered aeroplanes, 10% were owned by women. Aeroplanes could be bought at the larger department stores, in 1932 Selfridges had established an Aviation Department. There were some sixty Aero clubs with well over 5,000 members, and the largest membership was the London Transport Flying Club based at Broxbourne, Herts, where the Company subsidised the club subscription to a mere 6d a week for over a thousand of its employees! Gliding was flourishing as were Aero Modelling clubs, largely fostered by the Air League, and permission had been given to provide flying training for schoolboys aged over seventeen.

'Joy-riding' companies continued to operate at many seaside resorts; 5s for a ten-minute flight was the 'going rate'. Air services to most areas of the country, especially the popular holiday destinations, were readily available providing one had the inclination and the necessary cash! For the more venturesome a return to Paris could be obtained for just over a 'fiver', far cheaper than Imperial Airways and also about thirty minutes faster! Imperial was equally busy during the year, its fleet had flown more than $7\frac{1}{2}$ million miles but no European airline could compete with *Lufthansa*, which announced in September that it had carried its one millionth paying passenger, the 'lucky' person was presented with a portrait of the German Chancellor – Adolf Hitler! Imperial had taken delivery of two Short L.17 landplanes – *Scylla* and *Syrinx* – which proved to be heavy and difficult to handle and were not liked by the pilots. The accommodation for the thirty-eight passengers was spacious and quite luxurious although many passengers claimed that the airliner 'wallowed around like a small boat in a rough sea.' Furthermore they cruised at less than 100 m.p.h., further fuelling Imperial's reputation for 'slowness but reliability'. The airline also received its first DH.86 *Delphinus*, another eleven were delivered during 1935/6.

The fifteenth RAF Display took place on 30th June in glorious sunshine and attracted a crowd of 130,000. Sadly the occasion was marred by the first fatal accident at such displays. Sqn. Ldr. Collett, the Commander of No 600 (City of London) squadron and son of the Lord Mayor of London, was killed when he failed to escape by parachute; the engine of his Hawker Hart failed during a fly-past and crashed, bursting into flames. The Display continued but as one newspaper reported, '... the tragedy cast a heavy shadow over the subsequent events, which was a great pity for all the airmen taking part ... they must be complimented on the brave manner by which they demonstrated their flying expertise in such difficult circumstances.'

Excitement mounted as the day of the MacRobertson Race neared – 20th October; it was already being called 'the world's greatest air race'. The departure airfield was RAF Mildenhall, Suffolk, which had formally opened just four days earlier and as yet no bomber squadron was in residence. The rules did not limit aircraft to size and power, night-flying was permitted and there were five compulsory control points – Baghdad, Calcutta, Singapore, Darwin and Charleville. Within the overall competition there were speed and handicap prizes and all competitors had to complete the flight, 11,330 miles, within sixteen days. Of the original sixty-four entrants only twenty were starters and perhaps surprisingly there was not a single German competitor. The Prince of Wales flew in during the previous afternoon and later the King and Queen motored over from Sandringham to meet the competitors and view the aircraft. The three Comets resplendent in their 'racing colours' were the star attraction – the Mollisons' black/gold *Black Magic*, the scarlet/white *Grosvenor House* piloted by Charles W. Scott and Tom Campbell Black and the British racing-green Comet flown by Owen Cathcart-Jones and Ken Waller. Most were British aircraft – Puss Moth, Fairey Fox, Dragon Rapide, Airspeed Courier, Miles Hawk Major and M.3 Falcon; the latter was the Company's first cabin aircraft and had only flown just eight days earlier. These aircraft were all dwarfed by the two sleek commercial airliners, a Boeing 247D of United Air Line flown by the Americans, Roscoe Tanner and Clyde Pangborn, and a Douglas DC.2 of the Dutch K.L.M. piloted by K.D.

Parmienter and J.J. Moll, which also carried three passengers and a quantity of mail. Flt. Lt. Donald Bennett, later of Imperial Airways and RAF 'Pathfinder' fame, competed in a Lockheed Vega. Amy Mollison was not the only woman taking part; Jacqueline Cochran, a celebrated American racing pilot was flying a Granville R.1 monoplane, *QED*; twenty-nine years later she became 'the fastest woman in the world' flying a jet-fighter at over 1,200 m.p.h.!

The first competitor was due to leave at 6.30 a.m., the others followed at half-minute intervals. Despite the early start '... the roads for miles around Mildenhall were choked with motorists, cyclists and walkers ...' and it was estimated that over 70,000 had gathered to watch the start. Seventy hours and fifty-four minutes later Scott and Campbell Black in *Grosvenor House* landed at Essenden airfield, Melbourne to win the Gold Cup (valued at £500) along with the first prize of £10,000. Twenty-two hours later the D.C.2 arrived to claim second prize despite the two Dutch pilots getting a little lost over Australia. Close behind was the Boeing 234D followed by the Comet of Cathcart-Jones and Waller; the Mollisons had been forced to retire in India. Only another five managed to arrive within the allotted time, the Courier was placed third in the handicap section and perhaps the most

Charles W.A. Scott and Tom Campbell Black won the MacRobertson Race in DH.88 Comet, Grosvenor House.

valiant performance was James Melrose in his Puss Moth which gained him £1,000 as second on handicap.

Scott and Campbell Black returned by boat, as did the victorious *Grosvenor House,* but Cathcart-Jones and Waller flew their Comet back in style, arriving on 3rd November, having flown 23,000 miles in less than a fortnight. Scott and Campbell Black were feted on their return and awarded British Silver Medals for Aeronautics by the Royal Aero Club. It was, of course, a spectacular victory for British aviation and for de Havilland's in particular, but the Race had given a clear message to Imperial Airways and the British aircraft industry. Two virtually standard commercial airliners of American design had put up remarkable performances not greatly inferior to the Comet, which had been specifically designed for the Race. With cruising speeds of about 190 m.p.h. they changed the concept of international air travel.

On 8th December, Imperial Airways despatched their first regular weekly airmail service to Australia via Karachi and Singapore and the mail arrived in Brisbane on the 23rd. This was three days after the Government announced details of their 'Empire Air Mail Scheme' under which all first-class mail between parts of the British Empire currently being served by Imperial would automatically be carried by air rather than by sea. However, the Scheme was not scheduled to be introduced until 1937.

On the last day of the year Edward Hillman died of a heart attack. Only weeks earlier his airline had been awarded the contract for a daily postal air service between London, Liverpool, Belfast and Glasgow, he also had plans to extend his existing European services and his Company had 'gone public'. The death of this self-made man and colourful personality was a sad loss to commercial aviation, he had contributed in no small measure to make air travel more accessible and popular.

As the euphoria created by the 'Great Race' slowly receded, it was military aviation that frequently took centre stage during 1935. The renascent German Air Force was formally acknowledged, which directly led to yet another RAF Expansion Scheme, and in his Jubilee year King George V reviewed the Royal Air Force at Mildenhall. Two vital elements in the grim air-defence of the country during 1940 originated during the year. The investigation and development of RDF was approved and the Hawker Hurrricane made its maiden flight.

On 1st March the *Reichsluftwaffe,* soon shortened to *Luftwaffe,* was 'officially' formed and the date was thereafter celebrated as 'German

Air Force Day'. Eight days later Adolf Hitler acknowledged to the world the presence of the *Luftwaffe*, which already comprised some 1,800 aircraft, to which 200 were being added each month, and 20,000 officers and men. Within a year it would be almost equal in size to the combined strength of the British and French air forces. Hermann Göring, an ex-WWI fighter 'ace' and commander of the famous Richtofen *Geschwader*, was appointed Commander-in-Chief, but it was the German Secretary of State for Air, Erhard Milch, who had successfully developed and managed *Lufthansa*, who was the real architect of the powerful *Luftwaffe* of WWII.

All Churchill's warnings about a German Air Force had been proved right and there was a deep concern in Parliament and in the country that the RAF was lagging far behind. Lady Houston offered £200,000 for 'the air-defence of London', which she was convinced was utterly unprotected! In May, Parliament voted for Expansion Scheme 'C', which proposed a Home Defence of 123 squadrons by March 1937. This would require an additional 22,500 personnel, including 2,500 trained pilots to add to the existing 2,700, thus necessitating a large increase in the flying training programme and the provision of many new Service airfields. Spending on the RAF increased from a paltry £16.8 million in 1933 to £27.6 million in 1935, and this was just the beginning of a dramatic expansion of the Service.

In 1934 a Special Committee had been formed 'to investigate the possibilities of countering air attacks by utilising the recent progress of scientific invention'. It was really to investigate what the newspapers insisted on calling 'a death ray'. H. T. Tizard was appointed Chairman and one of the members was H. E. Wimperis, the Director of Scientific Research, and he sought the views of Robert Watson-Watt, a scientist at the National Physical Laboratory. His report submitted in February 1935 identified two specific areas for research and investigation. Firstly the re-radiation of radio waves to detect aircraft and also the possibility of devising a coded signal transmitted from friendly aircraft (IFF or Identification, Friend or Foe). Within weeks a Handley Page Heyford was detected flying over Salisbury Plain by radio beams transmitted from the BBC wireless station at Daventry. With commendable foresight £10,000 was allocated for further experiments at Orfordness, known as 'the Island', on a lonely stretch of the Suffolk coast, where a 75 foot high aerial was erected. The first successful 'interception' was swift, on 24th July three Hart light-bombers were detected by radio beams. To provide greater space and facilities Bawdsey Manor in

Suffolk was purchased as a research centre for Watson-Watt and his scientists and technicians, and it was from here that radar was born.

It was quite a coincidence that two aircraft produced and first flown in 1935 for the commercial and private markets would be developed into excellent military aircraft, each in their own way playing an essential role in the early years of WWII. The Avro 652 Anson was a small six-seater airliner ordered by Imperial Airways in April 1934; the prototype, named *Avalon*, first flew on January 7th closely followed by *Avatar* (re-named *Ava*). Both were delivered to Imperial in March and saw extensive service on the Croydon to Brindisi route until July 1938. The Air Ministry had noted its possibilities to operate on coastal reconnaissance duties and had placed an order for a prototype, which appeared at Woodford, Manchester on 24th March as a 652A; virtually the same as the commercial model but with different engines and the addition of a dorsal gun turret. The first production Anson I was completed on the last day of the year and when they entered the Service with No 48 squadron at Manston in March, it was a red-letter day for the RAF, not only was it the Service's first monoplane but it was also fitted with a retractable undercarriage – a rarity in those days. The Anson became one of the best loved aircraft in the RAF known affectionately as 'the Faithful Annie'; almost eleven thousand were built up to May 1952 – seventeen years – the longest production run of any British aircraft; Ansons continued in the RAF until June 1968.

Lord Rothermere of the *Daily Mail* ordered from Bristol Aeroplane Company a fast aircraft that would accommodate a crew of two and six passengers at a cost of £14,500. Bristol's Chief Designer, Frank Barnwell (another Australian), came up with the Bristol Type 142, a twin-engined metal-skinned monoplane named *Britain First*, which was first flown at Filton by Cyril Uwins on 12th April. It made an immediate impression for its performance and easy handling, proving to be 50 m.p.h. faster than contemporary fighters; the Air Ministry asked for an extended loan to evaluate it fully as a potential light-bomber. Lord Rothermere immediately presented it to the Nation and by September the Air Ministry had ordered 150 military versions – 142Ms; the prototype appeared in 1936 and the Blenheim I was born.

At the end of March, H. L. Brook arrived back from Australia in his Miles Falcon after his participation in the MacRobertson Race. His return flight had taken 7 days and 19 hours about a day faster that Jim Mollison's official record of 1931, although little interest was now being taken in such record-breaking flights – their lustre had rather

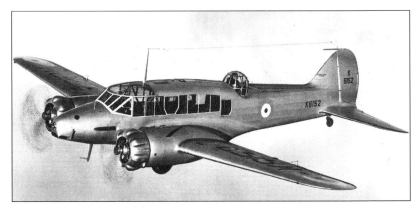

Avro Anson or 'the Faithful Annie'.

diminished. However, the return to Croydon on 29th April of Jean Batten did indeed make the headlines, after all she was the first woman to fly to Australia and back and she caused some considerable fashion interest when she emerged quite immaculate from her Gipsy Moth in her 'flying gear' – trousers, fur coat and black helmet. Although undoubtedly glamorous, Jean Batten eschewed publicity and her reserved and unassuming manner resulted in her being called the 'Garbo of the Air'. In November she flew a Gull, *Jean*, from Lympne to Port Natal, Brazil, equalling the flights of Bert Hinkler and Jim Mollison, but also becoming the first woman pilot to cross the South Atlantic. On her return she was awarded the Brittania Trophy; she had taken over the mantle from Amy Mollison as the leading airwoman of the day.

Once more Cobham's 'Flying Circus' set off in April on another grand tour of the country, it had become an integral part of the summer scene. From July it divided into two separate displays – Astra and Ferry Shows. When the tours were completed on 29th September, it was for the last time. Sir Alan had decided that the best days for these types of aerial displays had passed, he sold out to Charles W. Scott but not the rights to use his name. Sir Alan had become engaged on other aviation ventures, his Company – Cobham Air Routes Ltd – formed in May, was operating air services from London to Guernsey via Portsmouth, Southampton and Bournemouth; also, of course, he was involved with his in-flight refuelling experiments.

Hanworth had become a thriving aviation centre, although no longer

THE "BRISTOL" TYPE 142 "BRITAIN FIRST."

owned by National Air Services, which had gone into liquidation two years earlier. The flying club leased to the London Air Syndicate was known as London Air Park Club and the mansion re-opened in June as Hanworth Country Club. In the same month Flying Training Ltd established No 5 Elementary & Reserve Flying Training School for RAF reservists and nearby the Cierva Autogiro Flying School offered a complete flying course on autogiros for £35 – 'Learn to fly the Modern Way'! The General Aircraft Ltd leased the airfield, where its distinctive Monospar cabin monoplanes were produced. The name derived from the original strong but light cantilever wing designed by Swiss-born H. J. Steiger. The Company's first Monospar, ST-4, a four-seater had appeared in 1932 but the first to be built at Hanworth was the ST-10, which won the 1934 King's Cup at an average speed of 134 m.p.h. Two new models appeared in 1935, the ST-18 Croydon designed to carry ten passengers and the ST-25; the latter designed to commemorate the King's Jubilee and was later named the Jubilee. This rather angular five-seater was further developed and over twenty were produced. Also at Hanworth was British Manufacturing Co. Ltd. with their B.A. Eagle, a three-seater cabin tourer with a retractable undercarriage and the B.A. Swallow II, a two-seater open cockpit monoplane described as 'the safest aeroplane the world has ever known'! It cruised at 95 m.p.h. and was said to cost just 1d a mile to run. Originally priced at £725 its value and worth made an immediate impact with private and club

General Aircraft's ST.25 Monospar, Jubilee.

owners, and over one hundred were sold, most of which were British registered. British Aircraft also had premises at Hanworth producing their Drone VIIs.

Perhaps this hive of activity was one reason why the Royal Aeronautical Society moved the venue of their annual Garden Party to Fairey's Great West Aerodrome at Harmondsworth. It had become the foremost aviation gathering of the year attended by everybody of importance and fame in the aviation world. A wide range of aircraft were on display, from light planes to gliders, new military aircraft to civil airliners, and many gave flying displays. The aerodrome, some 190 acres, had been developed into a fine level and smooth grass airfield, with one of the hangars thought to be the largest in the world. The Garden Party was held on 8th May and over 2,000 attended, many had arrived by air with the omnipresent Moths in the majority. *The Aeroplane* (or rather Charles Grey!) was most impressed '... [it] was a success in every way, in entertainment, in atmosphere, in setting and in weather ... strawberries and cream in the shade of the marquees ... fashionable ladies in elegant dresses ... the Central Band of the RAF providing suitable music ... the steady drone of aeroplanes overhead ... the English aviation scene at its peaceful best ...'; an event that really epitomised these glorious and halcyon days of flying.

Despite unfavourable weather the second Empire Air Day on 23rd May attracted large crowds, not only at RAF and civil aerodromes but also at several aircraft factories, which had opened their gates to the public for the first time. Air Commodore Chamier was delighted with the public's response to his initiative and was especially appreciative of 'the enormous trouble taken by all Service ranks to give their visitors an interesting and entertaining afternoon ...' Almost in complete contrast the RAF Display at Hendon over a month later was thought to be '... a disappointing affair, the show was dull and there was nothing new or startling among the machines.' The fourth SBAC Show held on the following Monday, 1st July, would be the last to be mounted at Hendon. The organisers found that the task of cleaning-up the airfield after the large crowds had become far too onerous and the Society sought a new venue for 1936. Interestingly there were no Miles aeroplanes on display despite being the second largest producers of light aircraft in the country, and as yet the Company was not a member of the Society.

It was fitting that a Service originating during King George V's reign should be officially reviewed in his Jubilee Year. The King, accompanied by the Prince of Wales and the Duke of York, arrived at Mildenhall on 6th July and they toured the serried ranks of over three hundred and fifty aircraft lined up on the large airfield. It was quite clear why the RAF was jokingly called 'the Hawker Air Force' with squadrons of Hawker Hinds, Harts, Furies, Demons and Audaxes awaiting inspection. In the afternoon the King, accompanied by Queen Mary and the Duke and Duchess of York, visited Duxford, where they were treated to 'the largest fly-past in the world'. Seventeen squadrons took part including No 19, recently equipped with the newest fighter – Gloster Gauntlet – the last open-cockpit fighter. Although it was a most impressive display, nothing could disguise the fact that the RAF gave the appearance of an out-moded force – ponderous bombers, relatively slow fighters and all biplanes. Some harsh critics claimed that 'little progress had been achieved in the last fifteen years, except perhaps in the development of aero-engines.' Charles Grey earnestly hoped that '... His Majesty may live long enough to see his Royal Air Force leading the world in every way as Queen Victoria saw her Navy ruling the sea.'

King George V at RAF Mildenhall for the Jubilee review of the RAF – 6th July 1935.
(RAF Museum)

During the summer Imperial Airways was informed that it would lose the exclusive rights to operate services north of the London-Cologne-Budapest line to allow competition from other British operators. These smaller airlines were concerned about adequate finance, and amalgamation seemed to be the only long-term solution. With the agreement of their shareholders Hillman, United and Spartan Airways amalgamated to form Allied British Airways ('Allied' was quickly dropped) with the intention of commencing operations from Heston on 1st January 1936.

Amongst the plethora of air meetings, races and rallies, one was gaining in popularity – the International Air Rally held at Lympne on 25th August with echoes of the pre-war Gordon Bennett race. The Rally attracted a large entry of European aeroplanes and pilots, no less than thirteen from Germany, but the main prize, the Wakefield Cup, was won by a French Caudron Simoun racer, although the stars of the show were a small Focke-Wulf Steiglitz biplane and its pilot Herr Förster, which gave an outstanding display of aerobatic flying; it was the major *Luftwaffe* training aircraft.

By contrast the all-British King's Cup race was again held at Hatfield during 6/7th September, over a gruelling 1,300 mile course taking in Scotland and Northern Ireland. This year it was notable for being dominated by monoplanes, only two of the thirty entrants were biplanes, really showing how far out-of-step military aviation was compared with private/club flying. There were thirteen Miles aeroplanes competing and they demonstrated their superiority by taking four out of the top five places. The winner was Tommy Rose in a Miles Falcon Six at an average speed of 176 m.p.h.; it was an excellent tourer/racer selling at £1,325 and was advertised as having '... no equal.' The overwhelming success of his aircraft tempered Fred Miles' disappointment in not qualifying for the final six laps in his latest single-seat racing machine, M.5 Sparrowhawk, which had only appeared a few weeks earlier; the whole project had been supervised by 'Blossom' Miles.

The most amazing flying craze to sweep the country during 1935/6 was that of the *Pou-du-Ciel* or Flying Flea, as one contemporary observer declared 'the Flea craze was an astonishing revival of the

Pou-du-Ciel *or Flying Flea meeting at Ashington, Southend. G-ADPX produced by* E.G. Perman & Co. (via D. Brown)

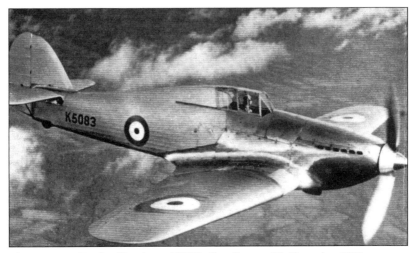

The prototype Hawker Hurricane, K5083, first flew on 6th November 1935.

spirit, which had earlier imbued the aviation pioneers.' This mania was all due to a Frenchman – Henri Mignet – who had long been experimenting with gliders and small flying machines. By 1933 he had successfully designed, built and flown his latest prototype – HM.14 and committed to print his instructions on how to build a similar machine. When the Air League translated his book *Le Sport de l'air* in 1934, the first edition of 6,000 copies sold out within a month. It was said that by the spring of 1935 over five hundred Flying Fleas were under construction by enthusiastic amateurs. The *Daily Express* invited Mignet over to England and on 13th August he flew his miniscule HM.14 across the Channel and began a tour of aero clubs, air meetings and displays. The Flea, twelve feet long, five feet high and with a wing span of twelve feet (when folded), was said to be easy to construct with the minimum of hand tools and expertise; it could be powered by a motor-cycle or a small Ford car engine. Sir John Carden adapted a Ford engine specifically for use in Flying Fleas, and the first British registered Flea flew at Heston in July powered by a Ford/Carden engine. Besides all the dedicated amateurs building their Fleas, several companies were formed to produce them at prices that ranged from £50 to £100; the most prominent was E. G. Pearman, founded in October. Groups and clubs were formed around the country, often arranging special Flying Flea meetings.

What might be described as moving from the ridiculous to the sublime occurred in November when two new aircraft appeared, heralding a major advance in private and military aviation – the Vega Gull and Hurricane. In June, Percival had clearly demonstrated the excellence of his Gull aircraft when he flew from Gravesend to Oran, Morocco and back to Croydon – 2,300 miles in less than a day – justifying the publicity that a Gull '. . . is a touring vehicle that treats continents as a car treats counties.'! His latest development – Vega Gull – the last in the series, was a four-seater fast touring/racer, which was very well-appointed and easy to fly. It cruised at 160 m.p.h. and proved equally suited to long-distance flying; ninety were produced up to July 1939.

At Brooklands on 6th November Hawker's chief test pilot, P. W. S. 'George' Bulman took the prototype 'Fury Interceptor' – K5083 – on its first flight. As he climbed down after the flight he remarked 'Another winner, I think'. The monoplane fighter had been designed by Sydney Camm, Hawker's Chief Designer since 1925, who had been responsible for many and various Hawker aircraft. Camm decided to use the recently developed Rolls-Royce PV (Private Venture) 12 engine (later the famous Merlin). The new aircraft was of traditional construction, wood and fabric stiffened by a metal-tube framework but with wings specially designed to carry eight machine guns as specified by the Air Ministry. The prototype went to the A.&A.E.E. in February for official evaluation trials and tests, where a top speed of 316 m.p.h was achieved. The Company were then utterly convinced that they had a winner on their hands and took the unique decision to produce six hundred before receiving an Air Ministry contract. It was christened the Hurricane and this legendary fighter ushered the RAF into a new and exciting era.

11
FLYING BOATS, GULLS AND HURRICANES
(1936–1937)

New monoplanes appeared with a steady regularity, all-metal construction largely replaced wood especially in military aircraft, and many famous WWII aircraft made their maiden flights. Speed became the order of the day and the seemingly innocent days of biplanes had all but vanished. The RAF began its dramatic expansion, it was fundamentally reorganised and provided with a genuine reserve. Moreover these were the days when the majestic Empire flying boats stole the thunder from 'mere' land-planes.

The cherished prospect of a regular passenger and mail service across the North Atlantic moved a little closer to reality, although as yet there was no British airliner capable of flying the Atlantic and the solution appeared to reside with long-range flying boats. In January 1936 Imperial and Pan American Airways signed an agreement, which was valid until 1942, that each would operate two weekly round trips between New York and Southampton with the first experimental flights targeted for early 1937.

On 20th January King George V died at Sandringham and on the following day the new King – Edward VIII – flew from RAF Bircham Newton to Hendon to attend a Privy Council meeting, thus setting a precedent as the first British monarch to travel by air. On 8th July he made a tour of inspection of five RAF stations – Martlesham Heath, Northolt, Kenley, Mildenhall and Wittering – another Royal first. He travelled in his Rapide and a week or so later he created 'The King's Flight', under Flt. Lt. E. H. 'Mouse' Fielden as 'The Captain of the King's Flight.'; it was based at Hendon under the responsibility of No 24 squadron. According to *Flight* '... this affords further evidence of King Edward's very real interest in and practical appreciation of the value of aviation.' Over the next six months the Rapide was used for over sixty Royal flights.

South Africa was the mecca for long-distance flyers in 1936. On 6th February two pilots departed on the same day. The popular and ebulliant Tommy Rose took-off from Lympne in a Miles Falcon Six and completed the 7,130 mile flight to Cape Town in three days and 17½ hours, arriving as fresh and cheerful as usual, and having broken the existing record by over seventeen hours. David Llewellyn started his Johannesburg flight from Hanworth and it was a much more pedestrian affair – some twenty-three days! Llewellyn was delivering an ultra-light aircraft, an Aeronca 100, to a customer. This aircraft was based on the American Aeronca C-3, which had first appeared in Britain in September 1935 and was produced by the Aeronautical Corporation of Great Britain. Considering that it was a small cabin monoplane powered by a 37 h.p. engine, which cruised at barely 80 m.p.h, Llewellyn's flight was impressive by any standards.

Early in March a small company was founded that would ultimately revolutionise military and civil aviation. Flt. Lt. Frank Whittle, with two former RAF officers, formed Power Jets Ltd to test and develop his turbo-jet engine. The development work was conducted at British Thomson-Houston turbine factory at Rugby and although Whittle was a serving officer, the Air Ministry allowed him to work on the project 'for not more than six hours a week'; subsequently he was appointed to the Special Duty List, which enabled him to devote his full attention to his turbo-jet engine. His experimental engine- 'Whittle Unit' – made its first test run on 12th April 1937. At the same time similar experiments were taking place in Germany by Heinkel A.G. and its He 178 was the first jet-propelled aircraft to fly in August 1939; Britain's first jet-aircraft, Gloster E28/29, made its maiden flight on 15th May 1941.

On 6th March the prototype of the most famous fighter of WWII made its first flight at Eastleigh aerodrome, Southampton under the control of Flt. Lt. J. 'Mutt' Summers, Vickers' Chief test pilot. Supermarine Type 300 – K5054 – was already known as the Spitfire, much to the disgust of its designer Reginald Mitchell – 'sort of bloody silly name they *would* choose'! The sleek all-metal monoplane with its distinctive elliptical wings housing eight Browning machine guns clearly showed its pedigree – the Schneider Trophy racers. It was powered by a 990 h.p. Rolls-Royce PV12 engine and tests at Martlesham Heath proved that 'it was easy to fly and had no vices' and at almost 350 m.p.h., was faster than the Hurricane. In June the Air

Ministry ordered 310 Spitfire Is but it took Supermarine almost two years to tool up for this contract; sadly too late for Mitchell to savour his aircraft's phenomenal success – over 23,000 in various marks – he died in June 1937 at the early age of forty-two. Even today the sight and sound of a Spitfire performing at air displays thrills the young and old alike.

Two other WWII aircraft also made their debut in March. On the 10th the Fairey Battle first took to the skies; a well-designed two-seat light bomber/fighter, which entered the Service in May 1937 but two years later became virtually obsolescent because it was under-powered and lightly armed, these inadequacies were grievously exposed in France during May 1940. Seven days later the Armstrong Whitworth AW.28 Whitley made its entrance, the first heavy bomber to be produced in quantity for the RAF; eighty had been ordered direct from the drawing board. The Whitley was steady, reliable, spacious and rather slow and soon became known as the 'Flying Barn Door'! Nevertheless over 1,800 were produced and they served in Bomber Command until 1942.

The latest Expansion Scheme – F – was presented to Parliament on 17th March, and proved to be the only one actually completed. It proposed 124 Home squadrons and 1,736 front-line aircraft to be in place by March 1939; Overseas squadrons were also increased and the FAA was raised to 26 squadrons. The cost was £50 million, by far the largest Air Estimates since 1918. The Service would require another 25,000 personnel and fifty additional stations. It was fully recognised that the aircraft industry would be under the greatest pressure to produce the necessary aircraft, so the Government prevailed upon motor-car manufacturers to extend their facilities to build aero-engines using their 'assembly line' technique, and this was later extended to the production of airframes. Austin Motors and Rootes Ltd were the first to respond to this 'shadow factory' proposal, followed closely by Daimler, Rover and Standard Motors.

In July the RAF was fundamentally reorganised. The 'Air Defence of Great Britain' was dissolved and replaced by four separate and functional Commands – Bomber, Fighter, Coastal and Training – each with a precise and specific role and divided into a number of Groups. Other than the addition of a few smaller Commands this was essentially the basic structure under which the RAF entered WWII. At the end of the month Lord Swinton, the Secretary of State for Air, announced the creation of the Volunteer Reserve, as a reserve for the

All eight of these famous WWII aircraft made their maiden flights during 1936/7: 1. Fairey Battle 10th March 1936; 2. Vickers Wellington 15th June 1936; 3. Armstrong Whitworth Whitley 17th March 1936; 4. Handley Page Hampden 21st June 1936; 5. Supermarine Spitfire 5th March 1936; 6. Bristol Blenheim I 25th June 1936; 7. Short Sunderland 16th October 1937; 8. Westland Lysander 15th June 1936.

regular Air Force, without separate squadrons of its own, unlike the Auxiliary Air Force. It owed its inception to Air Commodore A. W. Tedder, the Director of Training, who envisaged a 'Citizen's Air Force' designed to attract '... young men of our cities, without any class distinctions ... to open the new force to the whole middle class in the widest sense of that term, namely the complete range of the output of the public and secondary schools ...' Thus giving opportunities to young men, who never considered that they would be accepted for flying training.

The new recruits received flying training during weekends and bank holidays, as well as two hours 'ground training' each week at town venues, and were required to attend a two weeks' full-time training course. For this commitment they received travelling expenses and an annual bounty of £30. Flying tuition was provided by one of the Elementary & Reserve Flying Training Schools operated by civilian flying schools under contract to the Air Ministry. There were already nine in operation and by the end of 1937 twenty were instructing numerous Sergeant pilots, hitherto most RAF pilots were of officer rank. Recruitment for the VR commenced in April 1937 with the objective of producing 800 pilots each year, but it was far more successful than the Air Ministry's wildest hopes; on 1st September 1939 the RAFVR's aircrew strength was over 10,200, of which some 6,400 were pilots.

British Airways had extended its passenger/mail services to most large European cities. It absorbed another two British airlines, British Continental Airways and Crilly Airways, and by the end of the year its fleet of thirty airliners had carried over 28,000 passengers. It was perhaps a sign of the growing popularity of air travel that Imperial Airways felt compelled to issue passengers with details of some of the restrictions imposed on air travel; most of these are now so familiar that they seem to state the obvious! 'Whilst In flight passengers must remain seated for most of the time and, if standing, resume their seats instantly at the command of the pilot [lap safety belts did not become compulsory until October 1937] ... Luggage is restricted as to size and weight and passengers are required to be weighed before boarding ... [many found this experience to be 'the greatest indignity imaginable'!] ... no mid-air snacks or thermos flasks are allowed to be taken on board ... certain meals and drinks are provided on board'. A further indication of the increasing regulatory nature of air travel was the first court case of a passenger being fined £10 for smoking in the toilet, as one report suggested 'the severity of the fine was to deter others'!

Faced with increasing competition from British Airways and other European airlines, Imperial's salvation clearly lay with its Empire Air Mail and passenger routes. On 23rd March a weekly service to Hong Kong was started, although in the previous year only some four hundred passengers had been carried as far as India and beyond. It was scheduled to take ten days, compared with thirty-four by ship. In May, Imperial, along with Qantas, increased their service to Brisbane to twice weekly and endeavoured to maintain the timetable schedule of eight days. But Imperial's halcyon days were just around the corner with the imminent arrival of its first Short S.23 'C' class Empire flying

Short S.23 'C' Class Empire flying boat – Canopus.

boat. These splendid all-metal high-wing monoplanes were probably the most famous commercial aircraft of any nation during the late thirties.

Their *raison d'être* was the Empire Air Mail Scheme and Imperial's Technical Manager, Major R.H. Mayo, had drawn up a specification for a long-range flying boat with a heavy payload for passengers/mail allied to a high cruising speed, and Short Brothers were asked to submit a design. So impressed were Imperial with the final design that they took an unprecedented decision to order a fleet of twenty-eight at a total investment of £1.75 million! The flying boat had two decks, the upper for the crew and the lower for twenty-four day passengers or sixteen sleeping berths and $1\frac{1}{2}$ tons of freight/mail. The passenger area was divided into three cabins; the forward one was a promenade 'deck' where passengers could stand and look out of windows. The first flight of the prototype, G-ADHL *Canopus*, took place at Rochester on 4th July, followed seven days later by *Caledonia*. *Canopus* was delivered to Imperial on 20th October and two days later flew out to Alexandria via Rome; the remainder of the fleet were delivered at a monthly rate.

Although many maintained that the summer aviation scene would not be the same without Cobham's 'Flying Circus', Charles Scott's Flying Display attempted to fill the gap; indeed it was essentially a replication especially as it was organised by Dallas Eskell, Cobham's erstwhile tour manager. Scott had competition from his friend and fellow pilot, Tom Campbell Black, who had gathered together nine pilots and aircraft, along with four parachutists for his British Empire Air Display. It toured the country from 6th April to 7th September. One of its popular attractions was a Flying Flea flown by Bob Doig. Although everybody seemed to be talking about this diminutive machine during the year, several fatal accidents both abroad and in Britain had cast serious doubts over its inherent safety. The Air Ministry conducted tests at Farnborough and as a result refused to issue any new Authorisations to Fly – effectively a ban. In total only some one hundred and twenty Flying Fleas were registered but it was thought that another three hundred or more were under construction, many of which were abandoned after the Air Ministry's decision. Nevertheless a number of dedicated enthusiasts continued to work at creating a safe machine and the last fatal Flying Flea accident in Britain occurred on 29th September 1939.

Private and club flying continued to prosper with over seventy clubs as well as numerous flying schools and almost seven hundred new pilots' 'A' and 'B' licences were issued during the year. Fifteen new light aeroplanes appeared, several designed to capture the market created by the Flying Flea mania, with a few really no more than power-converted gliders. The two more successful low-powered machines were both based on foreign aircraft – the Hillson Praga and Aeronca 100. The Praga was based on a Czechoslovakian aircraft, the Praga Air-Baby, but now built under licence in Manchester by the woodworking firm of F. Hills & Son. It was a two-seater shoulder-wing cabin monoplane constructed almost exclusively of plywood, with a 36 h.p. engine produced under licence by Jowett Cars Ltd. After Llewellyn's successful flight in an Aeronca, Hillson's followed suit during May; H. L. Brook flew a Praga from Lympne to Cape Town in sixteen days. At the end of the month a Praga won the Hanworth to Isle of Man race with an Aeronca placed second. Both aircraft had demonstrated that they could be used for touring and racing and with each priced at under £400, they clearly provided simple and economical flying for those who could not afford anything better and faster; nevertheless only forty-nine in total were sold – twenty-eight Pragas and twenty-one Aeroncas.

The most successful new light aircraft of the year was designed and produced by Fred Miles. On 14th May he first flew the M.11A, a low-wing cabin monoplane in which the pilot and passenger sat side-by-side in some comfort. It was easy to fly, cheap to maintain and was

Hillson Praga, one of the cheapest light aircraft on the market. (via R. Smith)

relatively fast with a cruising speed of 130 m.p.h. It had been specifically designed to the order of Whitney W. Straight and as such became known as the Whitney Straight. Although mainly intended for use in the Straight Corporation's flying schools and clubs, it was generally available for sale at £985 and fifty were produced – one of Phillips and Powis' longest production runs of a purely private aircraft.

Straight was born in New York, the scion of the wealthy Whitney family, and had moved to Britain with his mother in 1925. He obtained his 'A' licence at Haldon aerodrome in Devon at the age of seventeen but after his time at Cambridge University he was drawn into motor-car racing. However, in 1935 he became a British subject and formed Straight Corporation to take an active interest in aviation. Over the next three years the Corporation controlled and managed airlines (especially Western Airways), many flying clubs and schools and several local authority aerodromes, providing excellent facilities for travellers and spectators alike. The Straight Corporation made an immense contribution to civil and club aviation during the immediate pre-war years. In early 1939 Straight joined the AAF, he flew in the Battle of Britain and ended the war as an Air Commodore.

It was again difficult to keep the ladies out of the limelight during 1936. Pauline Gower was the Chief Pilot of Campbell Black's Air Display and in early May Amy Mollison, conscious that her name was fast slipping out of the headlines, decided to try to better Tommy Rose's record to Cape Town. Edgar Percival loaned her a Gull Six because he thought it would be good for publicity. She made the journey there and back in record times, and there were large crowds at Croydon on 15th May to greet her when she returned – almost like the old days. *The Times* commented, 'This is no flash in the pan but an achievement in keeping with her aeronautical career.' This record flight

Miles M.11A Whitney Straight. (via L. Rowe)

proved to be the apogee of her flying career, by the autumn her
marriage was going through difficult times and ultimately she sued for
a divorce. In August another woman pilot came briefly to the fore –
Betty Markham. She was employed as Chief Pilot for Air Cruises Ltd
and was described in the press as '... twice married and twice
divorced, leading a most colourful life'! On 4th September she left
Abingdon in a Vega Gull, *The Messenger*, loaned by Lord Carberry, a
celebrated wealthy amateur pilot; some twenty-one hours later she
crash-landed in Nova Scotia so becoming the first woman to fly solo
across the North Atlantic from east to west. Then on 5th October Jean
Batten left Lympne in her Gull Six, *Jean*, bound for her native New
Zealand; crowds of reporters, photographers and fans gathered to see
her off. She made Australia in six days, beating the existing solo record
to Darwin by over a day. When she finally arrived in Auckland on the
16th it was to a 'huge and tumultous welcome'. She had crossed the
dangerous Tasman Sea, known for treacherous storms, in 10½ hours –
another solo record. Jean was feted in her home country and was
ceremoniously granted the Maori title, *Hine-o-te-Rangi* – 'Daughter of
the Skies'.

It was an eventful summer for aviation with June standing out as a
memorable month. On the 6th, Gatwick was formally opened by Lord
Swinton and the occasion attracted over 30,000 spectators including
over 200 special guests. The small airfield had been acquired by Alfred
Jackman in September 1933 and he formed the Horley Syndicate to
develop it into a civil aerodrome to rival Heston and Croydon. The first
step was achieved in March 1934 when a public licence was granted

and work commenced on the design of a terminal building that was to become the famous circular 'Beehive'. In the following year Airports Ltd. was formed and the land cleared, levelled and drained, the river Mole was diverted and hangars were erected. Southern Railway had been persuaded to build a new railway station on the nearby London to Brighton line and this opened in September initially named Tinsley Green, which was linked to the aerodrome by a subway. The Air Ministry granted a subsidy to Airports Ltd with the provision that Gatwick be kept open night and day with night landing equipment, Customs accommodation had to be provided along with sufficient passenger facilities as befitted a major airport. On 15th May British Airways moved in from Heston and two days later its first service left Gatwick for Paris. Although the aerodrome was then slightly larger than Croydon, its immediate future was not as successful as anticipated and British Airways was forced to move out temporarily to Croydon in February 1937 because the landing area at Gatwick was frequently flooded during the winter.

The indomitable Jean Batten – 'Daughter of the Skies'.

During the month four well-known WWII aircraft made their maiden flights. Two appeared on the same day (15th) – Vickers Wellington twin-engined medium bomber of WWII 'Wimpy' fame and Westland's distinctive high-wing or 'parasol' P.8 specially designed for Army Co-Operation duties, later named Lysander. Six days later Handley Page's H.P.52 Hampden, another twin-engined medium bomber, made its first flight and on the 25th the prototype Bristol Blenheim 1 also took to the skies for the first time. All these new aircraft (apart from the Blenheim) were on view to the 170,000 visitors to the RAF Display at Hendon on the 27th. These spectators also had the privilege of seeing for the first time a prototype Battle, Whitley, Spitfire and Hurricane. No small wonder that there were favourable comments about the Display '... Hendon certainly did us proud on Saturday ... the RAF has never put on a better show ... we saw flying worthy of the World's best Air Force ...'. In very marked contrast to all these

Fokker XII of British Airways alongside Gatwick's famous 'Beehive' terminal. (Via L. Rowe)

Hendon Air Display – June 1936. Left to Right: Hawker Hurricane, Supermarine Spitfire and Vickers Venom. (RAF Museum)

prototypes there was a fine and rare selection of historic aeroplanes – Sopwith Camel, Wright biplane, Blériot, Caudron and Farman – clearly demonstrating how 'the old order changeth ...'

Captain Edgar Percival had more reasons than most to be pleased with his Company's progress during 1936. The year seemed to be one of unbounded success for his splendid aircraft. Besides all the welcome publicity gained as a result of the successful solo long-distance flights, a Vega Gull, piloted by Charles Gardner, won the King's Cup at Hatfield on 10/11th July. Geoffrey de Havilland, the oldest competitor, was co-flying a DH.90 Dragonfly with his son Geoffrey – a unique partnership. It had first appeared in August 1935, as a smaller, faster and racier version of the Dragon Rapide; at a price of over £2,600 it was certainly in the luxury end of the market, which obviously existed as sixty-three were produced but only a third were registered in Britain.

The most disappointing aviation event of the year was the Schlesinger Air Race from Portsmouth to Johannesburg, South Africa held at the end of September. The Race was sponsored by Isaac Schlesinger, a wealthy South African industrialist, and timed to coincide with the Empire Exhibition at Johannesburg. He hoped to emulate the successful MacRobertson Race of 1934. However, the event, with total prize money of £10,000, was confined to British pilots and British aircraft, which immediately made it a rather

King Edward VIII inspecting RAF Mildenhall on 8th July 1936. Royal Dragon Rapide – G-ADDD. (RAF Museum)

'parochial affair', though *The Aeroplane* still considered '... in general, a thoroughly good event is promised ...' Unfortunately tragedy struck before the Race had even started when one competitor, Tom Campbell Black, was killed in a freak taxiing accident in his Mew Gull at Speke aerodrome, Liverpool in September. Finally nine aircraft lined up at Portsmouth Airport before dawn on 29th September – two Mew Gulls, two Vega Gulls, a Miles Sparrowhawk and Hawk Speed Six, a BA Double Eagle and an Eagle and last an Airspeed Envoy. They were flown by most of the leading pilots of the day – Tommy Rose, Charles W. Scott, Arthur Clouston, Max Findlay, David Llewellyn, Giles Guthrie, and Captain Stanley Halse. It turned out to be a tragic fiasco of a race. Only one aircraft, a Vega Gull piloted by Scott and Guthrie, finished the race to claim the first prize of £4,000. Tragically the Envoy crashed at Abercorn, Northern Rhodesia killing Findlay and Waller, both were flying instructors at Brooklands. The other entrants were forced to retire and four aircraft were written-off. It was perhaps not too surprising that this was the last major air race of the Thirties.

The latter half of the year was also somewhat overshadowed by a number of civil air accidents, which cast doubts on the safety of air travel and British airliners. On 10th August a Vickers Vellox of Imperial Airways crashed shortly after taking-off from Croydon and the crew of four were killed; there were no passengers on board. Two days later a British Airways DH.86 on a night mail service to Cologne crashed with two fatalities. In September and November another two DH.86s of British Airways were lost, killing five crew members including Captain Walter Anderson, the Airways' Chief Pilot. On 9th December there occurred Britain's hitherto worst-ever aircraft accident when a Douglas DC-2 of KLM crashed in fog shortly after taking-off from Croydon, killing the pilot and thirteen passengers, including Juan de La Cierva, the designer of the Autogiro. Four months earlier the world of aviation had mourned the loss of another pioneer airman – Louis Blériot – who died on 8th August aged sixty-four. In the following year Imperial Airways heralded its 40,000th crossing of the English Channel – such was the advance of aviation since Blériot's historic flight.

The country was shocked and dismayed on 11th December to hear the radio broadcast by King Edward VIII announcing his abdication. Within days the new King – George VI – sent a personal message to the RAF in which he assured the Service that he would maintain his close connections with them '... which has been such a happy feature of my life ever since I became a junior officer in the Service in 1918 ...' Thus the RAF had its third Commander-in-Chief in a space of less than twelve months, but this time it was vastly different because the new King had actually served in the Force and since June had held the rank of Marshal of the Royal Air Force. The year closed on a sad note when Lady Houston, DBE died at the age of eighty – '... this eccentric old lady was famed for the intensity of her patriotism ... and her fervour for, and unbounded generosity to flying for Great Britain and the Empire ...'

In January two Empire flying boats, *Castor* and *Centaurus,* initiated Imperial Airways regular weekly services to Alexandria via Marseille, Rome, Brindisi and Athens and thus ushering in a golden age for Imperial. These splendid flying boats were the wonder of the time, viewed in almost similar awe as the latter-day Concordes. They provided the air traveller with extreme luxury and the same high standard of comfort as experienced on Pullman trains or first class sea travel. Four course meals, silver cutlery, bone china, wicker seating, sleeping bunks, ample space to move around and a viewing 'deck'. The Captains were also encouraged to mingle with passengers rather on the same style as occurred on first-class sea journeys! An area of Southampton Water at Hythe was selected as the terminal pending a permanent base in Langstone harbour. Perhaps the only discomfort for the passengers was embarking and disembarking in rough weather. In March all Empire services were transferred from Croydon to Hythe with the African services departing on Tuesdays and Fridays and those to Australia on Wednesdays.

Passengers were convinced that flying boats were a safer means to travel over oceans, although this was hardly borne out by the experiences of Imperial during 1937. Three of its Empire flying boats were lost in tragic accidents and another two were damaged whilst at their moorings. In March *Capricornus* crashed over the French Alps and only the radio operator survived. The following month *Courtier* was wrecked at Athens and four passengers drowned and then in December (4th) *Cygnus* crashed in Brindisi harbour when a crew member and passenger were killed. Despite these tragic accidents it should be said that Imperial's fleet of Empire flying boats flew millions of miles without any other *serious* accidents.

In February the prolonged and hoary debate about the control of the Fleet Air Arm once more surfaced when the Admiral of the Fleet, Sir Roger Keyes, argued, 'The Navy cannot afford to be dependent on the Air Ministry any longer, for they have utterly failed to keep pace with the development of aircraft as in other navies and have never been able to fulfil the Admiralty's requirements ... much has been heard of the marvels of new RAF machines. But not once has mention been made of new types for the FAA. This is because no new type has been produced except one which is a combination of some old types.' It is presumed that Sir Roger was referring to the Fairey Swordfish, a carrier-based torpedo and reconnaissance biplane, which had first flown in 1934. The Swordfish entered the FAA in June 1936 and although technically obsolete three years later, it proved to be a highly versatile and doughty aircraft, fondly called 'the Stringbag'. This truly classic aeroplane performed with great distinction throughout the war. Nevertheless the FAA's first all-metal monoplane did make its debut on 9th February, flown by Flt. Lt. A.M. 'Dasher' Blake, whom at the age of forty-seven was the oldest test pilot. The Blackburn Skua was the Service's first purpose-built dive bomber and the first monoplane to fly from an aircraft carrier. Almost two hundred were ordered from the drawing board and they entered the FAA in late 1938. The RAF/FAA dispute, which one Service historian described as 'a storm in a tea-cup',

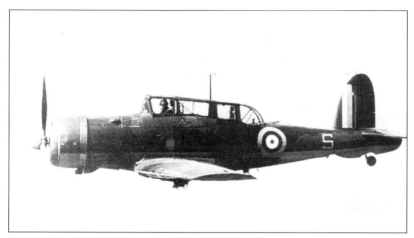

Blackburn Skua – the Service's first purpose-built dive bomber.

was finally resolved in July by Sir Thomas Inskip, the Minister for the Co-ordination of Imperial Defence. He recommended that the FAA be transferred to the Admiralty 'within the next two years' and on 24th May 1939 the Admiralty took over formal control of the FAA.

Woodley aerodrome was the venue, on 20th March, for the formal christening by Mrs 'Blossom' Miles of the first production Miles M.14 Hawk Trainer for the RAF. It was given the name Magister and the first were delivered to the Central Flying School in May. They became the Service's first monoplane trainers and the Air Ministry had, on this occasion, revoked its insistence on metal aircraft – the Magister was of all-wood construction. They remained in service until 1948 by which time over 1,300 'Maggies' (as they were fondly known) had been produced. The Magister was the first of a number of successful training aircraft produced by Miles for the RAF.

In March the public was saddened to hear of the demise of another 'Grand Lady' – the Duchess of Bedford. On the 22nd she left Woburn Abbey in her Gipsy Moth on a short triangular flight of eighty miles to complete her two hundred hours solo and she was not heard of or seen again. RAF aircraft from several airfields in East Anglia searched in vain for any signs of wreckage. About ten days later four struts were washed up on the East coast and they were believed to come from her Moth. Charles Grey wrote of 'A great lady and a charming woman … British aviation is much the poorer for losing her.'. For many she was more of a heroine than Amy Johnson and Jean Batten and one letter to *The Times* read '... If it had to be, the fading into the twilight of that courageous lady was sublime. We, of the same generation, following less adventurously in her footsteps, recognise in her pioneer flights, the dispelling of the old established belief that flying was for the very young alone.'

Later in the year another famous woman pilot would also disappear without a trace. Amelia Putnam (Earhart), whilst attempting to fly around the world in her red Lockheed Electra 10E, left New Guinea on 2nd July and apart from a final radio message 'we are heading north-east', she and her navigator Fred Noonan disappeared without trace. There was a massive search by American Naval vessels but her aircraft was never found. What their fate was nobody knows, it was assumed that a navigational error had been made, that they ran out of fuel and then crashed into the Pacific ocean; some people seriously suggested that she had landed on some inhabited island and was still alive. Before the flight Amelia acknowledged the dangers involved but maintained '... I want to do it because I want to do it! Women must try to do things as men have tried.'

Another celebrated American flyer was also in the news during the year, Charles Lindbergh. He and his family had moved to England in 1936 where he said they felt safe 'without worry from politics, the press of fantaticism'. He had borrowed a Whitney Straight from Phillips and Powis for a trip to Berlin and was so impressed that he asked Miles to build him a fast, comfortable and commodious two-seat cabin monoplane for his frequent trips to Europe. The Miles M.12 was specially designed for long-distance flying with a range of 1,400 miles and was powered by an American Menasco engine, which gave it a top speed of 190 m.p.h. Lindbergh chose black and orange colours because 'they show up most readily in all weathers' and named it *Mohawk*. He was delighted with the aircraft, he and his wife travelled in it as far as India and Russia until he left Europe in 1939. The *Mohawk* was then impressed into the RAF and it survived the war. In 1950 it was sold to a Spanish owner and twenty years later was found in a Spanish scrapyard, *Mohawk* was despatched to Orlando, Florida for restoration; its present whereabouts are not known.

A committee under Brigadier-General Sir Henry Maybury, formed in June 1935 to consider all aspects of civil aviation in Britain, presented its report – a heavy tome which contained no earth-shattering propo-sals and rather stated the obvious. Amongst its many recommendations one concerned the siting of a 'central junction aerodrome' somewhere between London and Manchester with radial routes to other English cities, Belfast and Glasgow; actually Birmingham (Elmdon), which opened on 1st May 1939 seemed to fit the bill nicely. It was proposed that local authorities should provide aerodromes for private and club flying, in fact many were already doing just that especially those managed by the Straight Corporation, and more would open in the next eighteen months. In the Committee's opinion 'aerial displays' should be replaced by demonstrations showing the practical application of flying, and in fact the days of 'flying circuses' were almost a thing of the past. It was also proposed that the existing seventeen internal airlines should become a single company to operate all internal air services. This never seemed to be a viable proposition, although in 1938 the newly formed Air Transport Licensing Authority did introduce some rationalisation into the air routes within the British Isles.

On 9th April the very first Japanese aircraft landed at Croydon. It brought an Address from the City of Tokyo to King George VI in his Coronation year. The Mitsubishi monoplane had completed 9,900 miles in just over ninety-four hours and there was a large crowd gathered at the airport to greet the crew. The aircraft was named *Kamikaze* (*Divine* or *Heavenly Wind*) but nobody realised what sinister connotations this name would have for the war in the Pacific. Eighteen days later the newspapers were full of the horrendous bombing of Guernica, which 'gave the world a new name for the horrors of War'. In less than three hours of sustained bombing this small Spanish market town well behind the front line was virtually razed to the ground with 1,654 civilian fatalities and 100s gravely injured. The bombing was universally condemned and the German government attempted to assure the world that 'no German airplane took part ...', but it was generally accepted that its Condor Legion, formed in November 1936 from six hundred so called 'volunteers', was responsible for this 'monstrous atrocity'. For the many people in this country that could still remember the Gotha raids of 1917/8, the thoughts of a future war became even more fearful.

As usual the summer aviation calendar opened on Sunday 9th May with the Royal Aero. Society's Garden Party at the Great West Aerodrome. Over 3,000 guests braved the elements, high winds and heavy rain, many were distinguished foreign visitors in London to attend the Coronation three days hence. Thirty companies exhibited

271

MILES MAGISTER I."

their aircraft in the hangars but the inclement weather rather marred much of the flying. The two latest long-distance record breakers were invited; the Australian Harry Broadbent had arrived from Australia only the previous week in a Leopard Moth in six days and eight hours, whereas H. L. Brook had reduced Amy Mollison's South African record by sixteen hours in a Gull. He complained that these sporting flights now seemed to claim scant recognition. Such had been the monotony of record-breaking flights that they had become a little passé now creating meagre public and press interest unless an attractive lady was involved!

British Airways, unlike Imperial, was not under any obligation to operate solely British airliners, its fleet already included some Fokker XIIs and Junkers 52s and in the previous year the airline had ordered American Lockheed 10 Electras. They were well-proven and had been operating in the States since 1934. The Electras carried a crew of two and ten passengers and cruised at 182 m.p.h.; they are now considered the most technically advanced of all pre-war airliners. British Airways held a press launch at Gatwick on 24th May and all the aviation experts were most impressed. Ultimately British Airways operated seven Electras and another nine Super Electras, they famously carried Neville Chamberlain on his three flights to Munich in 1938.

Empire Air Day was celebrated on 28th May and it seemed to have added import coming soon after the Coronation. Like that memorable

The Coronation Display at Hendon – 26th June 1937. Farman biplane flies over serried ranks of biplanes; the RAF was still mainly a biplane force. (RAF Museum)

day it was also blessed by glorious sunshine, which encouraged hundreds of thousands to cram the fifty-three RAF stations and many civil aerodromes. Such days as these confirmed the general belief in the country that the RAF was 'the Best Flying Club in the World'. Service life appeared to go along at a most leisurely pace, some stations closed down for annual leave and Wednesdays were almost solely devoted to sporting activities. Outwardly the stations gave the appearance of an almost gracious style of living – imposing entrances, elegant and spacious red-brick buildings, centrally-heated barrack blocks, tar-macked roads, neat lawns and ample sports facilities. Despite all the new monoplanes due to enter the Service, biplanes still reigned supreme and the pilots were largely recruited from public schools.

Perhaps it could be said that the pre-war RAF was epitomised at the Coronation Display held at Hendon on 26th June under clear blue skies. The King (in the uniform of a Marshal of the RAF) and the Queen

273

Gloster Gladiators: the RAF's last biplane fighters.

attended along with 200,000 of their subjects. Over six hundred aircraft took part in the various spectacular displays and nearly two hundred and sixty in five columns flew in the ceremonial fly-past. As one spectator commented, '... the sound of the engines seemed to beat the brain ... that shows what to expect in the next war. Fancy raids of that size coming over all day long!' Once again a display of WWI aeroplanes enthralled the crowds and some journalists suggested that little progress had been made since those days! The Display ended with an impressive set-piece battle on a large model 'port' which was attacked by Whitleys, Wellesleys and Blenheims and urgently defended by Gladiators and Demons – a splendid finale. Little did those watching the RAF in action realise that this eighteenth and most successful Display was the last ever held – another era had passed.

It was possible that some of the Service's critics had been influenced by witnessing the valiant efforts of its Demon and Gladiator biplane fighters, especially as the Gloster Gladiator was the RAF's latest fighter, having entered No 72 squadron earlier in February. Its design was a natural development from the Gauntlet but more heavily armed and provided with an enclosed cockpit; the Gladiator was the last and most advanced of the RAF's biplane fighters. Although all pilots agreed 'they were a delight to fly' nothing could disguise the fact that with the arrival of Hurricanes and Spitfires they were virtually obsolete.

At the end of June Flt. Lt. M. Adam regained the world's altitude record. He reached 53,937 feet in the all-wooden Bristol 138A monoplane powered by a special Pegasus supercharged engine. Britain had previously gained the record in September 1936 in the same aircraft when Sqn. Ldr. F. Swain attained 49,967 feet but this was surpassed by an Italian aircraft. The successful flight was not without incident, the cockpit canopy cracked and Adam was only saved by his special pressurised suit. It must be said that apart from aviation specialists the record made little impact on the general public.

The SBAC Show was held at Hatfield on 27/28th June; it was the Society's 21st anniversary and appropriately Frederick Handley Page (a founder member) was Chairman. Maybe in the light of the recent Guernica bombing he felt constrained to comment in his opening address '... We, aircraft constructors, are more concerned with the aeroplane as a means of bringing peace to the whole world than a weapon of destruction. The aeroplane is the best peace-bringing machine that has ever been invented. By it we can wipe down barriers between races and so bring widespread happiness.' Fine words and noble sentiments but the cynics were ready to point out that Handley Page was 'the doyen of heavy bombing', his Company had been, and would remain, in the forefront of bomber production right from the pioneer days of the 0/100 to the Halifax! On display was Airspeed's prototype Oxford, the military version of their small airliner Envoy; one had recently been added to the King's Flight. The Oxford had only made its first flight ten days earlier and in November became the RAF's first twin-engined advanced trainer. During its long service career (seventeen years) over 8,500 were produced and it acquired the name 'Ox-bow'. With dual controls as standard it trained not only pilots but navigators, radio operators, gunners and bomb aimers.

The undisputed 'star' of the Show was the most impressive de Havilland airliner – DH.91 Albatross. In January 1936 the Air Ministry had placed an order for either a twin or four-engined experimental Transatlantic mailplane that could cruise at over 200 m.p.h. in an attempt to compete with the Douglas DC-2 and 3, which had just appeared. The airliner was designed by a team led by Arthur Hagg, one of the last of his designs before he resigned from the Company he had served for over twenty-two years. It had first flown at Hatfield on 20th May and was a handsome, sleek and elegant aircraft considered by many to be the Company's finest design notwithstanding the two Comets. Imperial ordered five with a twenty-two passenger interior, the first being delivered in November 1938. The Society's guests were also treated to a fly-past by the Empire flying boat, *Calpurnia*; both fine aircraft showed the thriving state of the British aircraft industry. At the conclusion of the Show it was announced that the second day of next year's Show would be opened to the public but it turned out that 1937 was the last Show pre-war. It was another eleven years before public attendance became a regular feature – in September 1946 at Radlett; two years later the Show moved to its regular venue at Farnborough.

Somewhat against the current trend the Albatross was of all-wooden construction and Havilland's produced another small wooden aircraft – DH.94 Moth Minor. It was designed to capture the private/club market lately usurped by Miles and Percival but also the Air Ministry had intimated that they were considering abolishing the requirement for privately-owned light aircraft to need a Certificate of Airworthiness providing 'it was adequately designed and built'; in this respect de Havilland's felt that they had the very aeroplane. Geoffrey de Havilland made the first flight on 22nd June and this delightful small two-seater low-wing monoplane proved to be 'easy and docile to fly'. At a price of £575 (£690 for a coupé top) it should have made a greater impact on the private/club scene than it did, although the war did intervene. Nevertheless by September 1939 one hundred had been produced, though less than half were registered in Britain.

The first of the Transatlantic trial flights set off on 5th July. Captain

A flight of Airspeed Oxfords. (RAF Museum)

DH.91 Albatross, G-AFDI, Frobisher *sporting the famous 'speedbird' badge.*

Wilcockson, with a crew of three, left Foynes, Ireland in an Empire flying boat, *Caledonia,* and arrived at Botwood, Newfoundland fifteen hours later. He then flew on to Montreal and ultimately New York. On the same day Pan American's Sikorsky S-42B, *Clipper III,* left Newfoundland with Captain Grey and a crew of four, and it landed at Fownes twelve and a half hours later. It reached Imperial Airways' terminal at Hythe a day later. Newspapers on both sides of 'the Pond' heralded the flights as 'Imperial and Pan. Am. now lead the world and hold sway over the oceans.'! By the end of the year Imperial had completed five successful return flights and Pan American four, nevertheless neither airline yet had a flying boat capable of carrying out a commercial passenger/mail service.

Despite the unsettled European political situation many British and European pilots (including German) regularly met and competed in friendly rivallry at the International meetings held during the year. *Flight* considered 'these meetings and rallies clearly demonstrated that the close bonds of friendship of flyers of all nationalities knows no political boundaries'. In June the York municipal aerodrome, which had opened in July 1936, hosted a particularly successful International Rally that attracted large crowds. German pilots took most of the honours and there was a fine display of aerobatics by Henrich Wendel, a Chief Flying Instructor at a *Luftwaffe* training school at Jena. In the last week of August Lympne held its fifth International meeting, which took place over two days and over 20,000 people attended to witness a fine display of races and events. Hopes were expressed that these rallies and meetings would foster better relations between European countries; the events of 1938 showed them to be no more than wishful thinking.

The purely British affair, the King's Cup, held at Hatfield on 10th September appeared to be losing some of its allure, at least as far as the public was concerned. One observer thought that '...the sight of aeroplanes flying overhead no longer amuses them, the novelty has worn off ...' Charles Gardner won the Cup for the second year in succession with his Mew Gull with Edgar Percival in another being placed third. His new company, Percival Aircraft Ltd formed in late 1936, was now operating from premises at Luton's new municipal airport. *The Aeroplane* considered his success story '... Percival had built a flourishing business from very small beginnings. It had sprung from the sale of civil machines and has never to depend on military orders.' Percival now decided to break into a different market with the production of his Q.6 – his first twin-engined cabin aeroplane designed to carry four/five passengers and it certainly showed its parentage – the successful Gulls. The aircraft was a trifle expensive at £4,700 and only twenty-six were produced, of which nine were impressed into the RAF in 1940 when they were named Petrel.

In September Air Chief Marshal Sir Cyril Newall was appointed Chief of the Air Staff. Like all senior officers he had served with distinction in the RFC, having qualified as a pilot in October 1911. Newall was destined to preside over the RAF during a period of dynamic growth and is considered to be 'the prime architect of the wartime Air Force'. When he retired in October 1940 the Service had

DH.94 Moth Minor.

Percival's Q.6 prototype first flew at Luton on 14th September 1937.

attained its first major and most critical victory – the Battle of Britain.

The military version of the Empire flying boat, Short S.25 Sunderland, made its maiden flight at Rochester during October. This remarkable aircraft epitomised RAF Coastal Command during the war and when it entered No 230 squadron at Singapore in June 1938, it was the RAF's first monoplane flying boat as well as the first to be fitted with nose and tail turrets. The Sunderland cruised at about 115 m.p.h. and had an operational endurance of $12\frac{1}{2}$ hours. Over seven hundred were ultimately produced and they were not retired until May 1959 – the most successful and longest serving of all RAF aircraft.

The days of solo long-distance flying had not quite run their natural course. On 24th October Jean Batten arrived at Croydon from Australia in five days and eighteen hours, close to the existing record. She stepped out of her Gull Six in her renowned white flying suit and smiled for the benefit of the press photographers. A large crowd had gathered to welcome her and it was said to be '... reminiscent of the palmy days of record breaking'. She had decided that this was to be her last long-distance flight; in 1938 the F.A.I. presented her with its Gold Medal, the first woman to be so honoured, and she was later awarded a KBE. It remains somewhat of a mystery why, like Amy Johnson and

Pauline Gower etc, she was not recruited for the Air Transport Auxiliary, it may have been due to bouts of double vision she suffered as a result of an earlier crash. She never married and died in obscurity at her home in Majorca in 1982 aged seventy-three; the International Terminal at Auckland airport is named in her honour.

Almost a month later another long-distance flight ended at Croydon when the famous *Grosvenor House* Comet, now re-named *The Burberry*, landed from South Africa. It was flown by Flg. Offr. Arthur Clouston accompanied by Mrs Kirby Green; they had completed the flight to Cape Town and back in less than a week shattering Amy Mollison's previous record. As one newspaper commented, 'Such flights should no longer excite us as they once did but nevertheless for some unaccountable reason they still do! At least this flight has shown that Arthur Clouston is a first class pilot ... but we knew that already!' – after all he was a civilian test pilot at Farnborough.

December was a memorable month for the RAF when the first Hurricane 1s were delivered to No 111 squadron at Northolt; they replaced their Gauntlets. The first monoplane fighter to enter the Service and moreover the first to exceed 300 m.p.h. The Hurricane, like the Spitfire, would gain immortal fame in the Battle of Britain and over 14,000 were produced in Britain and Canada. However, just a month earlier a German Bf 109 fighter (an adversary in that famous Battle) sent shockwaves through the military aviation world when it established a new world speed record of 379 m.p.h.; certainly no Air Force had a fighter to match that speed.

12
THE WAR
CLOUDS GATHER
(1938–1939)

For much of the time it was impossible to escape news of military aviation, the endless talk of an approaching war and all the various preparations for that eventuality. A number of established aviation events fell by the wayside and the glamour and sheer enjoyment of flying was fast fading away as the war clouds gathered menacingly over Europe, casting ever lengthening shadows across the aviation scene.

However, on New Year's Day 1938 there was a bright and promising start when the Short-Mayo Composite made its first taxiing trials on the Medway near Rochester. This was an unusual but perfectly serious attempt to bring an early answer to the problem of a Transatlantic airmail service. It comprised a specially adapted Empire flying boat, *Maia*, carrying a small four-engined Short S.20 seaplane, *Mercury*. In 1932 Major Robert Mayo, Imperial Airways' Technical Manager, revived an idea that had first seen light of day in 1916; a small aeroplane launched in mid-air from a larger flying boat. After several years of discussion and persuasion the Air Ministry finally agreed to support the project and *Maia* first flew in July 1937 followed by *Mercury* in November. On 19th January the maiden flight of the Composite was made, and on 6th February the first mid-air separation was successfully accomplished. Now, providing further tests at the Marine Aircraft Experimental Establishment at Felixstowe were satisfactory, the first Transatlantic flight by *Mercury* could be attempted in the summer.

There was, of course, another solution to the Transatlantic problem – in-flight refuelling. Sir Alan Cobham's Flight Refuelling had continued its trials using aircraft loaned by the Air Ministry as 'the tanker-receivers'. During January the Company conducted experiments with Imperial Airways, using an AW.23 (the forerunner of the Whitley)

Short-Mayo Composite first flew on 19th January 1938

refuelling the Empire flying boat *Cambria*. Seventeen flights were carried out and they were so successful that Flight Refuelling offered a guarantee of 'service in any part of the world to deliver 1,000 gallons of fuel in ten minutes . . .' Imperial agreed a contract for a series of aerial refuelled Transatlantic crossings in 1939 and two flying boats, *Cabot* and *Caribou*, were duly modified to incorporate the refuelling device.

There was more encouraging news for Imperial when Armstrong Whitworth's A.W.27 Ensign airliner made its maiden flight from Hamble on 24th January. Back in September 1934 Imperial had ordered a large all-metal four-engined airliner, capable of carrying forty passengers and cruising at 200 m.p.h. The Ensign was designed by John Lloyd, responsible for the earlier Atalanta; in 1935 Imperial were so impressed with the completed design that they ordered twelve. The delay in the production of the prototype was largely due to the Air Ministry, who had pressurised the Company to concentrate on the production of Whitley bombers. The Ensign was the largest British airliner, providing spacious passenger accommodation in its elegantly contoured fuselage. Imperial extolled its refinements – large cabins, fully adjustable lounge seats 'the most comfortable ever constructed', two separate toilets and a fully equipped kitchen that could provide '. . . from a seven-course dinner . . . to drinks and snacks of all descriptions.' *Ensign* went into service on 27th October to Le Bourget and three more, *Egeria*, *Elsinore* and *Euterpe*, were used on the busy Christmas mail service to Australia. Sadly the airliner's performance did not quite live

AW.27 Ensign: the largest British pre-war airliner. (via R. Makin)

up to its early promise; crews were unhappy with the flying controls and its Armstrong Siddeley Tiger IX engines proved unreliable. They were returned to the Company for modifications.

Evidence of the growing number of aerodromes around the country could be seen by the largest number of delegates, over one hundred, attending the annual conference of the Aerodrome Owners Association held during January. In the last four years the number of municipal aerodromes had risen from sixteen to thirty-six and three well-known 'airports' officially opened in 1938 – Speke (Liverpool), Ringway (Manchester) and Luton. Additionally there were over one hundred private aerodromes of varying sizes, about a quarter owned by aircraft companies. Little did the delegates realise that their aerodromes would be requisitioned by the Air Ministry twenty months hence and all their present concerns about the provision of satisfactory radio approach facilities as required by the Air Ministry would be long forgotten.

On 10th February Hurricanes were headline news when Sqn. Ldr. J. W. Gillan, the Commander of No 111 squadron, flew one from Turnhouse near Edinburgh to Northolt, a distance of 327 miles in forty-eight minutes at an average speed of almost 409 m.p.h. The Air Ministry was quick to appreciate the publicity value of this high-speed flight, but many experts greeted the news with more than a little scepticism, the Hurricane could not possibly have attained such a speed. However, it transpired that Gillan had benefited from tail winds in excess of 60 m.p.h.

Luton Municipal Airport officially opened on 16th July 1938. (London-Luton Airport)

The Air Estimates, presented to Parliament in March, amounted to £103.5 million, double that of two years previously and yet another Expansion Scheme, L, was approved in April. The short-lived Schemes J and K, dating from December and January respectively were abandoned. This new Scheme saw the first significant increase in the number of fighters and it also gave priority to their production. This change of emphasis was largely due to Sir Thomas Inskip's view that the RAF's role should not be to deliver 'any early knockout blow' but rather 'to prevent the Germans from knocking us out'! However, the Munich crisis of September threw RAF expansion plans into disarray and in November Scheme M was introduced with a target of 2,500 front-line aircraft to be in place by 31st March 1942, which would include an additional twelve fighter squadrons. Though in truth it was no longer a matter of sheer numbers and gaining parity with Germany but rather that the Service's front-line aircraft could actually wage war. The new Air Minister, Sir Kingsley Wood, assured Parliament that 'the highest priority would be given to strengthening our fighter force.'

With such an accelerated rate of expansion came the pressing need for increased aircraft production, by April it amounted to 158 aircraft monthly. The industry had greatly developed with some 90,000 employed in aircraft and aero-engine production. Hawker Siddeley was by far the largest consortium including Hawker, Gloster, Armstrong Whitworth and Avro. Several companies were now controlled by ship-building concerns notably Vickers Ltd with Vickers (Aviation) and Supermarine and Swan Hunter owning Airspeed. The 'Shadow factory' scheme received fresh impetus with the Government providing new factories, which would be managed by aircraft companies on an agency basis. An exceptional turnaround was achieved, by September 1939 aircraft monthly production had reached 800, equalling German figures.

Nevertheless, in April 1938, the Air Ministry considered the situation demanded help from outside Britain and an Air Purchasing Commission, headed by Air Commodore Arthur Harris (later of Bomber Command fame), was sent to the United States to seek out 'suitable military aircraft'. There was a storm of protest from the SBAC and the press despite assurances from the Government that the Commission was merely making 'exploratory enquiries'. However, by June the Commission had placed orders for 200 Lockheed 214s, the military version of the Electra airliner, to replace Ansons on reconnaissance duties and the same number of North American NA-16s, a two-seater advanced trainer. The first Lockheed, named Hudson, arrived in

Lockheed Hudson: the military version of the Electra airliner, almost 2,000 served in the RAF.

December and in the following June the RAF received its first of almost 2,000 Hudsons; Lockheed also established a factory at Speke to assemble them. The North American Harvards entered No 12 Flying Training School at Grantham in December and they served the RAF until 1955.

Civil aviation experienced a difficult year. On 23rd February Imperial Airways despatched its first Empire flying boat service to India and Singapore, possibly the most heartening news for several months because the Committee, chaired by Lord Cadman, appointed the previous November to investigate certain alleged irregularities and mismanagement by Imperial Airways, made its report. It recommended that British Airways should be given the monopoly of European services except London to Paris, which would be operated by a separate company formed by British Airways and Imperial. It was also clear that the days of the two separate and independent airlines were numbered. On 4th July Sir John Reith, the autocratic head of the British Broadcasting Corporation, was appointed Chairman of Imperial Airways. He had no previous aviation experience and it was assumed, quite rightly as it turned out, that he had been selected to amalgamate British Airways and Imperial Airways into a public corporation. Indeed by the late autumn he had gained the agreement of both Boards for the merger, and had already selected the new name – British Overseas Airways Corporation. The proposal was put to the House of Commons in November and it was agreed that the requisite Bill would be introduced in 1939.

Imperial Airways had not only been frustrated by the delay of the Ensign airliners but also by their order for three larger G Class flying boats specifically designed for the Transatlantic service. Furthermore the airline's new London air terminal in Knightsbridge had been hindered by planning regulations, and although Croydon was still busy with nine British and seventeen European airlines operating regular services, its long-term future was in doubt. Because of the steady and increasing encroachment of housing the airport could not be overly extended. The Government was considering a new international airport 'out in the country' (Lillingstone in Kent), and the City of London Corporation had purchased a site at Fairlop, Essex with the intention of developing it into a major 'London airport'. Perhaps the best news of the year for Imperial was the delivery of its first Albatross airliner in October, named *Frobisher*, which entered into the Paris service in November, carrying for the first time Imperial's 'speedbird' insignia – later famously adopted by BOAC. It was followed by *Falcon, Fortuna, Fingal* and *Fiona*.

British Airways had finally managed to achieve a profit during 1937/8 – over £296,000. Some 3,600 staff were employed in thirty countries and it operated six weekday services to Paris and five on Sundays; the cost of a return was £6 6s and the flight took only ninety minutes in its Electras. During the year they took delivery of the new 14 Super Electras, which cruised at 225 m.p.h., and the Government had offered the airline a subsidy to establish services to other major European cites, besides Paris, Brussels, Copenhagen and Stockholm. With the encouragement of the Air Ministry, RAF pilots acted as co-pilots on services to Germany 'to make them familiar with that country from the air'!; *Lufthansa* had been suspected of doing the same for the last few years. In late May British Airways moved their operations to Heston, which the Government had owned since November although Airwork Ltd continued to operate the airport. Considerable improvements had been made to passenger and landing facilities and there were ambitious plans to develop Heston into a large international airport as an alternative to Croydon.

The Royal Aeronautical Society's Garden Party, which had became such a curtain raiser to the summer season, was held on Sunday 8th May. It was now fully accepted that '... the Great West Aerodrome is the place where one comes to see the newest and best in British Aviation ... but it is so much more than a pleasant and lively social gathering of aviation's great and good. It has become a flying display on the grand scale ...'! There was a sprinkling of new aircraft on show including imported machines and as a reminder of the 'good old days' – a Sopwith Pup, Hanriot biplane and a couple of Blériots. Besides all the other spectacular flying displays, three gliders gently soared around the aerodrome; they were flown by Phillip Wills, who had recently completed 206 miles from Heston to Cornwall, Dudley Hiscox, a celebrated glider pilot, and Amy Johnson. She had reverted to her maiden name and had failed to secure any flying post, so had turned to gliding.

Although the summer scene lacked the attraction of an RAF Air Display for the first time since 1920, it was somewhat compensated by another successful Empire Air Day held on 28th May; despite heavy rain 100,000s flocked to the various Service and civil aerodromes. As *Popular Flying* explained 'British crowds are attracted to aerodromes because they are more or less forbidden territory ... they seem to love poking their noses into hangars and workshops'! Martlesham Heath held 'a wonderful display of flying well worthy of Hendon at its best', which attracted over 15,000 visitors. At Hornchurch where a flight of Hurricanes performed for the large crowds, Jean Batten flew in to add a touch of glamour to the proceedings. RAF Cardington had a display of barrage balloons for the first time, less than four months later they would be seen in the skies over London. But inevitably the thought lingered – 'Would there be another Empire Air Day next year?'; more especially as the SBAC cancelled their Annual Show because 'it is not in the public interest to show the latest type of aircraft and aero-engines and the immense amount of work devolving upon the industry makes undesirable the diversion of time and energy to the organisation of such a display.'

Early in June the International Air Race from Hatfield to the Isle of Man was held and despite the unsettled political situation six German pilots competed as did two from Czechoslovakia. There were sixteen starters for the modest £125 first prize and each aircraft had to be capable of exceeding 100 m.p.h. The young and rising 'star' of British racing, Alex Henshaw, achieved the fastest time in his Mew Gull – 247 m.p.h. – but was placed second on handicap to S. T. Low in a Comper Swift. The Manx Air Derby held a few days later was won by John Rush flying the only biplane in the competition, a rather ancient Hawker Tomtit dating from 1928; a rare occurrence in these days when monoplanes ruled.

There was even more international flavour to the air display held at Gatwick on 25th June. It was sponsored by the *Daily Express*, '... in recompense for the loss of the RAF Display'; Lord Beaverbrook, the newspaper's proprietor, vowed it would be 'the Display of the Century'. Certainly it attracted huge crowds and the large temporary grandstand, bedecked with Union Jacks, was full to capacity. German, French and American pilots competed and the RAF supplied formation teams of Harts and Furies. Despite the fact that they were billed as 'secret War planes' a Lysander, Battle, Blenheim, Hurricane and Whitley were on show. The prototype Focke-Wulf Fw 200 Condor, *Lufthansa's* latest sleek airliner, made its first appearance in Britain. The Display ended with a bombing set-piece *á la* Hendon and finally RAF Battles wrote *Buy the Daily Express* in smoke across the sky. One spectator remarked 'it was an interesting day but lacked the excitement and the professional touch of the Hendon displays, which were something else'.

On 2nd July the King's Cup Race was held as usual at Hatfield, but, according to *Flight* it had become 'a most mundane affair'. The 1,000 mile contest comprised twenty laps from Hatfield to Barton airport, Manchester and Alex Henshaw was successful in claiming the Cup and a prize of £800 with his Mew Gull at an average of 236 m.p.h. – the fastest speed attained in seventeen years of competitions. It also completed a hat-trick of wins for these splendid aircraft. Edgar Percival was placed sixth on handicap although he recorded the second fastest time.

Twelve days later the American millionaire tycoon, Howard Hughes, with a four-man crew, landed at New York after flying around the world, 14,790 miles in three days nineteen hours, beating the existing record by almost four days. His aircraft was a specially prepared Lockheed 14-N Super Electra. For an entirely different reason another American airman captured the headlines on 18th July when he landed at Dublin airport. Douglas Corrigan, of Irish descent, had made the eleventh solo crossing of the North Atlantic in a rather dilapidated nine-year old Curtiss Robin monoplane. On landing he asked the Dublin officials 'Where am I? I intended to fly to California'! When they told him Dublin, he replied disarmingly 'I must have flown the wrong way'! He was immediately dubbed 'Wrong Way' Corrigan and when he returned to New York by sea, he was treated like a returning hero to a ticker-tape welcome. Clearly the American public had taken him to their hearts. Throughout his long life Corrigan stoutly maintained that he had made the transatlantic flight in error, claiming that his 'compass must have been wrong' or 'just shows what a bad navigator I was ...'!

The same certainly could not be said about the Australian, Captain Donald Bennett of Imperial Airways, who was the country's finest navigator holding 1st and 2nd class Navigator's licences in addition to publishing *Complete Air Navigator*, his comprehensive treatise on the science of navigation. On 21st July, Bennett, accompanied by Radio Officer Coster, flew *Mercury*, which was launched from *Maia* over Foynes, Ireland, to Montreal – some 2,930 miles in 22 hours and 20 minutes; it carried a consignment of airmail and newsreels. They then flew to Port Washington, New York before returning to Hythe via Newfoundland, the Azores and Lisbon. The flight was heralded in the press as 'a remarkable achievement for British aviation.' Bennett was now convinced that he could capture the world distance record in *Mercury*, providing he could obtain Air Ministry support. He was awarded the Johnston Trophy by the GAPAN for his flight. But the flight was rather overshadowed less than three weeks later when the Focke-Wulf Condor flew non-stop from Berlin to New York – 4,075 miles in 24½ hours.

During July the Air Defence Cadet Corps was formed; its intention was to encourage young lads to take an interest in aviation and the RAF in particular. The Corps could perhaps trace its origins back to 1927 when Charles Longman, an ex-RAF airman, formed the Young Airman's League at Bournemouth; but the new Cadet Corps owed much to Air Commodore J. A. Chamier, who described it as 'Venture Adventure'. It was an instant success and within a year there were almost two hundred squadrons throughout the country. In February 1941 it became known as the Air Training Corps (ATC) with King George VI as its first Air Commandant-in-Chief. The ATC was described as 'a broad highway into the RAF' and became the 'nursery' of RAF airmen and remains so to the present day.

But without a doubt the most innovative new Force introduced during the year was the Civil Air Guard (CAG). On 23rd July Sir Kingsley Wood, the newly appointed Secretary of State for Air, announced a scheme whereby 'healthy applicants of either sex between the ages of 18 and 50 years' could receive heavily subsidised pilot training, providing they agreed to serve in 'any aviation capacity at a time of national emergency'. The CAG was planned to commence on 1st September. Those flying clubs that entered the Scheme, required a minimum of twelve members to form a 'Unit' and would receive a £50 subsidy for each successful 'A' licence. Tutorial charges were set at 10s per hour at weekends and half that on weekdays.

There was an avalanche of applications, 35,000 in the first three months, of which some 6,000 were enrolled into the CAG and the rest placed on the long waiting lists at the sixty or so flying schools taking part in the Scheme. An initial fee of £14 was charged, which included helmet, goggles and membership of the Royal Aero Club. The CAG 'uniform' was a black flying suit with CAG wings attached and once the trainees had passed they were given a small CAG lapel badge with wings. It was estimated that for about £10 most would attain their 'A' licence. The Marquess of Londonderry was appointed the Chief Commissioner and Mrs F. G. 'Blossom' Miles the Woman Commissioner, and in 1939 Pauline Gower became a Commissioner for London and the South East. The CAG even had its own Pocket Book published by Whitney Straight Ltd at a cost of 6d. By May 1939 over 2,000 members had obtained their licences but by then they had been

The original caption of this publicity photograph reads 'Keen to get to the controls, enthusiastic girl members of the CAG rush to their machines at Chingford (Essex) aerodrome.'

individually classified in categories 'related to their prospective value at a time of war.'! Many would later serve in the RAF or the Air Transport Auxiliary.

British aircraft constructors, along with importers of European and American aircraft, saw the CAG as an ideal opportunity for their light aeroplanes to be adopted for training. The Belgian Tipsy B Trainer produced under licence by Brian Allen Aviation at Hanworth was a likely contender; it was amongst the last of the side-by-side open cockpit monoplanes and at £675 was a reasonable buy, but in the event less than twenty were produced. General Aircraft's GAL.42 Cygnet, an all-metal cabin monoplane, was provided with a tricycle landing gear but at £1,050 was a trifle expensive. The Chrislea LC.1 Airguard, a side-by-side cabin aircraft produced early in July and one of the cheapest on the market at £550, was probably not selected because of its foreign engine. The Luton LA.5 Major, another attractive small cabin aeroplane suffered the same fate. It was mainly Moth Minors, Hawk Trainers, Whitney Straights and BA Swallows that were used for CAG flying training.

In July the first production Spitfire 1s emerged from the Supermarine Woolston works near Southampton, although the main production was undertaken at a new factory at Castle Bromwich, where the Nuffield Organisation produced them on an agency basis. They were delivered to No 19 squadron at Duxford to replace their Gauntlets. On 4th

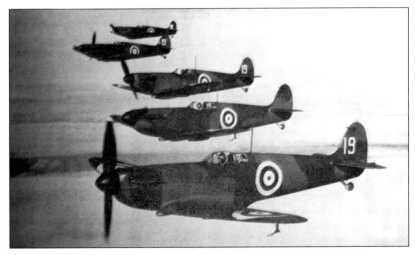

Spitfires of No 19 squadron in pre-war 'livery'.

August Duxford held a Press Day so that the squadron could proudly display their new Spitfires; two months later three Spitfires gave a display at the official opening of nearby Teversham (Cambridge) airfield. No 66 squadron, also based at Duxford, received their first Spitfires in mid-October. 'The aeroplane of one's dreams', as Douglas Bader described the Spitfire, had finally entered the RAF. Fighter Command was slowly taking on the mantle of a modern fighter force, already three squadrons, Nos 3, 56 and 111, were equipped with Hurricanes, but there was still a fair way to go with biplane fighters predominant in the Command.

The first ominous signs of gathering war clouds came in March with the German annexation of Austria and Czechoslovakia appeared to be the next country to be 'occupied'. But the more immediate concern was the bombing of Barcelona on 16/18th March mainly by Italian aircraft, which resulted in some 1,300 civilian fatalities and about 2,000 injured – close to the total number of British civilian casualties during 1914/18. The Air Raid Warden Service, which had been created in April 1937, recruited more volunteers – over 200,000 by June. As the summer progressed it seemed almost inevitable that Britain would go to war in defence of Czechoslovakia. On 10th September all foreign aircraft were forbidden to enter German airspace except by certain prescribed corridors. Five days later Neville Chamberlain, the Prime

Minister, flew from Heston in a British Airways Electra bound for Munich and the first of his three meetings with Hitler. After he had arrived back on the 24th after his second meeting the situation seemed dire and a State of Emergency was declared. The Air Raid Precautions services were mobilised and thousands of new volunteers came forward, basements were requisitioned for air raid shelters, trenches were dug in parks, sandbags appeared around government buildings, thirty-eight million gas masks were issued and the Government announced plans to evacuate two million people from London. Fighter squadrons were placed on a two-hour alert and aircraft were hastily camouflaged. Most people felt that war was only days away. Then on 30th September, after his third Munich trip, Neville Chamberlain

Neville Chamberlain's return to Heston Airport on 30th September 1938, after signing the Munich Agreement. Lockheed Super Electra in the background. (RAF Museum)

emerged from a Super Electra at Heston waving a piece of paper for the benefit of the newsreel cameras – one of the most celebrated images of the 1930s; this document he maintained ensured 'Peace for our time.' The crisis was apparently over. Of course it was nothing of the kind but the infamous 'Munich agreement' did provide valuable time to prepare and strengthen the country's defences, because according to the Service's official historian 'The Royal Air Force was simply not in a position to fight the *Luftwaffe* in the autumn of 1938.'

During this time Geoffrey de Havilland, along with his Chief Engineer and fellow director C. C. Walker, presented a project to the Air Council, which if it had received official support then might well have made a material difference in the early years of the air war. They tried to interest the Ministry in the concept of a twin-engined high-speed and unarmed bomber constructed of wood, which would carry 1,000 pounds of bombs at a speed of 400 m.p.h. – faster than any known fighter. The Air Ministry were less than impressed, after all military aircraft were now all-metal and as for a bomber being unarmed, such a thought was ludicrous! In any case it was thought that it was far too late to consider such a revolutionary design especially as war seemed all too imminent. To the RAF's and the country's everlasting thanks de Havilland continued the project as a private venture and with the dedicated support of one member of the Air Council, Air Marshal Sir William Freeman, the Director of Development and Production, the DH.98 Mosquito was born, arguably the most versatile and admired Allied aircraft of the Second World War.

The Air Ministry agreed to support Bennett's attempt on the seaplane distance record but the Munich crisis had delayed his flight; on 6th October *Mercury* was launched from *Maia* over Dundee. Bennett, along with Flg. Off. I. Harvey, planned to fly to Cape Town but they were forced to land on the Orange River at Alexander Bay because their fuel was low. They had been airborne for forty-two hours and had covered almost 6,000 miles – the seaplane world record but not the absolute distance record, which was then held by Russia. Although the RAF had designs on this world record.

During October two new military aircraft made their maiden flights – the Westland Whirlwind and Bristol Beaufort. The Whirlwind was the Company's first fighter and uniquely the first twin-engined fighter to be produced. It was a closely guarded secret when it first flew at Yeovil on 11th October. Although 340 were ordered in January 1940, it was never particularly successful, only 112 were ultimately produced

The prototype Bristol Beaufort – L4441 – first flew on 15th October, 1938.

equipping just two squadrons – Nos 263 and 137. By comparison the Beaufort, a torpedo/bomber, served Coastal Command well into 1943 with over 1,200 being produced. During the month the first production Wellingtons left the Vickers' Weybridge factory to enter the Service with No 99 squadron at Mildenhall. By the outbreak of war there were eight Wellington operational squadrons and along with Blenheims they opened Bomber Command's operations on 4th September, 1939. No less than 11,460 Wellingtons were produced, more than any other British bomber.

In November the RAF was again in the news when from the 5th to 7th two Vickers Wellesleys of the RAF's Long Range Development Unit at RAF Upper Heyford captured the world distance record. They were piloted by Sqn. Ldr. R. G. Kellett and Flt. Lt. A. Combe and despite adverse head winds flew non-stop from Ismalia to Darwin – a distance of 7,162 miles; a third Wellesley was forced to land at Koepang, Timor because of a shortage of fuel; it later completed the flight to Darwin. *The Aeroplane* commented '... whether we are justified in asking such young men to risk their lives hanging on to a single propeller and aero-motor can be argued ... but no praise can be too high for the nine young men who undertook this journey ...' The Wellesley, a light bomber, had entered Bomber Command in 1937 but was obsolescent by 1939 because of lack of speed and inadequate armament.

As the year drew to a close the last pre-war airliner made its maiden flight at Hatfield on 28th December – DH.95 Flamingo. Considering that the Albatross had only flown some twenty months earlier it was most commendable for de Havilland's to design and produce another airliner in such a brief time. The Flamingo was the Company's first all-metal stressed skin aircraft and designed to rival the Electras, carrying 12/18 passengers at a speed of 240 m.p.h. The Air Ministry was impressed with the aircraft, realising its potential as a troop carrier and forty were ordered under the name Hertfordshire, although only one was ultimately produced. The prototype Flamingo entered service with Guernsey/Jersey Airways in July 1939 from Heston and in total only sixteen were produced, seven operated with BOAC in the Near East and a couple joined the King's Flight in 1940.

By 1939 the universal relief experienced by the Munich agreement had all but dissipated and there were few people in the country under any illusions that war could be averted. Those that thought otherwise had their confidence severely tested when, on 15th March, Germany occupied the whole of Czechoslovakia. Nevertheless private and club flying still tried to present a brave face with the usual round of meetings and races whilst the country slowly and inexorably prepared for the impending conflict.

During the early summer five new aerodromes formally opened – Grangemouth, West Hartlepool (Greatham), Guernsey, Derby (Burnaston) and Birmingham (Elmdon). With perhaps a certain misplaced confidence and optimism several new light aircraft appeared for a market that suddenly disappeared in September. Perhaps the most unfortunate in this respect were the Mosscraft MA.2, the Taylorcraft Plus C and Chilton DW.1; the first two were two-seater cabin monoplanes. The MA.2 was produced by Moss Brothers of Chorley, Lancashire and was described as '... so very nearly the perfect light aircraft. ...' It was priced at £725 and surely would have attracted buyers in more settled times but only two were built. The Taylorcraft was a variant of the American Taylor Cub and produced in Britain by the recently formed Taylorcraft Aeroplanes (England) Ltd. The Plus C first appeared on 24th April and with a price of £480 it quickly attracted private and club buyers – over twenty. But its fame resides in the fact that it subsequently entered the RAF for AOP (Air Observation Post) duties, designated an Auster 1; over 1,600 in varying marks were produced during the war. The Chilton DW.1 was a single-seat low-wing monoplane first appearing in July; a remarkable little aircraft priced at a 'mere' £315, which certainly would have been produced in far greater quantities than four, had it not been for the war.

There were even echoes of the balmy days of Amy Johnson, Bert Hinkler, Jean Batten ... *et al*, when on 5th February Alex Henshaw left Gravesend aerodrome for Cape Town in a Mew Gull. He accomplished the outward leg in $39\frac{1}{2}$ hours and returned to Gravesend five days later in an almost identical time, both were new records by some margins. Doubts were expressed about the value of solo long-distance flights '... surely British aviation no longer has a need for such solo "jaunts", courageous though they be ... We have moved a long way forward since they were so lauded ...' Henshaw's was indeed the last solo long-distance flight thus bringing that particular chapter of pioneering flying to a close.

In mid-February the Air Estimates were presented to Parliament – a massive £220.6 million; mainly to the large orders of military aircraft. Civil aviation was also voted a larger budget – £4.7 million. This sum was intended to give additional support to the Empire Airmail Service and European services, increased grants to clubs operating CAG units and the further development of Heston.

Imperial Airways had now received most of its Empire flying boats, although five had already been lost and 1939 proved no better. On 21st January *Cavalier en route* from New York to Bermuda was forced to land on the open sea and ten of the thirteen on board survived the ten hours in an open boat. A few days later *Calypso* was forced down in the English Channel but a tug towed it into Cherbourg. However, these dramatic rescues re-affirmed the public's belief that flying boats offered the safest method of air-travel across oceans. *Corsair* was forced to land on a shallow river in the Belgian Congo because of a shortage of fuel but its hull was damaged. The subsequent ten-month successful salvage and rescue operations are well related in Graham Coster's book *Corsairville*. In May *Challenger* crashed at Mozambique and in the following month *Centurion* came to grief near Calcutta – a sad chapter for the airline.

British Airways, which had gained a certain publicity from the Prime Minister's three flights to Munich, added extra European cities to its scheduled services. Considering the volatile political situation it was perhaps a little surprising that on 17th April the airline introduced two new services – Berlin/Warsaw and Frankfurt/Budapest; it was the first regular British passenger service to Berlin since 1924. The airline was also not immune to tragic accidents. In August a Super Electra bound

Vickers Wellesleys of the RAF's Long Range Development Unit.

The prototype DH.95 Flamingo first flew on 28th December 1938. (via M. Morris)

Taylorcraft Auster 1. (RAF Museum)

for Zürich crash-landed in a field but the crew and nine passengers were safe. Four days later (15th) an Electra on the Stockholm service caught fire in mid-air, it ditched in the sea south of Copenhagen, four passengers and a crew member were killed but Captain C. Wright was rescued unconscious from the sea.

The German Air Force Day (1st March) was used by *Reichsmarshall* Göring to make a bombastic speech claiming that Europe was 'In fear of the German Air Force, the mightiest in the world ...' This, and the seizure of Czechoslovakia later in the month, caused the Air Ministry to order that all military aircraft be camouflaged and squadron markings removed to be replaced by two-letter codes. Service airfields were already being camouflaged and many adjacent public roads closed 'for security reasons'. *Flight* had commented in a February issue: 'Really this war scare business is getting beyond a joke. If the camouflaging of aerodromes continues at the present rate, we shall have a whole crop of accidents, through poor innocent aviators, service and civilian, landing in hedges because they think they are on aerodromes.'!

On 1st April the RAF celebrated its 'coming of age' – twenty-one years since its formation in the dark days of 1918. King George VI sent a celebratory message 'I have known the Royal Air Force from its earliest days and am proud that its spirit remains unchanged – a spirit that has enabled it to surmount many difficulties and rise, true to its motto, to even greater heights of achievement ...' Air Chief Marshal Sir Cyril Newall sent a personal message to his Service: '... I am convinced that if the RAF is called upon once more to defend our Country and the Empire it will maintain that reputation for courage and devotion to duty which it has so fully earned.'

The two Air Forces almost seemed to be vying with each other to gain favourable publicity and prove their superiority. On 24th February Flt. Lt. H. Purvis flew a special racer version of a production Spitfire at a speed of 408 m.p.h. The triumph was short-lived because at the end of March a Heinkel He 112H recorded an average speed of 464 m.p.h. and even this was surpassed on 26th April when a Messerschmitt Me 109R increased the world speed record to 469 m.p.h. As a counter to this publicity the RAF gave press displays of some of their latest aircraft during April. Lysanders of Nos 2 and 16 (Army Co-operation) squadrons performed at Hawkinge and Old Sarum as did Hurricanes at Northolt and Spitfires at Duxford. In addition the various aviation journals continually assured their readers that their Air Force was equipped with the fastest fighters and the most technically advanced bombers.

On 31st March Fred Miles flew the first production Master trainer from Woodley. It was a high-performance monoplane advanced trainer enabling trainee pilots to convert from the biplane trainers to Hurricanes and Spitfires and had originated as a private venture back in June 1937 as the M.9 Kestrel. With a maximum speed of over 240 m.p.h and similar handling qualities to the new fighters, the Master was yet another successful Miles trainer and almost 900 were produced.

The summer aviation scene, which proved to be rather truncated, opened on 14th May with the Royal Aero. Society's annual Garden Party at the Great West Aerodrome. Although the weather was unkind thousands braved the elements to witness a fine display of flying, which lasted for three hours. There was a rare mixture of aeroplanes on display from small light aircraft, such as the Tipsy and Cygnet, to the latest RAF aircraft. Two Blériots, a Sopwith Pup and a Deperdussin gave flying displays during the tea interval. As if to remind the Society's guests of the changed world, the day ended with an ARP demonstration! It was the last public air meeting at Fairey's airfield, six years later it became Heathrow Airport.

On 20th May sixty-three Service airfields and fifteen civil aerodromes

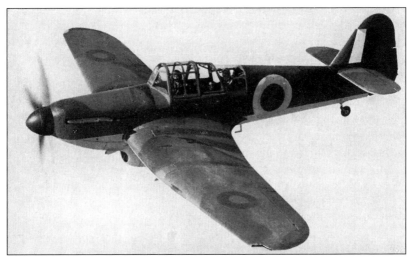

Miles Master 1 – yet another successful Miles' trainer.

Empire Air Day at RAF Biggin Hill – 20th May 1939. On display Hawker Hurricane, Fairey Battle and Handley Page Harrow. (via J. Adams)

opened their gates to the public (adults 1s and children 3d!) for what was the sixth and last Empire Air Day. Over one million attended, Northolt was the most popular with an attendance of 56,000; RAF charities benefited by £30,000. Despite this magnificent public response Air Commodore Chamier, the originator of the Air Day, was a little disappointed that the original concept was perhaps being lost: '... It was planned more on the lines of an 'At Home' than as a display – more as an occasion when Mr., Mrs., and the youngsters could wander around and see aviation from a new angle. Flying displays have been held since aeroplanes flew and there is no novelty in standing behind railings watching brilliant pilots perform dazzling manouevres ... But perhaps this swing to pageantry was inevitable ...'!

Towards the end of May Northolt again played host to visitors but of a very different hue – members of the Houses of Commons and Lords and representatives of Dominion countries – who were given the chance to see some of the RAF's latest aircraft. Wellingtons, Hurricanes, Battles, Blenheims and Beauforts were lined up for inspection and there was also a mini-Hendon flying display which included Gladiators, Henleys and Sunderlands.

In May Members of Parliament visited RAF Northolt. Fairey Battle in the foreground with a Hurricane in the rear.

The Whitsun Bank Holiday saw the start of the fourth International Air Race to the Isle of Man. Poor weather made flying conditions difficult for all the twenty-seven competitors. Geoffrey de Havilland, Jnr. won the race in a TK.2 at an average speed of 168 m.p.h. This aeroplane had been designed and built by the students of the de Havilland Technical College at Hatfield and had first appeared in August 1935. It survived the war and was racing again in 1947. Alex Henshaw, who was placed second in the race, gained some consolation on the following Monday when he and his father won first prize in the Manx Air Derby, beating Tommy Rose and Edgar Percival into second and third places.

For Imperial Airways there were two unresolved matters claiming the attention of the Board and its officials – the proposed Transatlantic passenger/mail service and the amalgamation with British Airways. Pan-American had successfully stolen a march on Imperial when on 30th March their new Boeing 314 flying boat, *Yankee Clipper*, arrived at Southampton via the Azores, Lisbon and Marseille on a trial flight. Meanwhile Imperial were conducting air refuelling trials with four Empire flying boats and it was clear that they would not be ready by 1st June – the agreed starting date for the new service. By mid-June Pan-Am. felt that they could not wait any longer and on the 26th *Yankee Clipper* left New York carrying nineteen VIPs and mail and arrived at Southampton two days later – some 1,970 miles at an average speed of

144 m.p.h. Quite a momentous aviation feat considering that it was a mere twenty years since Alcock and Brown had first crossed the North Atlantic. At the Savoy lunch Sir Kingsley Wood said that Imperial Airways hoped to commence their service from the beginning of August. Then on 9th July the first fare-paying passengers arrived from New York – the single fare was $340 (about £240).

Nevertheless matters were improving for Imperial. Their Ensign airliners, missing from its fleet since January, returned to operations in June. The long awaited Short S.26 G-Class flying boat, *Golden Hind*, was launched at Rochester on the 17th and made its first flight the following month. It was planned that *Golden Hind*, along with *Golden Fleece* and *Golden Horn*, would commence operating the Transatlantic service in early 1940. Imperial's new London air-terminal opened on 5th June, passengers were taken by bus to Croydon and by special train to Southampton Docks, where Berth 108 was now the established terminal for the Empire flying boats. The British Overseas Airways Act had passed through Parliament and Imperial was valued at £2.7 million and British Airways at £262,500; it became law on 4th August. In November BOAC was established with Sir John Reith as Chairman but the two airlines would not actually merge until 1st April 1940.

The admirable group of women aviators were not forgotten in all the flurry of military preparations. In May 1938 the Air Ministry had asked the Flying Section of the Women's Legion to identify and recruit

Boeing 314 Flying Boat – Yankee Clipper. (Smithsonian Institution)

women pilots who were likely to be useful to the RAF. As one air correspondent remarked '... this is the first official recognition given since 1918 to any part which women may be able to play in air defence.' Twelve months later Captain Balfour, Under-Secretary of State for Air announced '... In a National Emergency, women would certainly be used for ferrying aircraft for the RAF.' In late September 1940 authority was given to form a Women's Section of ferry pilots within the Air Transport Auxiliary and Pauline Gower was appointed to head this Section. The Air Council had already decided on the formation of the Women's Auxiliary Air Force, its members to undertake non-combatant duties with the Service and in particular to operate the numerous barrage balloon sites. On 28th June the WAAF was officially formed with effect from 1st July. Miss Jane Trefussis-Forbes was appointed Senior Controller at the rank of Air Commodore; by 1st September there were 234 officers and 1,500 airwomen.

During July flying boats took the centre stage. On the 2nd the Empire flying boat *Caribou* was successfully refuelled in flight. Then, of course, it was the turn of the *Golden Hind* followed closely by *Yankee Clipper*'s first passenger flight. Another American flying boat, Consolidated PBY-4, made a notable flight on the 13/15th by crossing directly from Newfoundland to Felixstowe, some 2,450 miles in $15\frac{1}{2}$ hours; the first delivery flight of a military aircraft from America to Britain. The M.A.E.E. were so impressed with the aircraft's performance and long operational range that fifty were ordered for Coastal Command where they were known as Catalinas. In total over seven hundred were purchased equipping nineteen squadrons.

Also in July, squadrons of Wellingtons, Blenheims and Whitleys flew over France as part of Air Defence exercises and also to demonstrate to the country's ally that the RAF was a highly disciplined force. The bombers flew in close formations and no higher than 6,000 feet; this provided the crews with practical experience of this type of flying over unknown territory. It had been accepted that formation flying improved the defensive capabilities of bombers, a lesson learned from the Gotha raids of 1917/8.

Almost as if all thoughts of war were furthest from their minds most of the eighty or so Aero Clubs continued to hold their summer meetings and events. The gliding enthusiasts were also busy during the summer especially for the week long National Contests in mid-July which were held at Great Hucklow, Derbyshire. The standard of gliding had so improved that no points were awarded unless a flight

Wellingtons of No 149 squadron over Paris on 14th July, 1939 (Bastille Day).

exceeded 1,500 feet or two hours duration; about a week earlier Phillip Wills had set a new British height record of 14,200 feet. Even in August when the days of peacetime flying were fast running out various air displays continued to be held. On 5th August, at Lympne, the Hon. A. Dalrymple won the Folkestone Aero Trophy in a Chilton DW.1 at a speed of 126 m.p.h – one of the last pre-war air races. Later in the month the Royal Aero Club 'regretfully' announced the cancellation of the King's Cup Race due to be held on 2nd November. A week later at Wilmington, the home of the Sussex Aero Club, three German pilots competed as well as a solitary Polish airman. Brooklands mounted its last pre-war meeting on the 20th, which brought to a close private and club flying at this historic aerodrome.

On 5th August Imperial Airways finally made its first Transatlantic mail crossing when *Caribou* under Captain J. C. Kelly-Rogers was refuelled in the air over Shannon Airport before setting out for Botwood, Montreal and Port Washington, New York; the entire journey took 36½ hours. *Caribou* returned to Southampton and three days later (12th) Captain Don Bennett in Cabot left on the second scheduled service, no passengers only mail. Imperial Airways had successfully cleared this final hurdle only to find that within weeks war intervened.

Whilst these historic flights were taking place the RAF was engaged from 8th/11th August on massive air exercises to test the effectiveness of the air defences. Over 1,300 aircraft took part along with RDF stations, anti-aircraft guns, searchlights and barrage balloons and a practice black-out over London and south-east England was imposed on the 11th. The following evening Air Chief Marshal Sir Hugh Dowding, A.O.C-in-C., Fighter Command, made a broadcast on the BBC to reassure the public of its safety from air attack: '... I confidently believe that serious attack on these Islands would be brought to a standstill within a short space of time ...' The country seemed to be poised on the very brink of war. Twelve days later (24th) Parliament passed the Emergency Powers (defence) Act because of 'the immediate peril of war.' All military reservists were called up, and fighter squadrons were put on a state of readiness. The aircraft were dispersed around the perimeters of airfields with pilots' tents placed within twenty-five yards of their aircraft. Despite the fact that Imperial and other European airlines were cancelling scheduled services, British Airways started a new service from Heston to Helsinki via Stockholm on the 28th; it would be very short-lived!

Hurricanes of No 87 squadron take-off over Blenheim 1Fs of No 29 squadron at Debden, Essex during the Air Exercises in August 1939. A last peaceful scene with war a few weeks away.

From midnight on 31st August a total ban on civil flying over the eastern half of the country was put in force and all civil flying banned except under the National Air Communications, which had been established to administer all the existing civil airlines. Croydon, the traditional gateway to London by air, and Heston, became ghost airports as airliners were moved away to Bristol (Whitchurch) and Exeter, although the Ensigns and Frobishers were dispersed to Coventry and various RAF airfields to be used to transport RAF men and equipment to their war stations in France. Imperial's Empire flying boats would later move from Southampton to their wartime base in Poole Harbour.

On 1st September, the day Germany invaded Poland, a State of Emergency was declared and a general mobilisation of the RAF was ordered. Private and public aerodromes were closed and many would

Blenheim IVs of No 139 squadron. (RAF Museum)

be requisitioned by the Air Ministry. Black-out regulations came into force from sunset, the full ARP services were put into operation and the first evacuations from London of children and adults began. On the following day ten Fairey Battle squadrons of the Advanced Air Striking Force flew to France and at all the RAF stations everybody was well aware that it was only a matter of days or even hours before 'the balloon went up'! At eleven o'clock on that sunny but fateful Sunday morning, 3rd September, when Neville Chamberlain gravely informed the Nation that it was now at war with Germany, perhaps no RAF station more keenly awaited the expected war signal than Wyton in Cambridgeshire; for three days a Blenheim had been on constant standby ready to leave on 'a secret mission'. Just after noon Blenheim IV – N6215 – of No 139 squadron sped down the runway and set out on the RAF's first operational sortie of the war; Flg. Off. A. McPherson and his two-man crew had orders to photograph the German fleet that was thought to be leaving the naval port of Wilhelmshaven. How Claude Grahame-White must have quietly applauded this mission after his practical demonstration back in July 1910!

BIBLIOGRAPHY

This is a small selection of the myriad of books covering British aviation up to 1939, which have proved useful as sources of information. They are my *personal* guide to further general reading but I fully recognise that the list is far from being conclusive.

GENERAL

Beaty, David. *The Water Jump: the story of Trans-Atlantic Flight*. Secker & Warburg, 1976.

Chant, Christopher. *Pioneers of Aviation*. Grange Books, 2001.

Cruddas, Colin. *In Cobham's Company. Sixty Years of Flight Refuelling Limited*. Cobham plc, 1994.

Cruddas, Colin. *Cobham: The Flying Years*. Chalford Pubs., 1997. (The Archive Photographs Series).

Cruddas, Colin. *Those Fabulous Flying Years*. Air Britain (Historians), 2003.

Culick, Fred C.C. & Dunmore, Spencer. *On Great White Wings: The Wright Brothers & the Race for Flight*. Airlife, 2001.

Duke, Neville & Lanchbery, Edward (Editors). *The Crowded Sky: An Anthology of Flight from the Beginnings to the Age of the Guided Missile*. Cassell, 1959.

Gibbs-Smith, C.H. *The Aeroplane*. H.M.S.O., 1960.

Gibbs-Smith, C.H. *A Brief History of Flying from Myth to Space Travel*. Science Museum, 1967.

Gibbs-Smith, C.H. *Aviation: A Historical Survey from its Origins to the End of World War II*, H.M.S.O., 1970

Gibbs-Smith, C.H. *Early Flying Machines, 1799–1909*. Eyre & Metheun, 1975.

Goodall, Michael & Tagg, Albert E. *British Aircraft before the Great War*. A Schiffer Aviation History Book, USA, 2001.

Grahame-White, Claude. *Flying: An Epitome and a Forecast*. Chatto & Windus, 1930.

Gwynn-Jones, Terry. *Aviation's Magnificent Gamblers*. Orbis Pub., 1981.

Harper, Harry. *Riders of the Sky: The Saga of the Flying Men*. Hodder & Stoughton, 1936.

Harper, Harry. *The Romance of a Modern Airway*. Sampson Low, 1930.

Harris, Sherwood. *The First to Fly: Aviation's Pioneer Days*. Macmillan, 1970.

Hooks, Mike. *Hendon to Farnborough, SBAC Displays, 1932–1972*. Chalford Pubs., 1996. (The Archive Photographs Series).

Hudson, Kenneth. *Air Travel: a Social History*. Adams & Dart, 1973.

Hurren, B. J. *Fellowship of the Air: Jubilee Book of the Royal Aero Club, 1901–1951*. Iliffe, 1951.

Jackson, A.S. *Imperial Airways and the First British Airlines*, 1919–40. Terence Dalton, 1990.

Jarrett, Phillip. *Pioneer Aircraft: Early Aviation before 1914*. Putnam, 2002.

Johns, W. E. *Some Milestones of Aviation*. Hamilton, 1936.

Johnson, Howard. *Wings over Brooklands: the Birthplace of British Aviation*. Whittet Books, 1981.

Learmouth, David, *The First Croydon Airport, 1915–1928*. Sutton Libraries & Arts Services, 1977.

Nash, Joanna, Cluett, Douglas (Editor). *The Great Days – Croydon Airport 1928–1939*. Sutton Libraries & Arts Services. 1980.

Oliver, David. *Hendon Aerodrome: a History*. Airlife, 1994.

Ord-Hume, Arthur W.J.G. *British Light Aeroplanes: Their Evolution, Development and Perfection, 1920–1940*. GMS Enterprises, 2000.

Penrose, Harald J. *British Aviation:*
1. *The Pioneer Years, 1903–1914*. Putnam, 1967.
2. *The Great War & Armistice, 1915–1919*. Putnam, 1969.
3. *The Adventuring Years, 1920–1929*. Putnam, 1973.
4. *Widening Horizons, 1930–1934*. H.M.S.O., 1979.
5. *The Ominous Skies, 1935–1939*. H.M.S.O., 1980.

Penrose, Harald J. *Wings across the World: An illustrated history of British Airways*. Cassell, 1980.

Rendall, Ivan. *Reaching for the Skies: The Adventure of Flight*. BBC Books, 1988.

Rinard, Judith E. *The Smithsonian National Air & Space Museum Book of Flight*. Firefly Books, 2001.

Rolt, L.T.C. *The Aeronauts: A History of Ballooning, 1783–1903*. Longmans Green, 1966.

Taylor, Michael J.H. *Milestones of Flight. C.843 B.C. to the Present*. Chancellor Press, 2000.

Taylor, Michael J.H. & Mondey, David. *Guinness Book of Aircraft Facts & Feats*. Guinness Superlatives Ltd., 1984.

Turner, C.C. *The Old Flying Days*. Sampson Low, c.1927?

Periodicals.

> *The Aeroplane*, 1919–1939.
>
> *Flight*, 1920–1939.
>
> *Flying*, 1938–1939.
>
> *Popular Flying*, 1932–1939.

SOME AIRCRAFT MANUFACTURERS

Allward, Maurice & Taylor, John W.R. *The de Havilland Aircraft Company*. Chalford Pub., 1996. (The Archive Photographs Series).

Barnes, C.H. *Shorts Aircraft since 1900*. Putnam, 1967.

Brown, Don L. *Miles Aircraft since 1925*. Putnam, 1970.

Davis, Mike. *AIrco: the Aircraft Manufacturing Co*. Crowood Aviation Series, 2001.

Dowsett, Alan. *Handley Page*. Tempus Pubs., 1993. (Images of Aviation).

Endres, Günter. *British Aircraft Manufacturers since 1908*. Ian Allan. 1995.

Gunston, W. *The Plane Makers*. New English Lib. 1980.

Hall, Michael. *The Blackburn Aircraft Company*. Chalford Pub., 1996.

Hall, Michael. *Sopwith Aviation Company*. Chalford Pub., 1997. (The Archive Photographs Series).

Hare, Paul R. *Aeroplanes of the Royal Aircraft Factory*. Crowood Aviation Series, 1999.

Holmes, Henry. *Avro*. Chalford Pub., 1996. (The Archive Photographs Series).

James, Derek N. *The Bristol Aeroplane Company*. Tempus Pub., 2001.

James, Derek N. *Hawker Aircraft Ltd*. Chalford Pubs., 1996. (The Archive Photographs Series).

James, Derek N. *Westland*. Chalford Pubs., 1997. (The Archive Photographs Series).

Munson, Kenneth. *Airliners Between the Wars 1919–1939*. Blandford Press, 1972.

Taylor, H.A. *Airspeed Aircraft since 1931*. Putnam, 1970.

Williams, Ray. *Armstrong Whitworth Aircraft*. Chalford Pubs., 1998. (The Archive Photographs Series).

AUTO/BIOGRAPHIES (some of the many!)

Berg, A. Scott. *Lindbergh*. Putnam, USA., 1998.

Boyle, Andrew. *Trenchard: Man of Vision*. Collins, 1962.

Brabazon, Lord of Tara. *The Brabazon Story*. Heinemann, 1956.

Bramson, Alan. *Pure Luck: The Authorised Biography of Sir Thomas Sopwith*. Patrick Stephens, 1990.

Bruce, Gordon. *Charlie Rolls – Pioneer Aviator*. Rolls-Royce Heritage Trust, 1991.

Cobham, Sir Alan. *A Time to Fly*. Shepheard-Walwyn, 1986.

Curtis, Lettice. *Winged Odyssey: Mary, Duchess of Bedford: A Flying Biography*. Air Research Pubs., 1993

de Havilland, Sir Geoffrey. *Sky Fever*. Airlife Pubs., 1979.

Ellis Peter B. & Williams, Piers. *By Jove Biggles! The Life of W. E. Johns*. W. H. Allen, 1981.

Fahie, Michael. *A Harvest of Memories: The Life of Pauline Gower*. GMS Enterprises, 1995.

Jenkins, Garry. *'Colonel' Cody and the Flying Cathedral: the Adventures of the Cowboy that conquered Britain's skies*. Simon & Schuster, USA., 1999.

Luff, David. *Amy Johnson: Enigma in the Sky*. Airlife, 2002.

Mackersey, Ian. *Jean Batten: The Garbo of the Skies*. Warner Books, 1992.

Verdon-Roe, Sir Alliott. *The World of Wings and Things*. Hurst & Blackwell, 1939.

Wallace, Graham. *Claude Grahame-White*. Putnam, 1960.

Wills, Phillip. *On Being a Bird*. Parrish, 1953.

MILITARY
General

Armitage, Sir Michael *The Royal Air Force: An Illustrated History*. Cassell, 1993.

Collier, Basil. *A History of Air Power*. Weidenfeld & Nicolson, 1974.

Coombs, L.F.E. *The Lion has Wings: The Race to prepare the RAF for World War II 1935–1940*. Alan Sutton, 1994.

Farrar-Hockley, Sir Anthony. *The Army in the Air: the History of the Army Air Corps*. Alan Sutton, 1994.

Grey, Charles C. *A History of the Air Ministry*. Allen & Unwin, 1940.

Hyde, H. M. *British Air Policy between the Wars, 1918–1939*. Heinemann, 1976.

James, John. *The Paladins: A Social History of the RAF up to the Outbreak of WWII*. Macdonald, 1990.

Nesbit, Roy Conyers. *RAF: An Illustrated History from 1918*. Sutton Pub./RAF Museum, 1998.

Robertson, Bruce. *The RAF: A Pictorial History*. Robert Hale, 1978.

Ross, Tony. (Editor). *75 Eventful Years: A Tribute to the Royal Air Force, 1918–1993*. Lockturn Ltd., 1993.

Slessor, Sir John. *The Central Blue: Recollections & Reflections*. Cassell, 1956.

Taylor, John W.R. & Moyes, P.J.R. *Pictorial History of the RAF. Volume One: 1918–1939*. Ian Allan, 1968.

Terraine, John. *The Right of the Line*. Hodder & Stoughton, 1985.

Thetford, Owen. *Aircraft of the RAF since 1918*. Putnam, 9th Edition, 1996.

World War I (not in France!)

Barker, Ralph. *A Brief History of the Royal Flying Corps in World War I*. Constable & Robinson, 2002.

Bruce, J. M. *Britain's First Warplanes: A Pictorial Survey of the First 400 Naval and Military Aircraft*. Arms & Armour Press, 1987.

Castle, H.G. *Fire over England. The German Air Raids in WWI*. Secker & Warburg, 1982.

Hyde, Andrew P. *The First Blitz: The German Air Campaign against Britain, 1917–1918*. Leo Cooper, 2002.

Mowthorpe, Ces. *Battlebags: British Airships of the First World War*. Sutton Pub., 1995.

Poolman, Kenneth. *Zeppelins over England*. White Lion, 1975.

Treadwell, Terry C. *The First Naval Air War*. Tempus Pub., 2002.

ACKNOWLEDGEMENTS

In this centenary year of manned powered flight I have attempted to outline the evolution and growth of British aviation up to the Second World War. Within the confines of this book it has been possible to include only the more memorable and significant events through these four exciting decades. I have sincerely endeavoured to maintain a proper balance between the development of private, civil and military aviation and I apologise here to any reader who feels that I have omitted an event that has a particular significance.

I am greatly appreciative of the countless number of authors who, over the years, have contributed to produce such a rich repository of aviation literature. I am also deeply indebted to several people for their kind assistance, especially Colin Cruddas, Roger Carter of the Chard Museum, and as always Norman G. Richards. I also acknowledge the constant patience, help and excellent editing of my wife Joan, who has once again made this book possible.

Graham Smith
Chelmsford, 2003

INDEX

Other aviation titles by Graham Smith available from Countryside Books include

Cambridgeshire Airfields in the Second World War

Devon & Cornwall Airfields in the Second World War

Dorset Airfields in the Second World War

Essex Airfields in the Second World War

Hertfordshire & Bedfordshire Airfields in the Second World War

Norfolk Airfields in the Second World War

Northamptonshire Airfields in the Second World War

Suffolk Airfields in the Second World War

The Mighty Eighth in the Second World War